SOLO executives

5 transformational strategies for leaders

overcoming isolation, anxiety, and fatigue in career transition

WAYNE BROWN

SOLO executives: 5 transformational strategies for leaders.
Overcoming isolation, anxiety and fatigue in career transition
is a non-fiction work, incorporating a fictional storyline

Hardback ISBN 978-0-6488136-0-6
Softcover ISBN 978-0-6488136-1-3
eBook ISBN 978-0-6488136-2-0

Cover artwork by Thorpe-Bowker Australia
Internal artwork by Fei Meng Chi (Faye)
Developmental and copyediting by Dr Renée Otmar and Carly Tenille

First edition 2021

10 9 8 7 6 5 4 3 2 1

Dedication

For all leaders who are suffering in silence
and struggling against the challenges of an
ever-changing business landscape.

100% of proceeds from the sale
of this book will be donated to the

Brain and Behavior Research Foundation,

for continued research into areas of mental illness.

BRAIN &
BEHAVIOR
RESEARCH FOUNDATION

Awarding **NARSAD** Grants

www.bbrfoundation.org

Contents

Acknowledgements

The characters, companies and settings in this book are fictitious, and any resemblance to a person you may have met is purely coincidental.

A special thank-you to those who have contributed to my career. You have helped me grow as a person and as a tribal leader. In writing *SOLO executives*, I sought guidance from many of these people, and their input has been invaluable.

Thank you to my wife, Franziska, and our daughter, Rochelle, for supporting me and providing me every opportunity to realise my dream of writing this book. I love you both dearly and cherish our lives together.

Thank you to the many people whom I've been fortunate to work with and call my friends. To those who have mentored and coached me, thank you for the lasting memories.

A special thank-you to the following for fact-checking and critiquing this book:

Rhonda Stuart, Matt Scanlan, Heinz Dickens, Warren Eves, Rodney Daniel, Rory Smith, Matthew Chelius and Pierre Njeim.

Finally, to the global elevator–escalator tribe, thank you for your participation in my journey, whether directly or indirectly. It's been incredible, and I hope to have the opportunity of meeting with as many of you as possible in the years ahead.

My sincerest regards as you embark on your future journey.

Preface

As I enter the final phase of my career, I want to contribute to the survival of leadership by sharing the knowledge I've been fortunate to gain from many incredibly talented people who have supported me. The elevator and escalator industry, like so many others, is at an important junction in its history.

Our industry has not adapted to change and new technologies as quickly as many others, and remains highly labour intensive. However the future of the industry will be considerably different, with technology enabling a revolution in development and delivery of services. I predict that within the next 10–15 years a convergence of multiple technologies and the associated exponential development will bring about a dramatic acceleration towards a new way of operating, with vastly different company structures and focus, thereby leaving behind the traditional practices and moderate advances seen over the past 170 years. In some ways, we will be catching up with those more advanced on their technology journey. Our industry will transform into one that will become purely commodity based: a 'plug and play world' on steroids, in which mechanical and electrical blocks of integrated equipment connect and are swapped and recycled rather than constructed and maintained.

If I'm correct, as an industry we face an increasingly rapid threat whereby knowledge of how to handle our business during such a transition will become extremely scarce and valuable. This period will call for cool heads. As the lure of cash and asset-rich organisations prosper in a world in which urbanisation continues apace, we'll witness the demise of rural living at the fastest rate in human history. We are likely to see new companies enter our market – companies attracted by the opportunity to leverage digital technologies with advances in material and information sciences.

Examining the elevator and escalator industry today, we might see collaboration across sectors, with increasing efficiency and optimisation of skills. The current product value chain marketing, research and development, manufacturing, sales, installation, servicing and product modernisation is destined to be a thing of the past.

Marketing and sales may survive but in a much different capacity to what we know today. Clients will pick and choose online, with instant price feedback. Computer systems will customise those requirements on the basis of standard product building blocks and forward specifications to workshops in which robots automatically upload the punching program to produce the desired result. It will be a seamless, process, almost without human labour. The product will be packaged and shipped, ready for assembly by the construction company.

Only after receiving the 'go-live' signal will teams of product commissioning experts become involved most likely remotely. These teams will engage their highly secretive programmed robots to run the checks and produce the test results. Once this production process is completed, the human involvement will be one of a parts wholesaler, swapping and recycling rather than maintaining.

Yes, I realise that this vision may seem a little over the top and reads like science fiction, but is it so hard to imagine this world based on the direction of the industry in recent years? I believe we are already on this trajectory, and whether it happens in the timeframe stated or five years later, it is most likely our industry's destiny. As such, this change offers vast potential and opportunity for companies that are able to stay up to date with technological and scientific developments and to adopt a flexible internal structure.

Leadership will be vitally important in steering and supporting people. Evolving customer demands and competitor innovations will require the capability to adapt to accelerating changes, through critical thinking and dynamic strategies. Only leaders capable of seeing this shifting landscape and developing agile businesses will endure. The 'naysayers', waiting for proof, will be left behind. The future will require a degree of courage, and a reliance on team collaboration rather than individual brilliance – in other words, a different breed of leader. In turn, it means leaders will need to seek advice, feedback, coaching and mentoring, and develop a desire for continuous personal growth through new knowledge and skills.

The structure of this book introduces a case-study approach with stories based on the lives of the fictional characters Tim, Maddie, Alan and Harry. The stories of Tim and Maddie illustrate those of the typical industry executive, who fumbles his or her way through a career overlain with moments of intent and purpose. However, learning as they go and through determination and persistence, they will find their way forward. Alan plays a significant support function throughout, as mentor and coach to both Tim and Maddie. He becomes an instrumental figure in their lives and careers.

Harry is the outsider as he isn't from our 'elevator tribe'; instead, he comes from a related industry. In Harry's story, the changes in roles and tribes highlight the similarities that exist a cross entire communities and industries. These similarities demonstrate that the strategies discussed can be applied universally.

Through these case studies, I introduce five transformational strategies that should be adopted and accompany all executives progressing through their careers, regardless of the company they serve or manage.
These strategies include:

1. Finding your mentor
2. Soliciting feedback and advice
3. Strengthening collaboration
4. Committing to a lifetime of continuous learning
5. Identifying the right coach.

Through these strategies I aim to showcase the need for partnerships and collaborations across company departments and multiple industry sectors – even the community at large. The need for executives to find a harmonious balance between their private and professional lives is highlighted. Ultimately, they should realise that every day presents an opportunity for those with a growth mindset, to seize the moment regardless of the situation, while maintaining an openness and transparency, a degree of curiosity, courage and a focus on continuous learning.

My hope in writing this book and sharing these five strategies is simple. We need a set of core behaviours embedded in our leadership DNA, which enable us to cope with a world of considerable and constant change. Advances in automation and the convergence of digital technologies, such as developments in quantum mechanics, information sciences, financial technologies and material sciences, are set to change our lives at an accelerating rate and on almost every conceivable level. Our niche industry will be no exception, and we need to provide some basic guide rails to support our leaders when faced with decisions that will influence and disrupt life and business as never before.

Without these five strategies it is likely that our leaders today, and into the future, will feel a compounding of past struggles. Working to overcome increasing levels of isolation, anxiety and fatigue while striving for connectedness. Desperate for opportunities to bond and share their troubles with family and work colleagues but denied the connection for fear of being seen as vulnerable.

Although presented here in the form of career strategies, these behaviours can stand alone to support both your professional and private lives. They can help you as an individual, whether that is as an executive, community leader or parent. Whether your challenge is engaging your client stakeholder base, growing in specific market segments or working internally to collaborate more effectively with cross-functional teams.

The characters in this book's stories will take you on a journey of learning and evolution, demonstrating through their adventures in the business and social circles how you, as an individualist – a 'solo executive' – may struggle to survive in tomorrow's world. The loneliness and isolation you may sometimes experience as an executive can be replaced by connectedness and support. The future requires that you live these strategies that promote courage and resilience. Whatever that journey is, you will need to understand the power of being vulnerable and learn to thrive through agility and continuous learning. All of which will become the new norm for coping with constant change.

In each strategy presented in this book, the lessons are crystallised by providing a 'how-to' guide that focuses purposefully on the behaviour introduced. In Chapter 16, the case study of Alan demonstrates how the five strategies can be interlinked and applied for a successful future.

Reading SOLO executives and adopting the strategies could provide enough knowledge to form the end of this journey for you. However, as recommended in Strategy 4, there will be an opportunity for continuous learning. As a bonus, in the back of this book you will find we are offering a free webinar series that steps you through the 'how to' in applying these strategies to your own life. Plus, we offer a companion webinar for learning about and dealing with change. Both are important additions for those wanting to deepen their knowledge in these vital areas.

Additionally, through our website at www.skills4executives.com you will gain access to blogs, podcasts, videos, Mastermind (F2F and virtual) workshops, online courses and coaching and mentoring programs.

I know you will enjoy the journey and look forward to discussing it with you on the other side.

Wayne Brown
1 October 2021

Prologue

Introducing Tim

Tim Henley lays motionless on his back, eyes fixed on the ceiling and sweat running off the sides of his face. Like most nights recently, he'd woken in sheer terror from the accident that had played out in his dreams. The nightmare had become a repeated event, ceasing at 3.00 am every morning, triggering an internal alarm and bringing the dream to an abrupt end.

Awake and startled, the scene halted at a specific moment, leaving Tim feeling confused and unsure about what happened next in the dream. Each morning after waking in this way, he would run through the scenario, trying to understand the meaning behind it. He worked hard to recall what was happening just before he woke.

Tim glanced across the bed. As usual, Janet was fast asleep and oblivious to the torment he was experiencing. He had considered confiding in his partner, Janet, but wasn't sure exactly what to share. He didn't know what was causing the nightmares and, more importantly, what to do about them. Was there a rational explanation? Or worse, could there be something wrong with him? Maybe with more time, the answers would present themselves. Tim decided to wait before sharing anything with Janet, at least until he had some answers himself.

Tim consoled himself momentarily by bringing his focus to the present moment – a skill he had learned at a recent mindfulness workshop. These nightmares were certainly providing ample opportunity for practice.
He grounded himself in the realisation that this was just another bad dream. But he was also aware that his mind was being used to play out a storyline as he slept. A figment of some unconscious thought process was utilising his creative imagination while he slept.

The nightmares began a few weeks ago, so Tim thought he could link their presence to a new project he had commenced a couple of months earlier. As was usual for him, Tim had taken on the project filled with confidence and he was 100 per cent committed to its success.

For the past two years, he'd proven himself as a resourceful and successful project manager. This new Sydney project was by far his most significant and challenging yet. At the handover meeting, Tim was informed about the importance of the project to the company and the focus that was needed from him to bring it to fruition. As his boss had suggested, Tim could plan on frequent visits and reporting requests from the global heads. He had, of course, been aware of the project from the sales team that was working on it and at one point, it seemed, most of the branch's management team were involved in some way. Still, their efforts had paid off when they secured the contract.

Technically, the project had included many 'firsts', both for the company and the industry. Tim's selection for the critical role of project manager had stemmed from what his boss and senior management had seen as his unique skill set. Having started in the industry as a service technician with a competitor almost seven years earlier, Tim had taken an opportunity to switch to Reldnihcs, working for 12 months as an adjuster before moving into project management. At the same time, with his company's backing, Tim had embarked on an ambitious program to achieve his PMI Project Management certification.

The project consisted of complex building structures, with more than 60 elevators and a similar number of escalators, spread across multiple banks and stages, and required a detailed project schedule. In addition, the product design called for collaboration with many parties – local and overseas suppliers, factories, external testing bodies and two separate testing towers. The research team was even engaging several universities to assist with solutions for building sway, air transfer between shafts, mass displacement and vibration calculations.

Tim had a large and dynamic group of experienced installers, for which he gave thanks every day, and a small, mostly inexperienced site management team, which he questioned just as regularly.

The project was stretching Tim's capabilities; however, he remained fully committed, putting in long days that often led to long nights. He consoled himself that this was a short-term issue until the project was stabilised and everyone was familiar with the main contractor's way of working. Although none of this was helped by the building's owner deciding to set up shop on the job site. This decision resulted in what seemed to be constant and increasingly outlandish demands, the least of which were daily meetings and impromptu intra-day safety walks through the jobsite to identify and correct potential hazards.

As usual on these projects, storage space was at a premium and required the use of an offsite warehouse, with after-hours site deliveries and materials hoisting booked for the early hours of the new day – typically between 2am and 4am. These issues were not insurmountable but required careful planning and came at a financial cost that wasn't budgeted for. Tim was not complaining, however, as he relished a good challenge.

Having built a reputation for finding ways to make money through actively pursuing change orders and variations to the contract's scope, he saw this as a means of demonstrating that talent.

There was something else, however, that was overshadowing this challenge. To date – in the first two months of the project – everything has been manageable, but deep down, something more perplexing is causing Tim's nightmares.

Take the journey through the following chapters as Tim learns, grows personally and professionally, developing his leadership capabilities and business acumen along the way.

Introducing Maddie

Sitting motionless in her office chair, eyes closed, listening to the sound of waves lapping at the shoreline, Maddie's tight facial features and slight smile are typical of her body language.

Relaxed and fully present, Maddie reflects on an unsolicited phone call she received three years earlier from her Melbourne branch manager at TYSO Elevators. The call led Maddie to accept the role of branch service manager, along with the challenges it presented. Challenges that both parties knew she was well suited to handle.

The managers' trust in her abilities at that time was very flattering and, more importantly, provided the chance for Maddie to return to the workforce in a new role after a one-year absence. During those 12 months, she had given birth to her son, Alastair, and since then had worked tirelessly to establish daily childcare routines and garner her mother's support to assist in managing this process. Although, to be fair, it was more a case of Maddie putting boundaries around an insistent grandmother and aspiring full-time, live-in caregiver who eagerly waited for opportunities to spoil her first grandchild. Therefore, Maddie felt comfortable and ready to return to work. Perhaps, she pondered, she had even been a little too eager to reignite her career.

The role provided an exciting challenge, accompanied by a good salary, which Maddie felt reflected the fruits of the hard work she had put in before her pregnancy. Supported by her husband, Paul, Maddie was determined to prove herself in the male-dominated environment. Paul was a political science professor at a leading Melbourne university and his salary was sufficient to help them through that year. Still, Maddie's return to the workforce and the additional income was indeed welcome, freeing them from some of their financial pressures.

Maddie's strong performance at TYSO is appreciated, although it has come at some cost to her home life. During the first year of her return, she encountered a state-wide industry strike, requiring management to cover all emergency service breakdowns for three weeks. During this period, Maddie's customer service background proved a blessing, as she handled call after call from disgruntled customers demanding the company's immediate response and support, according to the conditions of their blue-chip service agreement.

Later, after reviewing the minimal customer fallout following the strike, the state manager made a point of personally thanking Maddie for her performance and cool head during those tough weeks. He commented to the team that they needed to keep a close eye on any competitor interest in Ms Maddie Agnes. Maddie knew the comment was just a gesture in front of the group; however, the notion sparked something that resonated with her and bolstered her confidence immeasurably.

Perhaps Maddie's clients also saw something in her refreshing, customer-centric mindset, as the following two years had been particularly lucrative for the TYSO service business. Under Maddie's watch, the portfolio had grown a resounding 57 per cent and was now the most significant service operation in the Australian organisation. The growth had come from two directions: first, the internal handover on completion of several high-profile commercial and residential installation projects. Second, they had benefited from an active campaign that Maddie had implemented to regain previously lost units to competitors. Their approach had been so successful that the method was adopted by the Asia-Pacific management team as a best practice.

During that initial phone call three years ago, the branch manager asked Maddie to commit to the role for five years. Maddie instantly agreed, knowing this period would give her ample opportunity to effect change and demonstrate her ability. Now, here she is, three years into that period and, for the first time since commencing, she is allowing her thoughts to include the future. What might she do outside of this role? She has always been ambitious but until now has not truly known what direction she wanted to move in – or even what was possible. Thanks to her people skills, Maddie manages to balance a strong performance drive with her core values.

The trust she has established with her office and field teams is visible to senior management and a significant factor that sets her apart from her peers in other departments.

Yet, she was still not clear on how to utilise this strength and decided to seek guidance from the one person who could do something about it, her boss Terry. That decision and meeting changed her life forever and led to a meeting with Alan, a senior company executive whose guidance and friendship has greatly influenced Maddie's career.

Take the journey with Maddie in the following chapters, exploring a corporate world that leads her to many extraordinary achievements. Watch Maddie grow as a leader and learn how to let go of the idea of flying 'SOLO' in chasing her career aspirations.

Introducing Harry

As Harry Bloom stands beside one of his team members, studying a revised blueprint, he reflects on his career. It seemed entirely absurd that six months ago he was chosen to head up this handpicked team of experts. They were assembled to undertake two of the most ambitious projects ever attempted by the company, and now look at what they have achieved!. The team is just weeks away from launching the first product to an eagerly waiting world, one that promises to become a technology game-changer and that his company hopes to benefit from handsomely.

At this stage in his career, Harry is conscious that time is running out. If he is to make the next and possibly final move on the corporate ladder, he will need to move soon. He switched companies five years earlier to the role of digital production manager and was promoted once since then to head of production. In both positions, Harry has proven himself by elevating the team's performance with an improved, first-pass yield and a reduction in quality issues. At the same time, the company has experienced strong sales growth, leading to increased pressure on Harry's team for higher production output.

Harry's nomination to head up this current project has been somewhat of a surprise and, if he is honest, he isn't sure whether it was a good or bad thing for his future. The role and project are vitally important for the company, and the assembled team seems to support that case. Now, with the first project, the 'Symmetric Neuron' platform nearing release ahead of schedule and under budget, Harry will surely be acknowledged as a critical factor in this success.

The other significant project, involving digital-pairing technology with a revolutionary new engineering design platform, started two months ago. It is now at least another 9–12 months away from completion, but no less critical. The success of this development will secure his company as a world leader and design technology pioneer as it leap-frogs the current use of 3D BIM technology. In the process it will help to reshape the direction of multiple industries – from building architecture through automotive development, biotech industries to almost every conceivable design application in use today. Still, apart from Harry being a natural leader of people and a good team shaper, he credits his two core strengths as being a strategist and futurist. The combination of these two traits means that he needs to have a clear, mapped-out plan for his future, and when there isn't, he feels uneasy. With only 12 months remaining on these projects, what will be next? No one has approached him about a future role, nor does he see anything opening in the areas he is best suited to or interested in.

Harry's mind is preoccupied with these thoughts when he receives a call from his father, Robert, the now-retired but astute and globally sought-after economist who hails from the prestigious London Business School. The school itself is recognised as a leading academic institution, being the alma mater of 12 Nobel Prize winners. Although retired for many years, Robert, aged 74, is still very active in research and as an international guest speaker – typically to government and academic conventions.

Most recently, Robert has been a co-presenter at the World Economic Forum in Davos, discussing the next five-year outlook for employee skill needs as businesses worldwide confronted a growing reliance on information technologies and the disruption this is bringing to data systems and business analytics.

Even though Harry respects and appreciates his father's achievements, he has worked hard to live his own life outside the shadow of his father's success. People often privately and professionally compare his life and achievements to that of his father. However, with Robert's support, Harry decided early in life to seek out his own interests.

The reason for Robert's call is a surprise, as he is seeking his son's advice – a rare occurrence, indeed. Robert is to deliver a speech in Sydney and is thinking of bringing his wife with him on the trip. Since retiring from her career as head librarian at one of Oxford University's prized libraries, Claire has become quite ill, suffering a variety of ailments. When Robert first met Claire more than 50 years ago, his typical rational demeanour melted away as he found himself entranced by her. Aside from her beauty and elegance, Claire's intelligence, linguistic abilities and quick wit endeared her to Robert, and this has continued over the years they have been together. Claire was a dedicated professional and gave everything she had in support of family and the university.

Robert's call concerns Claire's health and whether she has the strength to make the long trip. It has been an unrealised dream of Claire's to visit Australia. She often tells the story of the one missed opportunity to attend a conference of librarians 'down under' due to a then-pressing engagement at the university.

As his father speaks, Harry recalls his mother's latest test results and the advice she was given by the family doctor to get more fresh air and exercise. Not surprisingly, that advice did not include anything about a travel risk. After some brief, but friendly banter with his father, Harry is pleased that Robert has agreed to seek the advice of their doctor before suggesting the trip to Claire. Both men know what will happen once she hears the suggestion – Claire will be on that plane regardless of medical advice.

Take the journey with Harry as he makes a major career decision and, together with his wife and children, embarks on a new chapter in his life. The journey is not without twists and adventures! In the process, Harry satisfies a lifelong ambition and finds true happiness by bringing many SOLO executives with him.

Transformational Strategy 1: Finding your mentors

Growth through your own experience is often significant and lasting but going it alone is not necessarily the best approach. Leveraging support from those who have travelled your path is a smart way to learn and develop quickly.

Chapter 1: Tim trades his solo lifestyle for mentoring support

Startled by a fist pounding the table, Tim's thoughts are interrupted and now focused clearly on his surroundings. Back to the reality of this regular Monday morning coordination meeting with his site manager, Dave. Ronald, the project head of operations for the main contracting company, Laezniam, is running the meeting with his usual aggressive style. It is commonplace as this prestigious project slides slowly but surely further away from the target completion date. For 18 months now, Ronald has sat in this room, filled with project and site managers from every contracted party, hoping to breathe life into a dying corpse. Trying his best to turn around what will be his swan song to a long career and well-earned retirement at age 65.

Having joined this gathering two months earlier, Dave and Tim are still in the honeymoon phase with Ronald, but there have been times recently when they felt that period might soon be ending. With desperation written all over his face, Ronald knows better than most that in this construction game you are only ever as good as your most recent result. He is using multiple tactics to ensure that those sitting around the table understand the gravity and seriousness of the current situation.

Dave has also been around for a long time, working on project sites for 28 years, and seeing many others come and go. While he is happy with his lot in life, he often wonders whether he should have thrown his hat in the ring earlier in his career and tried to run a few smaller jobs as the project manager. Dave isn't getting any younger, and his hip is starting to cause him pain, a legacy from walking all those stairs. The vast site footprint and

110 stories of this vertical 'Goliath' are going to prove a test for those hips, that much is clear. Which is why the opportunity to be a little more office-bound is beginning to look quite appealing. As always, Dave is close friends with the building's lift drivers, which enables him to at least move around the site as quickly as possible.

However, two other factors are presently playing on Dave's mind. He has never worked with Tim Henley before this project, and although he had heard good things about Tim leading up to it, he is yet to be convinced that Tim has the project under control. He hopes that this is due to Tim being cautious and wanting to start slowly, but that needs to change soon as the installation is gaining pace, and they have many component firsts to finalise and incorporate. Dave's second concern is the installation subcontractor they engaged to support their installers. He has worked with several of this company's supervisors on previous projects, and they know their stuff, but there is something about a handful of the crew that makes him feel uncomfortable. Over the years, Dave has learned to trust his gut instinct and right now, his gut isn't feeling so great. He can't put a finger on exactly what is bothering him about this crew so he resolves to keep a close eye on them.

'This main contractor is crazy,' Dave whispers as he leans in close to Tim. Never in Dave's career has he met with someone so obsessed with details and safety. Ronald's obsession is beginning to cause significant issues – not because of safety concerns, but rather because of the constant barrage of daily (two-hourly!) safety walks he is insisting on. These are mandatory, and it's putting pressure on Dave's ability to adequately cover the entire site and meet with his installation crews. At present, the five teams, are stationed in shafts spread across the site. The number of crews will grow to eight in the coming months as access to the escalator pits open. Plus, the first bank of four shafts, housing their prized 10-metres-per-second units are in planning right now and commanding a lot of Dave's input.

'Tim, one solution would be to appoint a safety officer to our team before the project starts to suffer,' Dave says. 'Not to mention my hip, which is already demanding an hour's soaking in the hot tub every evening,' he thinks. The two men look thoughtful and after careful consideration, Tim agrees and wonders whether one of his other team members could pick up the safety role. After all, the project is already under severe financial pressure, and one extra headcount wouldn't be an easy matter to get approval for.

Tim ponders his options – Robert, the draftsman, has been with Reldnihcs for several years and knows his stuff when it comes to elevator and escalator design. Still, he is not a 'go-to-site' guy for anything operational. Then there is Barry, the site administrator. Barry is responsible for keeping the mountain of paperwork under control. He works closely with Reldnihcs' branch office and the main contractor's finance team on all matters related to progress claims, document submissions, change requests and so forth. To date, Barry has had his work cut out for him and seems to be barely coping. He is working long hours. Tim has yet to arrive at the site office before Barry, and very seldom leaves after him in the evening.

That leaves only Jennifer, the media and communications intern. Jennifer is onsite three days a week – on loan as such – mainly due to the size and importance of this project for the company. She is really over-qualified to be an intern. Having decided to change careers in her mid-30s, she is shifting from her role as a reporter for one of the leading Australian news outlets to a communications role. Unlike in her reporting career, this current role enables Jennifer to do what she loves – researching and writing about significant events while far removed from the daily pressures of news deadlines or the travel insanity that dictated her work in the past. It was her husband who heard about this position and who used his influence to help Jennifer secure the role. He has been patient about her hardly being home since their marriage 10 years earlier, and when she is home, it seemed she is always working on her next big story.

'Dave,' Tim says, 'I'm considering something from left field. Could Jennifer be a possible solution to your time pressure and our site's safety needs? Could she be an option for this role?' Given her lack of experience on construction sites, they discuss whether she would even be interested. Both agree that they need more time to think it through.

Tim is also feeling uneasy. From an external perspective, the project is running smoothly – they are close to the targets shown on the installation schedule, with no significant product approval or production delays. The architect seems happy with the cabin finishes and landing fixture samples. The consultant has conducted the initial equipment inspections in their factory and has signed off on the progress. There are also no significant cost overruns at this early stage. However, Tim is struggling to settle into his typical routine due to the distractions – small niggling issues – that continue to surface.

With only Dave and himself as operationally capable, it means Tim is constantly running errands to keep the main contractor's team at bay and semi-happy. At one point he wondered whether these requests weren't part of a bigger plan by the main contractor to find weaknesses in all subcontractors that they could later exploit and use to divert the blame from themselves for any progress delays. But one of the things Tim is good at is understanding how to play this game and manage the tricks and tactics of his opponents – in this case, the main contractor.

As is Tim's habit, he's developed his project's progress assessment criteria. This is a simple checklist stepping through a range of critical considerations for the project and, where necessary, is modified to accommodate special activities. Tim insists on reviewing the checklist at several points during the project, and the first review for this project is only two days away – the 100-day milestone. Tim considers this milestone so crucial that he is insisting on stopping work for two hours in the morning and bringing the entire site team together to reflect on their progress, considering what is going well, what else needs to happen and what needs to be stopped. It typically takes only a short time for everyone to open up and start talking. As is often the case, his job as coordinator is tested with the need to control the team's enthusiasm. This week he has been priming his site team on what to expect and how to support the event by capturing what will be invaluable feedback and input.

Tim reflects momentarily on the past couple of months since they arrived on site to set up their office and storage areas. There were the usual feelings of excitement and anticipation of working together and setting up the equipment and materials that would support them through the next two years. There were many discussions and jokes about the journey that lay ahead and potential challenges, and notably, at no time was there any negative talk or apparent signs of a looming disaster.

At that stage, the Reldnihcs team had already been together for several weeks offsite, preparing documents, working with the different entities involved with product design and development, as well as with the factories and local authorities, and selecting the subcontractors. Overall, so far so good, Tim concluded. It is time now to start refininghis plans for the next three months and beyond. The thought of the big picture hasn't escaped him. This picture is the promise of a successful project and thenext step in his career.

This project, however, is demanding more of his time than he expected. Tim pauses at the realisation that it has been consuming all his time and energy lately. Not so useful for career planning – it feels like the success of this project might determine his future, and that is something too unpredictable for his liking.

It's evening and Tim goes for a run, passing through suburban streets lined with large overhanging trees that partially served to hide the enormous houses behind them. He reaches Taronga Zoo, his halfway point and the five-kilometre mark. This area is among his favourites in all of Sydney, and he has long dreamed of owning and renovating one of the old homesites.

On this night, however, the houses slip by without acknowledgement, his thoughts consumed by the future and what he could do to influence it.

As he turns into his street, a sudden sense of darkness comes over Tim, and his emotions turn to fear and sadness. He is dreading the nights far more than his daily schedule – these nightmares are starting to affect my personal life with Janet, he thinks.

Tim and Janet have been together for six years and are able to read each other's signals quite well. Tim knows that Janet has been worried for some time about the changes she's noticing in his behaviour but he hasn't found the right opportunity to sit down with her to discuss it. Janet has mentioned to Tim that he seems so preoccupied lately that it is almost impossible to have a normal chat for fear of upsetting him and making him angry. Janet is right to be concerned, and Tim needs to find a way to have that discussion. He decides then that tonight will be the night.

Tim arrives at the apartment complex, sweating and breathing heavily. It's clear that he needs more exercise, and he makes a mental note to review his schedule first thing tomorrow, to find a way to make that possible. While he is riding up in the lift, his mind drifts back to the emotions he felt while running. What was going on in his head? As he opens the apartment door, Tim is surprised to see Janet has already paved the way for their discussion. Soft lights and relaxing music, a bottle of his favourite red wine and a light snack are waiting. Tim remembers why they are together and are so deeply in love. Ignoring his smelly wet clothing, he goes to her and hugs her tightly for what must seem like an eternity to Janet, who has just come out of the shower. Still, she makes no effort to free herself from Tim's grip, instead gently guiding him towards the shower and gesturing that he should freshen up before coming to join her.

The night proves to be one of the best in their relationship for a long time. They talk for hours, reliving their past, taking about the future. Most importantly, they discuss the problems Tim is experiencing, including the nightmares. Janet is an accountant, not a psychologist but she knows Tim and understands how to be there for him. She is genuinely empathetic by nature, which serves particularly well this evening, as Tim reveals the story of the past few months. When they conclude their chat both are grateful to have such a loving and considerate relationship.

Tim knows his recent behaviour has been out of character, and that much of it can be attributed to his job. Therefore he sees it as a short-term problem – surely it'll be just a little bit longer before they turned the corner with this project? He prays for everything to return to normal. Tim genuinely feels sorry and apologises to Janet as sincerely as he can. After all, he loves her dearly and wants nothing more than to marry her and start a family. However, his grand plan of proposing once the project is bedded down at the end of the year is beginning to look doubtful. On top of that, he is still waking every morning at 3am from his recurring nightmare.

Sitting on the bus to the construction site, Tim reflects on his discussion with Janet. Last night they decided together that if the nightmares persist much longer, they will seek professional help. Tim considers speaking with his parents about his mental health but quickly dismisses the idea as too personal. He would feel more comfortable speaking with a stranger than divulging signs of weakness to his family. After all, his father is a leading heart surgeon and his mother a successful business owner running one of Sydney's leading fashion boutiques in Mosman. Perhaps he can open up to his twin sister, Rachelle? Rachelle is close to Janet, and the three of them have a great relationship. Rachelle is completing her postgraduate studies in law and economics at Sydney University and has access to professionals who may be able to shed some light on Tim's woes. At the very least, it seems worth a try. This idea of airing his troubles seems to lift some of the burden he has been carrying by himself until now.

As he stares out of the window of the bus, Tim can hear sirens in the background but can't work out the direction they are coming from. Still some 10 minutes before his stop, and due to the heavy morning traffic, it could be another 15–20 minutes. He is enjoying this time alone, thinking about the conversation with Janet and the persistent nightmare, which again woken him at 3am this morning. Tim thinks about how he admires Janet's ability to listen, and wishes he could develop this skill.

The blaring sirens are growing louder and appear to be heading towards them. Tim overhears someone on the bus telling their companion that the reason for the heavy traffic is the chaos caused by a fire. They are watching a live news report on their phone. It seems the fire is related to a new construction site – his construction site! As the realisation hits him, Tim's mind starts racing. He quickly opens his phone and searches for news. Sure enough, there it is: his building is engulfed with thick black smoke billowing from the top, as though coming from a tall chimney stack. The video footage on the news website doesn't provide much detail and it is hard to gauge the seriousness of the fire.

The resulting traffic jam is suddenly making this journey unbearable, so Tim readies himself to disembark at the approaching stop. He decides to take the rest of the trip on foot. The Law of Attraction at play again, he thinks with a wry smile, remembering his mental note at the end of last night's run – check the schedule this morning and find time to squeeze in more exercise. He has studied this topic recently and has notice how often his thoughts lead to something similar occurring. For the briefest moment, he forgets about the fire and welcomes the opportunity for some unexpected exercise.

Hopping off the bus, Tim starts walking as fast as he can through back streets, looking for short cuts to reach his destination as quickly as possible. Rounding the final corner to the site, Tim has his first clear view of the fire, and he goes pale as the blood drains from his face. Smoke is streaming from the top of the building, and he can now see flames on the upper levels. He starts running towards the burning building, dodging and pushing people out of the way. He is breathless by the time he reaches the police cordon.

The entire perimeter seems to be surrounded by firefighters and their trucks. Police officers are everywhere, sealing off the entrances and moving people away to ensure that access is unobstructed for the other emergency services that may be arriving. Tim fights his way to the front and shows his site-access badge, explaining his need to get on site and check the whereabouts of his team. Unfortunately, the police officer is not helpful, stating that only emergency services will be allowed to enter the site today.

Tim turns his focus to his phone just as an incoming call lights up the screen – it's Dave. Dave provides a quick update, advising he is onsite and confirming the safety of their entire team. The early report is that a welder caused the fire on one of the higher levels, with some of the hot slag igniting rubbish nearby. The fact that the upper floors are quite open means that the wind is fanning the flames and creating a challenge for the firefighters who are working their way up to the top through the internal staircase. It seems that no human life is at risk, but nonetheless this is a real wake-up call.

All members of the five installation crews are assembled at one of the three sections of the site, which is isolated from the trouble. 'We have reported to the section's fire warden and confirmed that the entire Reldnihcs team is accounted for and waiting together. We're now waiting for the all-clear from the emergency services before proceeding to survey the work areas closest to the fire, assessing any damage and the impact from the fire,' Dave says. How long they need wait isn't apparent yet but based on what Dave says and Tim can see unfolding in front of him, the flames appear to be growing not reducing. They estimate that it could be at least several hours, if at all today.

'Dave, I know you have been pushing for the additional safety person and I haven't acted on it quickly enough. Although the fire wasn't associated with our team, it is still a wake-up call and we need to get the issue addressed and a solution in place as soon as possible,' Tim says. He apologises for having dragged this decision on for too long. The only immediate solution he can think of is to ask Jennifer to take on a dual role and implement a more stringent set of procedures for their site works and the surrounding environment. These procedures should include a review of training and work practices, the use of Safe Work Method Statements and Job Hazard Analysis, among other smaller details. He intends to speak with Jennifer later in the day and see how she feels about the idea before moving forward.

During this phone discussion Tim continues walking around the site perimeter, heading in the general direction of the gathered crews. As he walks over, an idea comes to him about using this time to have their scheduled 100-day meeting with everyone already together. It will be one day early, but it seems a like good time, provided he can find a way in, as he knows the team won't be permitted to leave the site. Reaching the main truck entrance, he can see many workers standing in groups. It's clear that this area is one of the designated assembly points. It's also surprisingly easy, Tim discovers, to walk straight onto the site, as the security guards are preoccupied with helping the safety reps maintain some level of order with the growing number of workers arriving. Due to the noise and the number of people, the setting isn't going to be ideal for their meeting, but it is worth a try. At the very least, they can discuss safety and any issues that need immediate attention.

Upon reaching his team, Tim goes directly to his installers, checking all are safe and okay. While mingling, he notices that a couple of the subcontractors are not wearing their full Personal Protective Equipment (PPE) attire, and he makes a mental note to follow up on this later. Once he reaches Dave, they shake hands, Tim thanking him for bringing the teams safely out of the building and commending Dave on his leadership. They speak briefly about the idea of engaging Jennifer, and while Dave still has some doubts about her experience, he also can't see many other options.

Together, Tim and Dave scan the grounds for a less crowded area and find a small corner of the assembly area where they can relocate the team. Tim leads the team there while Dave goes to speak with the safety warden, letting him know what they are doing and where to find them. With the warden's approval, Dave heads back to join the others.

The immediate discussion is as lively as expected, with the first 30 minutes focusing on stories from the morning's events. Dave is impressed by Tim's ability to listen and engage with the team. It is clear that this isn't his first time facilitating such a discussion. Eventually, when it seems that the conversation has run its course, Tim moves the topic towards the project and three core questions: what is working well, what else do they need to do and what should they stop doing?

For the next two hours, everyone chats and toys with ideas about how to improve the overall installation process on this site – discussing topics such as equipment deliveries and placement, favourable unloading and cranage times, storage constraints and options for sharing of labour resources between the crews. Even the pros and cons of establishing a dedicated equipment management team responsible for deliveries, cranage, onsite and offsite storage, equipment preparation and distribution, guide-rail prep and door-frame assembly. Together with several other useful suggestions, the group identifies time-saving approaches that are immediately implementable and will enable Dave and the leading hands to focus on their main activities. Overall, both Tim and Dave feel hugely satisfied after the exercise and can see that the team also appreciates the opportunity to offer their input towards making the project successful.

Around 1.30 pm in the afternoon, the siren sounds and the all-clear is given to move back into the building for an initial damage assessment. Tim calls Jennifer and asks her to join them. Now that the teams are returning to the site, he doesn't want to waste any further time, and motions for Jennifer to join him as they head offsite to grab a coffee and wait for the crew's feedback on the site situation. Aside from the safety officer role, Tim wants to discuss the release of the communications related to the morning fire. During the impromptu morning meeting, Tim is happy to see Jennifer also providing input, and the group seems to have accepted her as one of the team. It is an essential ingredient and positions Tim well for the ensuing conversation.

It takes a full two weeks before everything is in place and to reach the point at which both Tim and Dave feel confident that Jennifer is in control of safety on the site. During that time, the management team has collectively given Jennifer an induction into her expanded responsibilities and have established, together with the installers and adjusters, safety protocols that will be adhered to for the remainder of the project. One initiative that comes directly from Jennifer is the idea of each crew sending through to Jennifer a standard series of pictures from the site, at the beginning of each morning's shift. These images will serve to demonstrate that the teams are fully kitted-up with their PPE, that the crews have discussed the day's work schedule and that they have reviewed associated Safe Work Methods Statements and have prepared any Job Hazard Analysis requirements. The team is now communicating and performing effectively.

Since their initial discussion several weeks ago and the fire at the construction site, Tim and Janet have had several lengthy discussions about Tim's nightmares and, as agreed, they have introduced Tim's sister Rachelle to the problem. Rachelle was quite surprised to learn about the nightmares. As twins they have always shared a special connection, and yet until now Tim has given her no indication of the problem he has been hiding for so long.

Naturally, Rachelle is pleased that they have chosen to confide in her. She agrees immediately to seek counsel from some professionals within her faculty or broader network if needed.

Having shared his feelings with Janet and now Rachelle, Tim is feeling somewhat relieved in the knowledge that this burden may soon be gone.

'Now, to start addressing another issue that is frequently on my mind,' he thinks, 'My career.'

Tim is getting the sense that his work project is coming under control. Seizing the opportunity, he has delayed his arrival on site and makes an unscheduled stop at the branch office to see his boss. Usually they schedule their face-to-face project reviews for a half-day once every second month, unless something urgent needs to be addressed. So, when Nathan sees Tim wandering down the corridor, speaking with different people and heading his direction, he is surprised. Their next face-to face meeting is not due for two weeks. The last time they met was shortly after the fire, when Tim briefed him on the situation and his plans regarding improved safety measures.

While Nathan is Tim's immediate boss, he is also the only person in the company Tim is close enough with to discuss this sensitive topic. Nathan has always been Tim's go-to guy and is the reason for his appointment to this project. He respects Nathan and knows that his boss has been through many challenges of his own during his career and has survived them, so Tim reasons that he is the right person to listen and offer guidance in this matter. Tim has rehearsed the conversation he wants to have several times before arriving at the office, and is still somewhat apprehensive about how to launch into it. He hopes that he is making the right decision and that Nathan won't think him too forward or aggressive in his approach. He also worries that Nathan might tell him that he can't help.

Tim knocks on the door and Nathan ushers him in, inviting Tim to sit. They exchange pleasantries and Tim finds the courage to bring up the reason for his visit. Nathan is clearly relieved that it is about Tim's future rather than a resignation. To lose Tim with this major project in full swing would certainly put immense pressure on Nathan and bring unwanted focus on his operation. As Tim speaks, Nathan leans in and listens intently. Tim thinks to himself that Nathan and Janet have a lot in common. Carefully laying all his thoughts on the table, Tim pauses to give Nathan the opportunity to digest this information and respond.

Great advice often comes when you least expect it, and you need to be ready to receive that advice or you may miss it entirely. In Tim's case, however, he is hopeful and ready, albeit not knowing exactly what to expect. Still, as he has hoped, it is immediately evident that Nathan won't disappoint. Nathan shares a secret about many successful people:

> *They don't do it all by themselves. It can be a very lonely world for those who go it alone and an even more solitary world when they inevitably fail. In contrast, most successful people have a team of supporters at work and in their personal lives.*

Nathan continues and names a few well-known gurus in leadership and business, both in Australia and abroad. To illustrate the point, he explains that the path these gurus choose and their subsequent success is as much about having the right team as it is about the leader's competence and skills. Tim reflects on a conversation with his mother some time back when they were discussing what it takes to be successful in business. Her advice then was much the same as Nathan is sharing right now. Successful people surround themselves with successful people, and they build a team of experts around them that can bring value in the ways and areas the leader may not be able to.

Their unscheduled meeting lasts a full hour, and Tim thanks Nathan repeatedly for his insights and tolerance while listening to his career wish list. As a closing suggestion, Nathan provides a lasting and insightful comment:

> *Many leaders today have a team of senior mentors within and outside the organisation who they confer with regularly. Typically, these mentors are experienced leaders themselves and willing to share their knowledge for the price of a coffee. Mentors come in all shapes and sizes, and can support you in business or your personal life.*

Nathan shares details about his 'group of three', who have guided him for many years on business, personal finance and fitness. Tim listens in wonderment, trying to understand why he hasn't even considered this angle before now. Nathan picks up the phone and makes a call to Jim

Wallace, his business mentor and good friend. Nathan asks Jim if he knows anyone willing to mentor a young, bright future CEO from their organisation. Jim promises to make some inquiries and call him back within the week. Tim is excited and his mind is racing. How has he been so blind not to realise this himself? The challenge now is to capitalise on this wealth of new knowledge immediately.

Leaving Nathan's office, Tim pauses and says, 'Thanks, Nathan. I have just realised that you are always playing the role of my mentor and I appreciate that immensely. I'll act on your suggestions immediately.' As the bus ferries him to the job site, he sends Janet a short but excited message: 'Great meeting with Nathan. Will discuss more tonight. Very excited! By the time he reaches the site, he has already mapped out in his notebook two pages of possible actions. As he enters the site office, Tim is still smiling to himself. Only a few weeks earlier, it seemed his world was about to collapse around him, and he was unclear about his future. Thanks to a series of events, he is now feeling confident and back in control of his life. More importantly, he has just mapped out a quick strategy, which he senses is the beginning of something bigger than he has dared to dream of before now. Among the actions in his notes, Tim has heavily underlined, 'Find more mentors!'

In their meeting Nathan suggested to Tim that he needs to find people he is comfortable sharing with and being open about his future – at both the career and personal levels. Now, sitting at his desk and looking over the notes he has written on the bus, he realises that Nathan has in fact been acting informally as his mentor. Tim decides to start searching for dedicated mentors and is already clear on the first area to focus on. Delaying any search for business guidance until he hears back from Nathan's mentor, Jim, he moves to the second most pressing area of need: a more profound, broader knowledge of financial matters. Given that Janet is an accountant, Tim has shied away from speaking about money in the past for fear of seeming incompetent. He knows his contribution to planning their financial future has been inadequate.

Tim opens his laptop and starts searching the sites Nathan suggested. He is also considering those within his network who might be able to begin the process for him. After 30 minutes, Tim sits up in his chair and stretches his arms and back with a sense of satisfaction. He has successfully narrowed his search to three sites and has added two connections he could approach. One is a friend, the other a senior colleague. He reflects on his mentoring list one more time before heading over to the construction site for afternoon inspections and again, is smiling broadly.

Suddenly he doesn't feel alone and isolated from the world, fearful of the night or tomorrow. For the first time in what seems like many months, Tim sleeps through the night, free of nightmares.

Chapter 2: Maddie secures a career mentor

Maddie is sitting with her eyes closed, headphones covering her ears. It's her lunch break and she is listening to meditative, relaxing music on her phone, having finished her lunch quickly so she can enjoy a part of her day she always looks forward to. It's her secret to recharging in the middle of the day.

Maddie's life is probably no different to that of many other businesspeople with family responsibilities. She starts each day with the alarm set at 5.30 am, first preparing herself mentally by reciting her mantra: 'Another beautiful day full of opportunities,' and by reflecting on five things she is grateful for in her life:

1. Her religious beliefs
2. A healthy, loving family
3. The careers she and her husband enjoy
4. The financial security they have achieved
5. The lifestyle they are blessed with.

Together with a short meditation session, this usually takes Maddie 15–20 minutes but is worth the investment of time because it helps her to set up her day perfectly. A quick shower and preparation meant she is preparing breakfast for three by 6.30 am at the very latest. The other family members usually begin to stir around that time. Her son, Alastair, comes to greet her in the kitchen, followed, most often by her husband, political sciences professor Paul Agnes. By 7.15 am the entire family will be rushing out the door, albeit in different directions. Paul heads to the Metro station, bound for his university. At the same time, Maddie is buckling Alastair into the child seat of their Lexus and drops him off at kindergarten before reaching her office around an hour later.

That usually places Maddie exactly 15 minutes ahead of the first staff member's arrival. During that 15 minutes she has time to open her laptop, take a brisk walk around the office to check the 6S quality status of desks and general areas, review her daily task list, which always includes the maintenance schedule, and to check in with the call centre for an update on any leftover issues from last night. Maddie has practised this routine since returning from maternity leave three years ago, and it is so well rehearsed and intrinsic to her day that missing even one of those steps tends to upset the rest of her day.

By 8.30am Maddie puts in a call to the technician on after-hours duty, to chat about the previous night's calls and anything that needs to be attended to during the day. On some occasions, when a unit has been shut down overnight, her second call is to notify the customer and assure them she is working on resolving the problem and will reconnect a little later that morning with details on the actions being taken. Her customers love Maddie's efficiency and professionalism, and it is rare for any customer complaint to filter beyond her level.

Today, Maddie's morning produces nothing unexpected or particularly troubling, and so she is able to take the opportunity to relax deeply. Her office team enjoys working with her and are appreciative of her lunchtime refresher sessions, as it means their afternoon is likely to be filled with fun moments. Maddie has a reputation for singing when she's happy, and her calming demeanour, together with frequent impromptu coaching and feedback sessions, makes the office a popular place to work.

As she sits in silence, Maddie's thoughts drift to her career and what her future direction might be. In recent times she has been considering her career and aspirations, thinking about her next possible move.

The challenge is that, as the Melbourne service department manager, she needs to either 'move' sideways into another field operations department, to broaden her knowledge, or to relocate to a new branch for the opportunity of a promotion. There are pros and cons to both. For one, she loves where they live and Paul is enjoying his job at the university. There's no indication of her boss moving on anytime in the foreseeable future, so to get a role of branch manager Maddie would need to relocate to a different city, or even a different state.

Maybe the better option, at least for the moment, is to pursue an opportunity as an installation sales manager or installation operations manager. Her background suggests she may be better suited to the sales role; however, she has often considered what she might do differently in an operations role to bridge the worsening divide between these three functions. The New Installation Operations manager, Barry Wolanski, is often heard shouting into the phone, or to anyone who will listen, about the latest challenge he is facing in that role. It is possible that these challenges stem from his clients, subcontractor teams or his suppliers, or any number of problems Barry claims sales has caused by accepting a contract with atrocious conditions.

As is common within the industry, Maddie and Barry have had their moments of conflict. The handover process when an installation project closes, and the responsibility for maintaining those new elevators or escalators, is transferred to the service department, and this often comes with challenges. In this industry, producing the finished product is not like when an automobile rolls off a factory production line. Every elevator installation project site is unique and is built from below the ground up. In the case of the elevator product, the components themselves (control systems, machine, rails, ropes, cabin, doors, shaft and pit equipment, landing and car fixtures, electrical cabling and all the small associated pieces) come as separate packages and, in many instances, from multiple supply sources. Most often, the components are assembled for the first time into a complete unit on that job site. Therefore, the site's environment and the workings of many other contractors who fall outside the control of the installation project manager play a very influential role in the success of that finished product.

Several other factors also influence the handover process. The sales-installation contract requires completion of the installation within a nominated timeframe. Access to the site and commencement of the installation work are dependent on the builder providing a waterproof elevator shaft and machine room and, ideally, with three-phase power available. The likelihood of this occurring as scheduled are usually slim, and even less so within the required construction tolerances. As a result, program compression is standard, meaning there is less time for the site crews to do what they must do. On top of this, the industry provides a warranty, sometimes referred to as 'free maintenance', since the service department receives little to no funds to maintain the units during that defects- liability period. This period commences upon completion of the installation and can stretch anywhere from one to three years. The first 12 months of operation tend to be a settling-in period for this newly assembled equipment. Therefore, the need for regular adjustment and chances of the component failure are high. The most obvious areas where failures occur are around the mechanical moving parts such as the landing and car doors, which open and close with every start and are subject to external influences such as being blocked or, worse, being knocked and interfered with by users.

The industry has worked hard to improve the entire installation process as it is the pivotal point in the value chain. High-value installation projects with small margins and comparatively high-risk contracts often attract a lot of fanfare but compare less favourably to the more lucrative and stable service operation. Getting the process wrong can have a great effect on the overall bottom-line result. Even worse, if the project is not installed and finished off properly, the pain is felt in the service operation, and the rectification costs can escalate.

So, while Maddie has learned to deal with Barry's ways and has established a reasonable working relationship, she still believes that the process can be handled differently. Therefore, she sees this as an opportunity to test herself and make a significant difference to the Melbourne operations. She has heard whispers that Barry might be moving on, and she has decided to approach her boss, Terry Ranger, with her ideas. Terry is a seasoned veteran in the industry with a strong personality – he is a 'no-fuss', straight-talking kind of guy, a bit rough around the edges, who doesn't pull any punches. Terry either likes you or he doesn't, and there seems to be no grey area in between. People often joke that even the strong union officials have their work cut out dealing with Terry if they manage to upset him. Fortunately for Maddie, she managed to impress Terry from day one, unlike some of the others under his watch. Her ability to manage people has been among the best he had seen and her decision to return to the company after 12 months of maternity leave has proven to be beneficial for both Terry and the company.

Maddie's call comes as a pleasant interruption to Terry's busy schedule, and he agrees to make room in his day for a chat. It isn't the first time this has occurred, as Maddie is ambitious and often approaches him with her questions and ideas. Still, he likes her and the opportunity to offer some guidance is a pleasure.

As usual, Maddie arrives punctually and knocks on Terry's door at precisely 3pm, as agreed. Terry is on the phone but motions for her to enter and have a seat. As soon as Terry finishes his call and looks up, Maddie starts speaking and unloading her ideas.

'Terry, I've been giving a lot of thought to my future, as you know, and I've decided on a couple of things that I'd like to run by you for feedback, please. The first is that I feel, at this point in my working life, I would benefit greatly from having a mentor. Someone senior within the organisation who has worked their way through the business and can offer guidance and become a sounding board for my thoughts. I'm aware that our company has a mentoring program and so I would like to know whether it's possible to apply.'

Terry listens intently and is once again impressed by Maddie's willingness to improve herself and put forward possible solutions rather than solely unload her problems. It is a rare trait among her peers, who mostly come to Terry to air their grievances.

Without pausing for a response, Maddie moves to the second topic.

'I know that when you offered me this service role, you asked that I stay for at least five years. The first three years have now passed, and the department is in good shape. Our projection for the remainder of this fiscal period is well above budget, and we have embarked on a couple of new initiatives that should dramatically reduce our G&A expenses even further. I'm enjoying the role and have a great team, so everything is in order. But as you know, I'm ambitious and like to seek out challenges where I believe I can bring something new and different to the game, which brings me to my point. I've heard a whisper that Barry might be moving on and I would like an opportunity to take on that position. It's no secret that Barry has issues with many of his peers, his team and his suppliers and, not to bad-mouth the guy because I know it's a tough job, but I also believe it doesn't have to be this way. I'd love the chance to show that it can be handled differently.'

This comes from left field for Terry, as he until now he has not considered Maddie for this position. Her intel is accurate – he is working to move Barry out of the role. Terry is also considering other moves, and has considered shifting Maddie to the new installation sales manager role, but this new suggestion is immediately appealing. Indeed, it is something to think through. Terry realises he needs time to process a range of influencing factors.

Terry smiles as Maddie pauses for breath. It seems she has said what she wants Terry to hear and is now ready and eager for his response. Terry immediately picks up the phone and makes a call.

'Hello Alan, I'm calling for a favour. I have someone here that I'd like you to mentor for me, please. Don't worry about the details just yet, other than to say that you won't regret it, as the person is potentially our future boss. You're interested? Great! We'll get some information through to you and set up the first meeting formally in the system. Much appreciated, and thank you!'

Maddie knows that her mouth has been open as she sat there listening, but she now she is truly without words.

Terry looks up. 'Okay, so that was your first request dealt with.'

'That was Alan Wright, our Australian new installation vice president. As you could probably tell, Alan and I are good friends and he's one of the best mentors we have in the program.'

Maddie manages a nod. She is aware of Alan Wright's reputation and that he is highly sought after as a guest speaker at industry and commercial events. Has a vast knowledge of the industry and has an engaging and interesting style. As she contemplates the idea of him as her mentor, it seems like a dream about to come true.

'And as for your second question,' Terry says, interrupting Maddie's thoughts. 'Tell me more about your ideas about how you would approach the operations role. It tends to be a boy's game and, I must confess, I hadn't considered you for the job but I know you well enough to understand that when you are determined to achieve things, we should at least hear you out.'

Maddie is flattered. Until now she has only thought through her approach at a high level and hasn't considered how to explain the detail to Terry.

Taking a deep breath, she explains her impression of the current situation as the 'perfect storm' – it seems that everyone is at odds with each other, pulling in their own and opposite directions. As a consequence, the projects are getting caught in the middle and are suffering as a result.

Her idea is to 'calm the waters', first by focusing on the four areas that will have the most significant effect – the relationships between the sales team, the manufacturing team, suppliers and, very importantly, the installation crews, including subcontractors. She gives Terry a few more examples and concludes that her strengths are in building high-performing teams rather than destroying them. 'While I know the reputation of the construction world is as a rough industry, I am not daunted,' she says. 'I am keen to give it a shot.'

Terry agrees to give it some thought and come back to her with a response.

Instead of returning to her office, Maddie chooses to go for a walk along the river, pausing for a rare late-afternoon coffee. Her head is spinning as she thinks through the conversation with Terry and what might be to come. She is eager to contact Paul at work but knows how he frowns on this practice unless it is an emergency. Sitting in the coffee shop, she starts jotting down ideas and actions that she could begin working on as soon as they settle Alastair into bed this evening. There are so many things! She has known about the mentoring program for a couple of years but never really considered being part of it until now. Terry has provided her with a link to the program's site, where she can log in and read more about the whole process.

Racing home after collecting Alastair and, after a quick look in the refrigerator, Maddie decides that the family will eat out at the local bistro, which is only 450 metres down the road. She settles her 4-year-old to working on his STEM activities, calls and made a reservation for three, and then sits down at the computer in their study.

Scanning through the TYSO mentor site, Maddie makes notes about the critical aspects of the program and how to extract the most from the opportunity. The program brings together senior executives with nominated executive talents in a 12-month engagement, with a meeting frequency of not less than once a month. She is quick to realise that she needs to start preparing for precisely what she hopes to achieve from this valuable gift. As such, she needs greater clarity about the mentoring concept and so starts researching the topic.

Maddie can feel the excitement building inside. Just four weeks ago, when she first heard the rumour about Barry leaving and started thinking about taking on the role, she was struck by the realisation that she probably lacked the necessary skills and experience. That's when her soul-searching and pursuit of answers lead her to the idea of requesting a mentor. She had not dreamed that it would become a reality so quickly and, as a result, she now feels unprepared.

Maddie begins to pour her energies into answering a series of questions about her career aspirations over the short, medium and longer terms. She considers her personal values, potentially limiting beliefs and thinks about the realities of achieving those aspirations in the context of her family and work commitments. That much at least she is clear about, and the exercises reinforce the need for guidance. Now, the big question remains how to best utilise this opportunity. She closes her eyes for a moment and gives thanks to God for watching over her. She prays for His guidance as she sets off on this new journey.

The practice of asking powerful questions has a way of turning up unexpected and timely answers. And this is the case for Maddie as she finds multiple sites from which she is able to piece together the bare bones of her approach. From what she knows of Alan Wright's reputation, he is enthusiastic and genuinely enjoys the role he plays in helping others achieve their goals. It has been rumoured that he and his wife head to Africa for two weeks each year to serve with charity organisations. Alan is also considered an industry expert in field operations, the same field in which Maddie is now hoping to broaden her expertise. So, before their first meeting and perhaps during that meeting, Maddie resolves to ensure she:

- Provides Alan with a short dossier, including:
    - an overview of her personal and career backgrounds;

- her top five strengths, as identified through the Clifton Strengths (Rath, 2007) assessment and underlined by her personality traits;
- her career goals, leveraging the SMART template so that there is clarity in her thoughts and aspirations; and
- her values and potentially limiting beliefs she would like to address.

- Learns what she can about Alan's background, education and any common interests. She hopes this will help her to establish a close relationship with Alan and enable them to develop trust quickly.
- Prepares a series of questions related to the mentoring practice and anything Alan might expect from her during the engagement. In other words, based on Alan's experience, what are the key things Maddie needs to be doing to ensure she gains the maximum benefit from their 12 months together?
- Seeks feedback from Alan at every session, related to anything he observes that Maddie needs to address. She hopes that Alan will stretch her to operate outside of her comfort zone.
- Clarifies the preferred location, time and method for their sessions and identifies how best to submit any requested actions before each session.

When that first day arrives for her scheduled meeting with Alan, Maddie knows she will be ready and prepared to engage in the process.

Alan Wright is as eager to meet Maddie as she is him. Terry and Alan have met since their brief call phone while Maddie was in Terry's office last week. At that meeting, they discussed the mentoring assignment and what Terry believes, or hopes, Maddie could gain from it. Terry was unusually strong in his praise of Maddie, which Alan knows is uncharacteristic so, for the first time in as far back as he can remember, he sits down to do his own preparation ahead of their meeting. It doesn't take long for him to understand Terry's enthusiasm.

Maddie agrees to meet Alan at a large coffee shop for their first session, not far from the Melbourne office. Alan arrives 10 minutes early to scout out a private spot for their discussion and is surprised to find Maddie already sitting in a secluded corner with her materials placed neatly on the table. He checks his watch to confirm he isn't late, then makes his way over to introduce himself. Halfway there, Maddie spots him, smiles and stands to greet him. First impressions are lasting, and Maddie is undoubtedly succeeding in making a positive impression. As she stands, Alan notices how elegant and composed she appears. There is something entirely different and unexpected about this woman.

During the one-hour session, the two chat over an array of topics. Maddie is so engaging with her questions and conversation about Alan's background and interests that he has lost track of time. Alan is also fascinated with Maddie's preparation and believes he is about to learn equally as much from this assignment as he knows Maddie will. It is clear that Maddie is a polished, empathetic 'people person', and her eye contact, posture, facial expressions and genuine smile are infectious. By the end of the hour, Alan has barely touched on his prepared material and regular mentoring introduction, so they agree to spend another 15 minutes running through some of the program's formal requirements. Alan briefs Maddie about what to expect from the engagement and makes an offer that he has never done before on a first meeting. He tells Maddie that, in addition to the scheduled monthly sessions, he would be more than happy to receive any questions by email or phone. That way, their scheduled meetings could be more fluent and productive.

As they stand to leave, Alan looks at Maddie and asks whether she follows any influencers or thought leaders on social media. Alan himself is well-recognised, at least in Australia, as one of the thought leaders in the industry. Still, he suggests this as a powerful way to keep up to date with events and developments on a much broader level. If Maddie is willing, Alan suggests, she could search for people who are shaping their world through their expertise and try to understand the differing views and opinions. He suggests she follow these people and, for the next month, rigorously monitors their posts, even contributing to them herself. It could be her 'homework' and she could introduce those activities at their next meeting. Maddie is no stranger to social media and so this idea resonates with her. She accepts the challenge gladly. It is an area she knows she can improve in, and as Maddie walks away from the meeting, she feels pleased to have this challenge. Identifying influencers and thought leaders in her field is interesting enough, but to purposely select those in other industries is a more significant challenge.

In her preparation and research for their first meeting, Maddie read about a trap that mentees should avoid. It's not unusual for people in positions of power to manipulate the lives and careers of their subordinates, as they work to increase their influence and develop those around them in the ways that work for them. Rather, the mentor should create a strategy that fits the mentee – based on their needs, talents, skills and desires, and to stretch them outside of their comfort zone, helping create a better person rather than a clone of themselves.

Alan's homework request to Maddie suggests that he certainly isn't trying to clone himself; in fact, quite the opposite by asking her to explore as many people of interest as she desires. To understand their opinions and to engage with them. It is an interesting project, but where to start? There are so many social media channels available: YouTube, Instagram, Twitter, Facebook, LinkedIn, even blog sites and podcasts.

In the evening, Maddie speaks with another thought leader in his field, her husband. At the age of 22, Paul completed an undergraduate thesis on 'The evolution of social media and its influence on an unprepared political world'. His professor at the time was nearing retirement and hadn't fully appreciated Paul's insights, which today are playing out in front of the world through some of its most powerful leaders. In the 14 years since graduating, Paul has continued his research in this area, focusing on and publishing research papers on the topic. Then came the revelations of widespread social media manipulation that influenced the outcome of the 2016 election in the United States, which proved a turning point in his career. Overnight, Paul became a sought-after expert, making regular appearances on local, national and even international news channels. It affected his standing and popularity at his university, where he lectured in political science. Seating availability for his lectures had suddenly become a highly prized commodity, and even more senior seasoned academics began to seek out his opinion on a range of related matters. There was no question that the United States president's Twitter feeds, which were spreading globally to other leaders, continued to be an excellent ally for Paul's career. This increase in popularity coincided with Maddie's return to full-time work, so they both were swamped with work and in high demand.

Maddie now needs her celebrity husband all to herself at this moment while she explains her new assignment and seeks his guidance on how best to start. Naturally, Paul is flattered and feels his status on the home front somehow escalating. Together, they draft a list of Maddie's areas of interest in her career and personal life. Paul is surprised by how little he knows about his wife's interests lately and makes a mental note to stay more attuned and connected with her activities in the future. While there is no question about their love for each other, political events in recent years have meant Paul has plenty of distractions to occupy his thoughts. Two of the great awakenings as they prepare the list is to learn that Maddie is a Liberal Party supporter and is passionate about reading Greek philosophy.

Perhaps now is not the time to embark on a debate about these two interests, but it is something he would like to return to and discuss later.

Paul recommends that Maddie starts with LinkedIn in her search for business influencers. From here, she might branch out to Instagram and, if needed, Twitter. Most thought leaders and social media influencers operated multiple accounts on different platforms, he explains. In many instances, the value they bring is not so much from regular, short posts but through the blogs, podcasts and associations they provide. To demonstrate his point, Paul searches for Bill Gates on LinkedIn. Gates is a regular contributor to articles related to his philanthropy. He also shares lists of books he has read and found to be valuable, together with details on areas of groundbreaking scientific and medical research, in which he is in some way connected or supporting through the Gates Foundation. By following just this one person, you can be instantly introduced to multiple associated areas of interest. Continuing with the Gates example, Paul then explains how even Bill Gates follows other thought leaders and has long-established relationships with other powerful influencers. One of the most well-publicised is his friendship with Warren Buffet. Paul explains that if you have an interest in financial matters or technology, then following Bill Gates will introduce you to Warren Buffet and several current Silicon Valley company CEOs. Through this example, Maddie can see how an influencer's network expands. From the connection with Buffet, comes access to the people he associates with and follows. The theory of six degrees of separation, which states that everyone can be connected within six moves or relationships, has certainly gained momentum with this explosion in social media.

Maddie marvels at the ease with which Paul finds his way around the different platforms. They are both of the Millennial Generation and, therefore social media and smart technology are not foreign to them. Still, Paul has maintained a stronger connection through his own social media presence, with a following on Instagram of over 150 000 and 120 000 followers on Twitter. She also wonders about Alan and how he has managed the transition, being in his late 50s. Then she realises that the adage 'If you want to be successful, you need to surround yourself with and study those who are already successful', has been around a long time and she guesses that Alan is proof this practice needs to become a part of a leader's DNA.

Once she has identified and starts following several highly successful industry and non-industry influencers, Maddie is overcome with an overwhelming sense that she needs to refine her initial broad list and focus more intently on those that can bring more business-related benefits to her. Her next move is to subscribe to the key influencers' channels or posts, ensuring she is kept informed every time they publish anything – be it through books, blogs, podcasts, video or social media – wherever they may be active.

As Paul has advised, LinkedIn proves to be just the tip of the iceberg. Aside from the usual social media channels, Maddie starts to get creative, looking for book summaries on related topics, identifying podcasts and scanning for live events, webinars and so forth. Becoming a subscriber to just a handful of people has triggered an avalanche of mail to her inbox, which she hadn't anticipated. Gradually, however, she begins to find her way through the mire and enjoys the process. Podcasts can be played while driving, webinars are scheduled around other activities and, on the rare occasion an event on a topic of real interest or importance arises (most typically from someone she is following in the United States), she sets her alarm and gets up in the early hours of the morning to participate.

After two weeks, however, Maddie still hasn't completed the project assigned by Alan. So, she begins to explore deeper the idea of who these influencers or thought leaders are following. 'Everyone learns from someone else', she remembers him saying, and this is where the connections become really distracting. Maddie is now so deep into this complicated web that she feels it starting to affect her work and private life. With the weekend just around the corner, Maddie decides that she needs to dedicate some serious time to getting this whole process sorted, once and for all. Paul decides he will take Alastair for a little father–son time to a local play centre on Saturday morning and then visit the university and friends in the afternoon, so that Maddie can have some free time to create order from the chaos.

Not wanting to waste a moment, Maddie is seated behind the computer by 5.30am on Saturday morning and a long, draining 11 hours later, she has successfully researched, subscribed or unsubscribed from multiple leaders. She has also reviewed specific areas of interest that each leader is discussing and has posted comments, which she hopes might spark a response. She has refined her podcast library down to seven influencers who seem to be active in producing an episode at least bi-weekly. She has explored and, in two cases, registered for online courses. She has made a list of books or papers they have written and videos they have produced. Maddie orders several books and then settles back to summarise what she has learned from the entire exercise. Aside from feeling exhausted, she feels at peace with the knowledge that she has gained and should continue to benefit from long into the future. It is still an hour before she expects Paul and Alistair to arrive home, so she runs a hot bath, grabs her phone and headphones, and settles in for a relaxing 20-minute recharge.

As her mind drifts and her thoughts race, she is able to centre herself through meditation, focusing on how she can utilise this new practice. One thing she is sure of is that it will be instrumental in taking her to a higher level of knowledge and perhaps skill set. She is passionate about growing as a person and believes in this for her team. The combination of having Alan as her business mentor and his assigning of this one project alone is seemingly reshaping how she will approach her career. This has already helped her to see and grow way beyond her initial thinking and, so far, she has found boundless opportunities to explore new perspectives and set new horizons. Were these limitations in her thinking and behaviours that obvious to Alan from such a short meeting? It is undoubtedly a question she intends to ponder and discuss further with him.

Another thought occurs to Maddie. Could she attend a live event with one or more of these leaders? She knows that these types of influencers owe a large portion of their success and following to their willingness to appear and engage with their followers on stage. They often travel globally, and Melbourne is a destination that attracts many of them. She visualises what it would be like to sit in the same room and listen to them. To have the opportunity to meet them and establish a personal connection, face- to-face rather than virtually. It is something she resolves to explore as her very next step.

Bringing her thoughts back to the present, Maddie leaves the warmth of her bath and proceeds to get ready for the evening's activities. The calm and tranquil feeling that engulfs her at this moment is surreal and beautiful. It is as if she is floating, free of any daily distractions, gliding effortlessly around the house. An image of her father suddenly appears in her mind and she imagines his face as she remembers him before his illness. Their minds connected and she had smiled at his loving gentleness as he stared intently. At that moment, Maddie knows she needs to call her mother. She reaches for her phone and begins to scan her recently dialled numbers.

Chapter 3: Harry benefits from working with mentors

Many refer to it as the ultimate test of endurance that only the strongest and fittest can achieve: the Ironman Triathlon – a series of long-distance races comprising an ocean swim, a cycling race and a marathon run. Ironman athletes compete mostly against themselves for the sense of pride that comes with the achievement of having willed their bodies to push through the pain and mental fatigue that comes with this extreme competition. Champion ironmen typically complete the race in less than eight hours and the champion ironwomen in under nine hours. It's a feat the average person cannot imagine. Still, for a growing group of athletes, albeit a tiny minority around the world, it is their life's calling – a challenge that when conquered heralds their uniqueness and invincibility to the world.

Competing in the Ironman Triathlon, Harry can see the beach as he rounds the final buoy. Only 300 more strokes to go before he will need to start running towards his bicycle station. He feels the muscles burning in his arms and legs, having swum more than 3.5 kilometres, it is normal and expected. His build-up to the race in the past several months has been excellent. Last night, as he sat and ate his regular pre-race meal and completed his final body and equipment checks, he was confident and hopeful of achieving a personal best. This is the longest of the triathlons on his annual calendar and the only full Ironman event he plans to race this year. Harry is hoping to make it something special; that's how it had started. Over a light breakfast this morning, together with his team coach, section mentors and other club members, the coach announced, as he always does, the club's favourite for the fastest race time. For the first time, his prediction was for Harry Bloom to run a personal best time and come in ahead of his teammates. It came as a surprise as there are some extremely successful athletes in the club, but the coach saw something in Harry that inspired him to announce his favourite for the race.

Harry exits the water and immediately begins pulling on the silk tail tied to his wetsuit's zipper. He releases his arms and feels the much-needed breeze against his bare chest and tired limbs. Taking the opportunity to glance at his watch, he checks his time and vitals. Passing the water station, he snatches a cup and downs its contents without missing a stride. Harry scans the station to find his bike, gauging his performance by the number of bikes still waiting for their rider. He quickly removes the bottom half of the wetsuit, pulls on his cycling outfit, shoes and helmet from a plastic bag, fits them swiftly and mounts his ride. He pushes forward, locking his shoes onto the pedals and reaches for another drink as he passes the last drink stand. In almost in the same motion he locates, unwraps and consumes an energy bar from his supplies before standing onto the pedals and setting off for a pleasant 180-kilometre ride.

The bike race covers hills and sharp bends. Of the three legs of the triathlon, this is his least preferred. Harry's cycling mentor has devised the series of mental games that he now runs through while settling himself into the journey ahead.

The first is to pick out a competitor ahead of him and focus on chasing him down, repeating the process one after another. He also notices how beautiful the countryside looks as the sun's rays bounce off the hills and trees that line the course. 'So far so good,' he says aloud as he glances at the signal for the halfway mark. He is pleased that the hilliest portion of the ride is now behind him, although the race organisers usually sneak in one last killer hill towards the end of the race. Today Harry is feeling particularly strong and is looking forward to closing out the cycling leg and moving onto the 42-kilometre road run. He finishes off his first water bottle and reaches for the second, then finds another energy bar and devours it. The flatter section of the road provides a perfect opportunity to take in some much-needed hydration and allow his tired muscles a moment to relax. With a further two-and-a-half hours of cycling ahead, followed immediately by almost three hours of running, it is critical that he feeds his body and listens to it for any telltale signs of fatigue. Starving it now would lead to certain dehydration and a rapid decline in performance.

Looking at his watch, Harry estimates that he is on target to improve on his personal best time considerably. 'Don't get excited, just stick to your race plan, and everything will go smoothly,' he chides himself. When he once again pushes his legs to propel his bike towards the small incline ahead, his mind goes to his safe place, as he has been trainingto do. He reflects on his swim leg, recalling those moments when he felt most at ease.

Since the age of nine, Harry's parents have encouraged him to swim. First, with swimming lessons at the local club and later they would often spend a half-day over the weekend at the municipal pool to allow Harry to splash and enjoy the water. Gradually, they guided him to practise his swimming, and he found it was something that he truly enjoyed. It was not surprising, therefore, that he developed an affinity with the sport. As Harry grew, he joined the local swim club and became competitive in several strokes, with long-distance freestyle being his favourite. By age 14, Harry was the regional champion for the distances of 400 metres and 800 metres. While he enjoyed these distances, he had set his sights on tackling longer distances as his body matured and, by age 17, he swam in his first event for the 1500 metres and finished second. This greatly encouraged him and led to his commitment to adding that title to his list of victories. It wasn't long before he eclipsed this goal and became well known around the region,even attracting a gathering of supporters.

During today's swim, Harry felt quite relaxed and was fortunate to be swimming besideothers who weren't crowding him or causing him to lose the fluency of his stroke. Everyone struggles to come to terms with the waves and chop created by the thrashing of feet, which is often the most draining part of the swim. Each swimmer wants to stay as close to the inside path as possible, to take the most direct route between each buoy and reduce the distance they had to swim. For the good swimmers, the first leg is usually a sprint as they try to put distance between themselves and the crowded field. For some reason, Harry has been able to avoid many of them today, and is keen to check the recordings later to understand why it has worked out this way. He guesses that, somehow, he has been fortunate by managing to stay behind those of equal or faster speed.

Sure enough, as he nears the completion of the bike leg, Harry encounters the final hill. It is long, steep in parts and winding. The worst combination, which does not allow the racers to settle into a rhythm. The typical circuit that Harry avoids on the cycling machine at the gym. Strangely, today he still feels like he has plenty left in the tank, which after 170 kilometres and almost six hours of exercise without rest, is unusual. As a distraction to the hill, he focuses his mind on the run ahead, visualising the course and stepping through his pace plan. He knows his body is likely to hit the wall around the 28-kilometre mark; it always does. He has been working recently with a marathon mentor on ways to prepare his mind and body just before that stage. Together, they have developed a personal mantra. Harry has converted each keyword into a mini verse that he has recounted so many times that it has become internalised.

Harry's mentor filmed him over several training sessions when at his peak on different high-energy exercises. They took those short clips and aligned them with the relevant words of the mantra, thus creating Harry's inspirational video that he can visualise whenever he needs to. Most often, that is around the 27-kilometre mark.

As Harry rounds the bend, he is surprised to see the transition station one kilometre ahead. He quickly prepares for a speedy changeover from riding to running, easing himself off the seat for one last time before ditching his cycling helmet and shoes for his road runners. It feels great to be able to stand up straight and stretch his body after sitting hunched over handlebars on a narrow and uncomfortable seat, or standing semi-upright for almost five-and-a-half hours.

Snatching a drink as he makes his way out of the station and back onto the isolated road, Harry looks around to see who he might team up with for some company during the early stages of the race. In the distance, he sees a group of three runners and decides that they would be his best chance to catch without breaking from his pace plan and overall strategy. It takes a full five kilometres before Harry is able to reel in these runners and he knows that he is stretching himself a little more than agreed with his mentor for this early stage of the long run. However, he wants to test himself today, and this seems like an excellent opportunity.

So far, he has clocked two personal bests, first in the swim, where he again broke through the 60-minute 'holy grail' and finished in 59 mins and 19 secs – 14 seconds better than his previous best. Then, on the cycle, his personal best (PB) was 5 hours, 56 minutes and 23 seconds. Harry has shaved off an impressive 17 mins and 11 seconds! His personal best time in any marathon is a very credible 2 hours, 54 minutes and 28 seconds, and in a triathlon 3 hours and 12 minutes. His target in this race is to break the 3-hour mark, and he is feeling today might be the day.

Racing past the 20-kilometre marker, Harry feels his body starting to tire. His legs are aching, and his arms feel as though they have weights tied to them, but he isn't about to give up the challenge just yet. Instead, he digs deep, asking his body to do the impossible. He visualises his family, who are waiting to cheer him on at the finish line. He pictures those who may have already completed the gruelling course and are now recovering. Numerous champions are running this race today: national, European and world champions – legends from his era to the current day all of whom he idolises. Harry wonders how many of them have already finished or are pushing hard to cover their final 5 to 10-kilometre stretch. They are seasoned professionals and know what it takes to push through the pain to reach their objectives. With one-and-a-half half hours remaining, Harry also recognises the feeling he is experiencing now. He knows that he can and must endure it before he traverses the remaining distance and can begin to enjoy the enormous satisfaction of having tested himself and succeeded.

He refocuses his attention on the race and those in front of him. In the far distance, he spots what appears to be a runner wearing his club's colours. Is it possible that one of his friends is enjoying even greater success than he has so far? Harry's coach's comments from breakfast flood his mind. Being identified as the choice for today's fastest club competitor is a rare but encouraging incentive for Harry and, sensing a threat to that spurs him on. Reflecting on his pace plan and assessing the likely impact of pushing himself at this moment in the race, he sets himself the aim of closing the 500-metre gap over the next 30 minutes. With that target clearly in sight, he channels his energy and hits 'play' in his head to start his inspirational video.

As it turns out, the person he identified is not from his club, but the exercise has driven Harry to run the distance at a new personal best time and to complete the distance in under three hours. In total, his time of 9 hours, 36 minutes and 46 seconds slashes a full 30 minutes and 55 seconds off his last year's result. For a 50-year-old, non-professional in the sport, this is an incredible result. Most importantly, Harry's focused build-up to this year's event has paid off as he exceeds all his pre-race targets.

Following last year's successful race and setting PBs, Harry decided to compete for one more year and to utilise the section-mentors offered through his club. It has undoubtedly taught him a lot about the value of leveraging from those with knowledge and expertise in a chosen field. By tapping into that resource, he has been able to improve his preparation tactics, adopt additional endurance practices and develop mind-focusing techniques that he can utilise at will during difficult stages of the race.

Later, he will look back on that lesson and wonder what might have been possible had he taken this path 10 or 15 years earlier. Perhaps he would have been able to compete with his idols.

The value provided through mentorship is not new to Harry. He entered the workforce at the relatively young age of 18 as an intern, having finished high school and embarking on his engineering degree the following year. Harry chose a different trajectory to his academic parents. He enjoyed the typical teenage upbringing, with one exception: everyone knew of his parents. At school, this had often led to moments where well-intentioned teachers compared his performance with that of his acclaimed parents. As a result, Harry had felt that he was always living in their shadow. Growing up, he would often try to hide who he was when starting something new, but inevitably word got out and he was soon being compared again.

By moving in this direction, Harry had hoped to provide himself with the freedom to develop as an individual, based on his own merits. Besides, his interests had been in tinkering with electronics and understanding the latest technologies, weaving them together in the design of new products. Therefore, during his university years he had been keen to grow his knowledge about industries that supported his ambitions. The internships he undertook were with companies known as leaders in both engineering and technology. He spent his first year of his degree working in the automotive industry, his second year and third year with industry giants in the field of information technology, before accepting a position in automation as a design engineer. He shifted companies only twice more during his 27 years, into the roles of electronics manager and then digital production manager.

Mentors soon became an integral part of Harry's experience and growth in the first of these appointments. The automotive group had long run a mentoring program for those in their talent pool, and Harry's capabilities and desire to develop made him an obvious choice for inclusion into this program. The program was somewhat unique in that it tapped into internal senior executives but also leveraged external mentors such as in engineering. In that regard, they worked closely with the Royal Academy of Engineering. Having two mentors from different disciplines and focused on various aspects of his role greatly assisted Harry in striking a balance in his own perspectives.

Possibly one of the most valuable and lasting takeaways from this mentoring was Harry's understanding that every problem has a solution waiting for someone to identify. As an engineer, his mentor worked with him to understand process and structure as essential ingredients in resolving problems. From his executive mentor, he learned to consider the business aspects and the effects any solution might have on financially and operational aspects. Over the course of his career, these two lessons would support him, time and time again. As his problem-solving skills developed, so did his ability to refine his approach, eventually adding a third element into the equation: the importance of the team members in bringing additional variables into the discussion, thereby producing multiple options before deciding on the solution. As Harry polished this skill, he became the go-to guy when people needed assistance. His logical and practical outlook endeared him towards management and his colleagues.

He even took the opportunity at one time to establish a lunch-hour activity called 'Problem Corner', where individuals or groups were encouraged to think of challenging business scenarios that needed solving. The activity became quite popular among the company's budding thought leaders and some of the more liberal-minded senior executives who saw the value of such a practice. Typical of Harry's style, the activity commenced with little structure and evolved rapidly. Within the first six months, a full blueprint for running this activity as a formal program was produced. Harry established an introductory eLearning platform, facilitator guidelines, process flowcharts, standardised templates and even support videos.

The group built a database to which all submitted business problems could be registered and given a unique case number. Each problem's project files were stored and the testing process recorded as evidence that a real root cause had been identified. From this, multiple options could be tabled and trialled before settling on a final solution. The company gradually came to see the benefits of such a scheme and adopted it into the curriculum, so that all engineering and leadership personnel would participate. This later morphed into a set of company-specific, computerised business simulations. Harry being the subject expert on the topic, was asked to train a small group of facilitators who would be responsible for cascading the program across the different locations where the company operated.

More recently, Harry came to realise that the world of mentoring was starting to be turned on its head. Once the domain of the elite – those more senior and respected personnel who had years of experience, having developed through a hands-on, trial-and-error approach and often failing before succeeding in their field of expertise – the role of mentor was now expanding. Today's business transformation from rigid, top-down structures, driven by documented procedures and processes, were starting to give way to the information era, in which technology dominated and agile strategies have become the new normal. Being an experienced senior executive was no longer seen as an advantage nor a guarantee for finding a solution. Instead, the younger generation – known as 'digital natives' – were being called on to support the transformation from internal legacy data systems to the deployment of cloud-based networks. This generation is considered 'hot property' today and is often called on to enlighten their senior colleagues.

Right at this moment, there appears to be a balance in demand between the older experienced individuals and technology-centric young adults. The writing, however, is clearly visible on the wall for all who choose to read it. With each passing year, demand for youth will win over the practised, greying and hard-won experienced practitioners. The latter form of experience being substituted by machines capable of crunching data to generate predictions from which decisions will be made. As Harry considers the next five years and assesses his skills, he imagines that there might be a significant gap if he does nothing to remain current. His primary differentiator, the one thing which he has become known for –

his problem-solving skills – are hugely at risk of becoming redundant as organisations driven by artificial intelligence rely heavily on information and data analysis to guide their operations.

To this end, Harry knows in his heart that he is at a crossroads that does not favour his generation. He considers his three children and the fields they have chosen to study. Each is making the selection themselves, but each is equally influenced by their upbringing.

All three are heading in their own direction. But, as the saying goes, 'the apple doesn't fall far from the tree'. His eldest daughter, Charlotte, is following in her grandfather's footsteps, studying economics, his son, Travis, is pursuing an engineering degree and Peg is choosing to follow her mother into the world of fashion.

Were they right or wrong – who could say? Harry only hopes that they too can sense the shifting, disruptive nature of the future world and remain agile enough to flourish. The topic has plagued Harry for some time, and he decides to seek the guidance of the most pragmatic observer of current and future scenarios he knows: the renowned British economist, Mr Robert Bloom – his father.

The family has long held fast to a tradition of meeting one Sunday every month for a lunchtime get together at Harry and Sandra's home. It is an occasion which has become as much about both sets of grandparents getting to spend time with the grandchildren as it is about being a stable family unit. Like countless other times, before embarking on any attempt to garner advice from his longest-serving and most critically opinionated mentor, Harry sets about doing his preparation well in advance. He researches the latest economic information coming from the World Economic Forum and scans media reports from leading countries, making sure to include England, regardless of that country's downward slide in recent years.

Harry reads up on technology, the predictions of business into the future, even going to the extent of identifying those writers who have studied this topic at length and propose their own views about how our world might function five, 10 and 20 years from now. In the process, he thinks of a brilliant question to ask his father: 'As one of the leading economists in the world, what are the resources Robert Bloom relies most heavily on to make assumptions and predictions?' Harry concludes that if he can obtain an understanding at this level, then he might himself be able to conduct similar research and draw his own conclusions. The idea seems rational, but he checks his wording of the sentence, looking for the slightest error that might derail the conversation and set the afternoon spiralling into a heated debate.

Sunday comes and goes, and much to Harry's surprise, his father seemed distant and reluctant to share his thoughts on the subject. It was indeed an anticlimax, given the work he had put into his preparation. Still, conducting the research gave him some insight into the immediate future and again triggered a secret desire to transition his career towards becoming a professional sports and life coach.

He has thought about this idea numerous times in recent years, but this year's triathlon and his experience with the club's mentor and coaching team has rekindled that desire. He is inclined to focus on the niche sports of running; be it cross-country, short, medium or long distance, and even triathlons. He knows there are already many legends who have pursued a similar path but he has identified what he believes to be a gap. His gut tells him that there is a demand from those amateur and semi-professional athletes for coaching and mentorship. Still, at this moment, he can't see a way of taking the dream any further towards reality.

As he lays in bed on Sunday night, Harry decides to set his subconscious mind to work while sleeping, by asking it a question: 'What are the critical steps I need to take to turn my dream of coaching into a reality?'

With that thought on his mind, he tries to visualise the joy and happiness he might experience should he be able to succeed in achieving the coaching dream. He sleeps soundly and, in the morning, awakes feeling bright and ready for the week ahead.

Strange as it was, the thoughts of the night before are no longer on Harry's mind. Instead, his focus has returned to driving the current project he is leading at work to a successful conclusion.

Transformational Strategy 1: Mentorship

I propose mentorship as our first strategy, because it is perhaps the oldest and most tested resource. The practice of mentorship dates back to Greek mythology and the origins of many religions. It was introduced as a formal practice in business halfway through the 20th century and today, whether formal or informal, it is typically one of the more common ways in which we learn and develop. Despite its ubiquity, however, it is no less important than other strategies and is not standard practice in the vast majority of companies.

The traditional approach is to seek guidance and support from those who have journeyed your path before. Whether it is a colleague or senior executive, they have tended to be older and more experienced, thereby able to impart knowledge, wisdom perhaps, from their own experiences. However, while we still see this traditional role of mentor today, we are also becoming accustomed to seeing digital natives called upon to offer their expertise and guidance where technology is involved. This is a trend that will continue as the business world moves towards an information-driven, data- analysing operation.

For 'SOLO executives', finding one or more mentors to support you on your journey should be one of the first actions you take as a leader. The corporate world is a tough breeding ground and with new technology it is going to become even more so into the future. There is zero shame or weakness in acknowledging that you don't know everything.

Demonstrating a degree of vulnerability is liberating and fosters greater trust.

Five key steps to finding your mentors

1. Identify the area/s in which you could use some support.
2. Define the level of support you need in each area.
3. Consider the resources you already have available to provide this support.
4. After completing steps 1, 2 and 3, start looking at whether working with a mentor might be the answer to obtaining this additional support.
5. If the answer is yes, then seek out options within your organisation and, where necessary, search external sources online, through social media or the local community.

Choosing the right mentor depends on where you are in your life or career, and your needs. As shown in the adventures of our three characters, Tim, Maddie and Harry, who each having slightly different requirements, resulting in different selection criteria for their mentors. Tim requires guidance on his future career moves into management, plus education in finance. Maddie is seeking support in finding direction for the next leadership move in her career. Harry relies on the expertise of mentoring professionals in sports, career development and potential career transitions.

You will find on the following pages a series of powerful questions titled 'Preparatory questions before engaging with a mentor, which you can ask of yourself to help determine what you need to address or gain from your mentor, and questions you can ask of the potential mentor or influencer to ensure they align with those needs.

The final section in this strategy provides a 4-part mentoring guideline on what you can expect from the mentoring engagement: the process, the roles and the responsibilities of both parties.

Powerful questions to support Strategy 1

Learning to ask questions helps the leader and the recipient to consider their resources so they might find answers and solutions that may otherwise have escaped them – asking the right questions cannot be overstated.

Question pool 1: Ask of yourself

1. What are the expectations of my current role, and do I have the capabilities to succeed?
2. What is the direction I wish to take my career?
3. What are the barriers to achieving clarity with questions 1 and 2?
4. What are the issues currently troubling me that I'm unable to resolve?
5. How do these issues conflict with my purpose, identity and values?
6. What, if any, of my limiting beliefs drive these issues?
7. How have I experienced these issues before? What did I do to resolve them?
8. For the current issues, what have I done already to resolve them?
9. What resources do I have available that I haven't considered but would help to address the issues?
10. If I do nothing to resolve the issues, what is the worst that could happen?
11. If I were able to resolve the issues, what would be the solution?
12. If I were able to resolve the issues, what might be the future?
13. What immediate actions can I take to address the issues?
14. If I could work with a mentor for advice and guidance, how would it assist me?
15. What specific experience and capabilities should the mentor have?

16. How can I connect and learn from any influencers related to these issues?

Answering some of these questions comprehensively may require additional study. On completing your answers, you may have a sense of 'what next'? If so, it's time to move towards the solution by utilising those resources you have identified above.

Question pool 2: Ask of the mentor

(during the selection process or at the first meeting)

1. What is your experience in working with others as a mentor?
2. What are your key areas of expertise and how have you applied those in your career until now?
3. Do you follow any standard practices or processes while mentoring to monitor or measure a mentee's progress?
4. Do you have any guidelines on the role of the mentor versus the mentee?
5. Are our conversations treated as confidential or is the information shared?
6. How do you sustain the mentoring momentum after multiple sessions?
7. What are your expectations of me during and after the sessions?
8. What is your preferred way of running each session: face-to-face, in person, virtual or over the phone?
9. How long can I expect each session to be?
10. Is there any restriction on the number and frequency of sessions?
11. What is the duration of the mentoring program?
12. Is our mentoring relationship possible outside of the scheduled sessions? Can there be informal communications if needed?
13. You may ask yourself additional questions when selecting the leaders you wish to follow on social media. It's essential to be selective in determining which people you are interested in, as the practice can

consume a considerable amount of your time and provide little in return if not focused.

Question pool 3: Ask yourself

(when selecting social media influencers and thought leaders)

1. How much time do I wish to dedicate to social media activities?
2. Does this time include my social presence or just those I am following?
3. Do I have a preference or objection to any particular social media platform(s)?
4. Have I chosen leaders with a specific purpose, and what could I contribute to their discussions?
5. Have I explored who these leaders are following? Are they of interest to me?
6. Have I explored all the benefits each leader brings to the table: articles, blogs, podcasts, videos, books, courses, webinars, events, associations etc.?
7. Am I prepared to actively engage with the leader and comment on their platform?
8. If not, what is stopping me?
9. To what extent am I willing to listen and learn from the leaders I have chosen to follow?
10. Have I chosen to follow these leaders solely because they offer opinions close to my own?
11. Have I selected a balanced range of differing perspectives to stretch my thinking and help me grow?

Through the lives of Tim, Maddie and Harry, we have introduced how they are able to bring the concept of using a mentor into their lives. Below is a program overview of what you might expect when you pursue this part of the journey yourself. Think of it as a short guide on the process, roles and responsibilities for both mentor and mentee.

Introducing the three typical phases of mentoring

Mentoring is generally provided over a set period of around 12 to 24 months and should involve the following three phases.

Phase 1: Getting to know each other

Establish a relationship and build trust.
Define the process that will be followed.
State the expectations of both parties.
Formulate goals ensuring there is a means of determining they are achieved.
Clarify organisational requirements (if doing this through your company).
If required, prepare a mentoring agreement (usually a good idea).

Phase 2: Action phase

Participate in regularly scheduled meetings (one per month is a good idea).
Introduce topics to address the formulated goals.
With your mentor, jointly reflect on topics introduced.
Define the next steps and possible actions.
The mentor shares practical knowledge and experience using measures discussed in everyday work to analyse the effects of your actions.
Monitor your progress, review your goals and, where necessary, adapt them and add new topics for discussion.

Phase 3: Conclusion and outlook

Jointly evaluate and reflect on the journey and learning experience.
Discuss open points and the need for future development to sustain results.
Provide two-way feedback on the mentoring process.
Mutually agree to end the formal mentoring process.
If appropriate, discuss the informal continuation of the relationship.

Ground rules of a mentoring relationship

The mentor's role is to respond to the mentee's needs as appropriate, but there are limits and boundaries that the mentor must operate within.

Confidentiality and trust

Mentoring is a special relationship between the two individuals, based on a mutual desire for development towards formulated goals. Both parties need to be clear about the confidential nature of thc mattcrs discussed. Everything that passes between the two parties must remains confidential and should not be disclosed without the agreement of both the mentor and mentee.

Mentoring is not a performance assessment

The aim of mentoring is to assist in the development and growth of the mentee. The mentor should use any observed progress to help the mentee further develop and improve towards the achievement of their goals.

However, if the mentoring program is being conducted within the organisation, the activity and results should not provide input for any professional appraisal process, nor should it function as a method of performance assessment.

The roles and responsibilities of the mentor

Mentors make time to meet with their mentees, time they always treat with respect. In this process, mentors share informal knowledge, typically based on their own experience. In their relationship with the mentee, mentors perform the following tasks.

- Encourage mentees to reflect on their strengths and areas for development.
- Motivate mentees to develop their skills and talents.
- Support mentees actively in their careers.
- Reflect on situations and events jointly with mentees, through questions.

- Give mentees clear and specific feedback on their ideas, expectations, andattitude.
- Provide encouragement and advice to mentees during challenges.
- Share their knowledge, experience and professional history with mentees.

Here are some sample questions you might expect from your mentor during the first meeting.

- What have you done so far in your working (or private/sporting) life?
- How do you feel about your progress to date?
- What was your most significant achievement in the past year?
- What situations have you enjoyed the most?
- From what relationships have you benefited?
- In which types of situations do you learn the most?
- What has been your most significant learning experience?
- What do you care about? What motivates you?
- What frustrates you the most in this area?
- Where do you see yourself in five years?
- What should we know about each other from the start?
- What are your biggest current challenges?

The roles and responsibilities of the mentee

In a mentoring relationship, the mentee benefits from the experience of the mentor. The personal discussions also allow informal knowledge to be shared. The experience shared by the mentor improves the mentee's understanding of the situation. Reflecting on the mentor's views and standpoints opens new perspectives for the mentee.

Two characteristics of a good mentoring relationship are trust and honesty. Mentees can expect personal, constructive feedback from their mentor on their visions, values, goals, behaviours and external perceptions. As a result, mentees can enhance their profile and develop their attributes.

Mentees also receive a clearer idea of the professional path they wish to pursue. More specific goals and expectations are clarified between mentor and mentee at the start of the mentoring relationship and goal achievement is reviewed during and at the end of the mentoring process.

Mentees must be willing to reflect openly on their behaviour as part of the mentoring relationship. By doing so, they can make more effective use of their time with their mentor. In their relationship with their mentor, mentees take responsibility for proactively driving the process, which means they:

- define their topics and goals for mentoring
- organise meetings with their mentor
- prepare meeting content
- contribute their questions and experience openly
- see constructive/critical feedback as an opportunity for further development
- ask critical questions and listen actively
- speak openly to clarify potential misunderstandings in the mentoring relationship
- reflect on each meeting and complete agreed development actions
- document goals, measures and findings where appropriate (e.g. learning diary).

Transformational Strategy 2: Soliciting feedback and advice

© S4E Publishing

There is tremendous value in asking someone for feedback or advice. Not only about your performance but also on ways to improve the business from those working with you. Create trust and engagement by learning to ask and listen. It's a powerful practice for all leaders.

Chapter 4: Harry learns to trust in the advice and feedback he receives

'It's a great idea, Robert, and will do both of you a world of good. Getting out of London, this polluted city, to the comparatively fresh clean air of Sydney will be fantastic for your health. Likely the only risk will be that your heavily soiled lungs will struggle to accommodate that high oxygen intake.'

This is the response of Jonathan Wilts, the family's doctor and head of the hospital's outpatients department.

'And you are sure that the long flight won't be too taxing on Claire?' Robert responds. 'She's not getting any younger you know, and she struggles with her sore hips when sitting too long in the one spot.'

'Look, if you're flying business class, just make sure that you both get up and move around every so often while you're awake. Exercise those joints by taking a walk to the bathroom or down to chat with the air stewards. That ought to at least ensure your heart is pumping and blood circulating.'

Jonathan adds, 'Try to take some time off while you're there as well, so you don't fly immediately back home. A couple of weeks of R&R should be just the ticket to freshen up that ageing old brain of yours? With any luck, it might even keep you both going well towards the century mark.'

Having received the call from his father a week earlier about the possible trip, Harry decides to accompany his mother to see Dr Wilts and ask some questions himself. It would at least ease his concerns about his parents' ability to travel that distance to Australia. The private conversation between Harry and his parents' doctor goes along much the same lines as it had the previous day with Robert.

'Both of your parents will have the time of their lives, provided they take a few basic precautions during each leg of the flight and while relaxing in Sydney,' Jonathan says. 'The holiday element will be great from both a mental and physical perspective.'

Harry asks whether there is any medication his parents can take with them to address the basics such as anxiety, travel sickness, joint pain or treatment for any of the ailments his mother has suffered in the past 12 months. At least, he reasons, that will give everyone some peace of mind that his parents will be able cope with the unexpected.

On the day Robert announces that Claire will be accompanying him to Sydney, he arranges for Harry and his family to join them for lunch. Harry's wife, Sandra, bakes a celebratory cake, while the three adult children, Charlotte, Travis and Peg, are all present to witness their grandmother's surprise. It is, indeed, a day to remember. The customarily composed Claire Bloom is reduced to tears, clutching her husband's hand so tightly that it brings back memories for him of his time in the delivery room when Harry was born. As Robert has anticipated, her mind immediately swings into preparation mode.

With agreement from his university, Robert will deliver a lecture to the economics faculty of Sydney University, including students and distinguished guests of the university, two days after their planned arrival, providing a brief opportunity to recover from the flight. Then, following the lecture, they will enjoy a three-week holiday, exploring the sites of Sydney and surrounding areas. Claire is so thrilled that she struggles to sleep for days.

On the day before their departure, Harry and Sandra spend time with Claire, running through preparations and ensuring they tick every item on her list, including packing medication for easy access and ensuring Claire is fully conversant with the picture function on her new smartphone (a travel gift from Harry) and especially how to access emergency contact numbers easily.

When the day arrives, the entire family turns up to farewell the couple. As Robert and Claire pass through customs, they turn to give everyone a final wave. Harry sends his wife and kids off home, insisting on waiting around himself just in case something unexpected arises before the flight's departure.

Arriving home later that evening, Harry is feeling exhausted but happy. He knows his mother has longed for this holiday for a large part of her life and is pleased the day has finally arrived. He is reminded of a time when he was in primary school, watching his mother as she moved around their house, smiling and singing. Seeing her so happy yesterday brought back many emotions he had long forgotten – feelings of happiness and great sorrow. A horrific car accident in which Claire had lost both of her parents had changed their lives and, while his mother had recovered and learned to deal with her grief over the years, she was never quite the same happy-go-lucky person again.

The next morning, the phone rings; it's Claire calling in as agreed during their brief transit in Singapore. Sandra hears the excitement in Claire's voice as she recounts the trip so far. The beautifully dressed women, the size and newness of the terminal compared to Heathrow; a free massage while waiting for the next leg of the flight. Sandra realises that this is going to be a trip she will be hearing about for many years to come. The remainder of the flight passes uneventfully.

Harry can tell by the images Claire is sending back or posting online that she is enjoying the experience. He can't see the same excitement in his father's eyes but guesses that Robert is a little preoccupied with his thoughts in preparing for the lecture he is about to deliver. Harry returns his thoughts to the challenge ahead of him. The second of his game-changing projects, which incorporates digital twin technology on a new revolutionary platform, has hit an unexpected glitch causing his entire team to be scratching their heads for a solution. Harry welcomes this distraction, which provides a break from worrying about his parents.

It isn't the first problem the project has been thrown their way, and he guesses it won't be the last. It's perplexing all the same, and required Harry as the project lead to marshal the strengths of everyone involved and systemically work through the issues, using a problem-solving technique that he has perfected over the years. Drawing on Albert Einstein's rationale, he had realised that every problem has a solution. The secret is to have a process equal to the challenge, which draws on both critical and creative thinking techniques, to explore multiple options, test hypotheses and a degree of intuition. Having worked together for the past 12 months, his team has come to respect Harry's no-nonsense approach to problem-solving. His confidence at the beginning of every new challenge like this is set by the belief that the solution is waiting for them somewhere out there, they just need to track it down.

It doesn't help, however, that his company, Snemeis, has already gone public with both major projects. Flashy presentations and graphical wizardry were used to illustrate the potential effect of this second invention on everyone's lives, not to mention within the digital world at large. It has added considerable pressure as well as pride to the project team, and so far, thankfully, they have been able to deliver. Development of the first project, the Symmetric Neo platform concluded successfully, and the release is now in full swing, with many industry experts singing its praises. Harry had been on stage numerous times at launch events with other company experts, speaking about the product from a technical perspective and detailing its capabilities.

The breakthrough comes the next day as one of the team members suddenly exclaims, 'I've found it!' As the group huddles around, their interest collectively turns to concern. If what he is saying is proven correct, they will be set back approximately two months in re-designing several of the components to accommodate this issue. To make things worse, before they can start on that rectification, they need to find evidence for this new theory and calculate how that might influence the remainder of the project. By late morning, the group has determined the likelihood of this discovery being correct as 'very probable' and are discussing their plans on how to start delving deeper to analyse the root cause. Harry knows he must share the bad news with his boss, Daryl Ratcliff, who had been riding high on the back of the first project's success. Harry knows Daryl well enough to know that he doesn't receive negative feedback very well, so he considers his approach and thinks about ways to put a positive spin on this unwanted information.

Only four months ago, the company rolled out a training program through its internal academy, in partnership with Cambridge University. The program focuses on establishing a culture in which leaders learn to seek, receive and deliver feedback. It is a useful training for everyone but, of course, there are always naysayers; people knocking the initiative as a waste of their precious time. Daryl was one of those who had been vocal about soliciting feedback from his team in this late stage of his career. Harry had felt quite uncomfortable during this outburst as he was part of that team and, therefore, any future attempt was sure to be a struggle. Even after the program, Daryl had continued his assault on the idea, making it known that he wasn't expecting any of his team to actively participate in such a ridiculous practice.

These words echo in Harry's head as he makes his way upstairs to Daryl's office. As he rounds the corner of a corridor, their eyes lock and, momentarily, they both look away as if hoping that they haven't seen each other. Daryl knows that Harry isn't a huge fan of his and seldom comes to see him, so he gathers that there is likely a problem. Immediately, Daryl starts cursing to himself that he has such an incompetent team that can't do anything without him. Harry reaches the door, regretting the need for this meeting the moment Daryl's body language and facial expression confirm his mood.

'What brings you upstairs, Harry? Problems again?' Harry is about to answer when Daryl continues. 'Seems your team got lucky on that first project, but I'm guessing you're here with bad news?'

'Yes, as it happens,' replies Harry, outlining the challenge. He sees the colour in Daryl's face starting to change to a darker shade of red. His high blood pressure means he always looks flushed and, due to his overweight frame, it is clear that he's a high-risk candidate for early retirement. Harry suddenly feels a vibration in his jacket pocket and reaches for his phone. Seeing it's his wife, he excuses himself from Daryl's office for a moment to take the call. If nothing else, he hopes it will allow Daryl to cool down.

Sandra sounds alarmed. 'Babe, sorry to disturb you, but it's your father. He collapsed after his lecture and was rushed to the hospital. Your mum is with him, but the hospital needs you to call them urgently. I'll text you the contact details as soon as I hang up. But Babe, they said he suffered a massive heart attack and may need surgery.'

'Harry?' Sandra probes, 'I'm so sorry, are you okay?' Harry mutters that he'll call back as soon as he learns more from the Australian doctor.

Harry is visibly shaken as he returns to Daryl's office. He gives Daryl a quick explanation about the phone call and apologises that he needs to deal with the matter urgently and will return once things are under control. Rushing downstairs to his own office, Harry collapses momentarily into his chair. Then, sitting upright, he reprimands himself; this is not the time to fall apart. There will be plenty of time for that later; right now, the doctor in Australia needs to speak with him.

A heavily accented voice on the other end of the phone greets him. 'Good evening, Cardiac Division, how can I help you?'

'My name is Harry Bloom. I believe my father, Robert Bloom, was admitted today? I've been asked to call Dr James Henley. Is he available, please?'

'Ah, yes. Mr Bloom, we've been expecting your call. Just a moment please. I will connect you with Dr Henley.' After what seems like an eternity, a mature male voice comes onto the line.

'Good evening, this is Dr Henley. Am I speaking with Mr Harry Bloom?'

Yes,' Harry responds anxiously.

'Is your father Robert Bloom and your mother Claire Bloom, from London?'

'Yes.' Now Harry is a little more frustrated than panicked.

'Apologies for all the questions, but I need to ensure I'm speaking with the right person. Mr Bloom, this afternoon around 6.30 pm local time your father collapsed offstage, having just completed his lecture at Sydney University. He suffered a heart attack and slipped into unconsciousness. Fortunately, I was in attendance at his lecture with my daughter, a student at the university. I was able to care for your father and stabilise him until the ambulance arrived. We transported him here to the cardiac ward. He is sedated and a nurse is stationed in the room with your mother. We're monitoring his heart and are ready to respond if anything changes.'

Harry listens as the doctor outlines the details of the treatment, trying to take it all in. Dr Henley continues, 'Your mother has asked that we contact you to discuss the procedure and seek your approval to operate if that need arises. By the way, your mother is doing fine. She provided us with Dr Wilt's contact details and we have been in liaising with him to analyse your father's medical history.'

After several questions, Harry asks if he could speak with his mother before giving a response to the doctor's request; though he realises they have few options. While waiting for his mother, he begins searching his computer for flights to Sydney. The earliest will be leaving around midnight.

Claire speaks into the handset, 'Hello, Harry? Sorry about bringing this news to you via the phone. It seems your father has some blood clots, which triggered a heart attack. The doctors are doing what they can to avoid surgery; however, it appears likely that they will need to do a bypass. I have every confidence in the ability of the medical team here, but I wanted to listen to your thoughts before giving my consent.'

Harry notices the calmness in his mother's voice and wonders how she is managing to put up such a brave front. Harry enquires about her health and asks how she is coping. Then he asks if she has spoken with their doctor in London. Without waiting for a response, Harry suggests that he makes a quick call to Dr Wilts himself and promises to call Claire back on her mobile.

After hanging up, he calls Dr Wilts, who has been expecting his call. Jonathan Wilts repeats the prognosis, adding that they are fortunate Dr Henley had been present at the time the heart attack occurred. He tells Harry about the reputation of Dr Henley and advises that he has already contacted the university's medical staff and two leading UK cardiac experts. All knew of Dr Henley and his research, confirming his surgical practices are world-class.

'What's your suggestion about the surgery if it's required? Do we have any other options?' Harry asks. Dr Wilts outlines the process in detail and explains the potential risks. It seems that the surgery is complicated and not without risk, but they have few options. If the treatment doesn't significantly reduce the blockages, then surgery will be a necessity. Dr Wilts promises to stay in contact with Dr Henley's team throughout the day and to consult with experts locally about ways to prepare or minimise the risks involved. Harry realises that this gesture was for his benefit and to help Claire and him feel as much at ease as possible.

Harry thanks him and hangs up, immediately calling his mother to update her. After a short discussion, he agrees that they should provide their consent for the surgery if it becomes necessary. He speaks one last time with Dr Henley to clarify the process and when the operation is likely to happen if that decision is made. Dr Henley advised that they'll continue with attempts to break down the clots for several more hours and will have a clear understanding of the need for surgery after this.

'As a precaution, we have scheduled the operation for 11.00 am our time, meaning within the next 8–10 hours.' Dr Henley, who will be the surgeon, is heading off to get some rest so that he can be well prepared in the morning. In the meantime, his staff will maintain a constant watch over his father and ensure that Harry's mother is comfortable and resting. The surgical procedure will take 4–6 hours, depending on their findings. He asks Harry if he plans to come to Sydney and Harry confirms that he will book the next flight available and be there as soon as possible. Dr Henley records Harry's mobile number and promises that he or his staff will keep him updated. He finishes the call with a reassurance to Harry, 'Your father looks strong and your mother is holding up well. We will take good care of them both before your arrival.'

Harry hangs up and calls Sandra with a brief update. 'I need to book the earliest flight available to Sydney. Apart from my father's condition, I'm worried about Mum.'

Sandra tells Harry she has already taken care of the flight, booking the first available, at 10.00 pm – in just a few hours. All Harry needs to do is come home and freshen up before they head to the airport. 'I've arranged with my company to take leave and come with you. My parents will come and stay with the children.'

Next, Harry speaks with his deputy manager, Frank Chi, and briefs him to take over the running of the project for an indefinite period. 'I'm not sure exactly when I will be able to make contact, but it will most likely be a few days at best. Are you okay with everything here? I'll arrange with the IT team to provide you access to the project files, and you'll find everything you need under the folder with the project name.' Frank is a little surprised but confirms that Harry need not worry and, that instead Harry should channel his focus on helping his family. 'Unless we have an absolute disaster with the project, Harry, you won't hear from me,' Frank says.

Harry packs some essentials to take with him from the office and notifies Daryl about his father. Harry introduces the immediate requirements for Frank to manage the project over the short term, adding that he will touch base as soon as possible once he has things sorted in Sydney. Surprisingly, Daryl is calm and very understanding.

'Harry, it's unfortunate, but these things happen. The most important thing right now is for you to be with your mother and father. Please take care of yourself as well, as your parents will need to rely on you being strong and helping them through the recovery. We will look after your project until you get back.'

Harry is surprised but thanks Daryl. On the way home, he calls Sandra again to check whether she has everything they need. By 6.30 pm they are loading their luggage into a taxi and heading to the airport. On the way, they receive confirmation that the surgery is scheduled for midnight their time. Sandra and Harry hold hands all the way to the airport, speaking little and, for the most part, both lost in their own thoughts. Harry reflects on his day and is pleased that he has been able to listen to the advice offered from multiple sources, despite a feeling of helplessness. Harry acknowledges to himself that in some way his career has prepared him to receive this information and, instead of shutting down or falling apart, a certain calmness has set in, enabling him to discuss options with experts in their field. He recalls how relaxed his mother seemed to be over the phone. Perhaps his behaviour and observations during this testing moment had their origins in his family and his upbringing.

Harry's phone buzzes with a message from Dr Wilt. Robert is now in the surgery prep room. They may shift him to the theatre about an hour after Sandra and Harry's flight is due to depart. Dr Wilt says he will leave a message on Harry's phone after the surgery, with an update on his father's condition.

Chapter 5: Tim and Harry seek feedback and commence a lifelong friendship

Harry

After an agonising 22-hour flight, Harry and Sandra touch down at Sydney's Kingsford Smith Airport. Harry is anxious to hear how his father is doing after surgery. In transit at Singapore they managed to connect with the hospital to confirm that the surgery had been successful and that Robert was in recovery. Harry checks the messages on his phone. His mother, Claire, reports that Robert's surgery has gone well and the doctor believes he should make a full recovery. Dr Wilt's message confirms that all has gone to plan and that Robert is now stable and in recovery. A third message is from the surgeon, Dr Henley, also confirming that everything went well during the procedure and he expects Robert to make a full recovery. He asks Harry to contact him once they arrive at the hospital.

They clear customs and find their way to the taxi stand, from where they headed directly to the hospital, which the driver says is less than 30 minutes away. Given that it's peak hour, it's a pleasant and short trip. Harry and Sandra can't help noticing the clear sky and how warm and fresh the air seem. They left a cold and bleak London late on Tuesday evening, and now they're in Sydney on a bright Thursday morning.

Arriving at the hospital, they identify the location of the cardiology ward and make for the elevator. As they get closer to the ward Harry feels an increasing sense of anxiety and breathlessness. Sandra takes his hand as they step out of the elevator, dragging the two large suitcases behind them. At the reception desk, the nurse looks up and, recognising the combination of their accents and the suitcases, steps forward with a smile.

'You must be Harry and Sandra. Hello, I'm Veronica. We spoke on the phone a couple of days ago. That was a quick trip from the other side of the world! You must both be exhausted. Let me take you to someone who will be very happy to see you.'

Something about her demeanour immediately puts Harry at ease and, for the first time in more than two days, he feels like things are going to be okay.

Approaching the room, they meet Claire in the corridor, taking the opportunity to stretch her legs while the nurses bathe Robert and changed his dressing. Apart from appearing tired, there are no apparent signs of concern on Claire's face. If anything, she seems happy. They embrace and Claire leads them to Robert's room, where they look in on him and have a chat with the nurses. Then they leave their the luggage in Robert's room and take Claire to the hospital's canteen for a coffee and to catch up on events from the past 24 hours.

As they sit talking, two people approach their table: it's Dr James Henley and his daughter, Rachelle. Claire smiles as they approach. Harry shakes hands with James, thanking him for everything he has done for his parents.

'Rachelle is the reason I happened to be at your father's lecture,' Dr Henley says with a smile.

Rachelle says she has been an admirer of Professor Bloom's theories for years, since first studying his papers as an undergraduate.

The Henleys are here to offer accommodation for Claire, Harry and Sandra for as long as they need to while in Sydney, including Robert when he is discharged from hospital in a few days. Hotels in the area are expensive. Rachelle is living by herself in the Henleys' large apartment, which they recently renovated, and would enjoy some company. 'Besides, how often does a student get to meet with such a legend in her chosen field?' Rachelle says.

Once Dr Henley has explained the recovery process and what they could expect from here on in, he returns with them to the ward to check in on Robert. The plan is for Robert to remain sedated for another two days, so the doctors can observe his recovery from the bypass surgery, and then they plan to slowly bring him back to consciousness, when the recovery and rehabilitation process can commence in earnest.

A full 30 minutes of questions later, Harry, Sandra, Claire and Dr Henley step outside the room to find Rachelle waiting. She has been busy cancelling their hotel bookings and clearing her schedule for the coming days. Enlisting support from her brother, Tim, and his girlfriend, Janet, she has mapped out a tentative itinerary to help ensure that the family is not stationed in the hospital room for the entire time they are in Sydney.

Their first stop is a 5-star hotel near the famous Sydney Harbour Bridge in the Rocks area, where Claire and Robert were staying before Robert was hospitalised. Rachelle knows the staff at the hotel well as she has worked there as intern during the semester breaks. With Claire's permission, she has arranged for the hotel to pack up the couple's luggage and to have it waiting in the lobby when they arrive. Claire simply needs to finalise the account, and they will be on their way to Rachelle's apartment. Fortunately, Rachelle has the use of her mother's 7-seater SUV.

The next stop is the apartment in Coogee, where they will be set up temporarily in relative luxury until Robert is strong enough to consider returning to London. As they quickly discover, the word 'apartment' is somewhat misleading. Turns out it is a free-standing, multi-storied terraced mansion, with 180-degree views overlooking the Coogee Surf Life Saving Club, a vast stretch of beach and the Pacific Ocean out to the distant horizon. Bookshelves laden with books on every subject imaginable line the walls of the lounge and study. The furnishings and drapes are a blend of the ultra-modern and traditional colonial. It is a mansion in every sense of the word. The Blooms are speechless and in awe of the generosity of this Sydney family they have only just met through these extreme circumstances. Rachelle watches their expression as she introduces them to their new home away from home.

'Please make yourself comfortable, freshen up and let's meet back here around 1.00 pm for a quick lunch,' Rachelle says. She suggests that Claire stays in the bedroom nearest to the elevator so that when Professor Bloom arrives he won't need to climb the stairs.

While the Blooms settled in, Rachelle drives to the city, picks up Tim and Janet, who have both finished work early to meet the Bloom family. Between the three locals, they plan to share the task of ferrying the Blooms around Sydney, but for now they will all take a stroll around the corner for lunch at a little fish n' chip restaurant on Arden Street.

In Rachelle's absence, Harry and Sandra looks around the property in wonderment. Standing on the balcony and allowing the fresh ocean wind to blow directly onto their faces was invigorating, to say the least, and helped to rejuvenate their tired bodies.

Over lunch, the six get to know a little more about each other. Tim tells them about his parents and their family. Sandra is excited to learn that Cynthia Henley is a fashion designer while Harry lights up when he hears about Tim's and Rachelle's fitness routines. Rachelle promises to drag Harry out along the beach and on her hill-running circuit as soon as he is ready. He agrees that it might be a useful way to dust off the jet lag. Not to be outdone, Tim insists on showing the family around the Sydney sights and giving them a special tour from high above the city; a climb to the top of the Harbour Bridge. Claire politely declines the offer, instead preferring to stay home when not visiting her husband in hospital.

After lunch Tim, Janet and Rachelle introduce the Blooms to the local public transport system, purchasing travel cards and showing them where and how to catch the nearest bus to the doorstep of the hospital. While Rachelle and Janet head off to attend to some grocery shopping, Tim ferries the Blooms back to the hospital, where he catches up with his father while they visit Robert.

A couple of hours later, Harry and Sandra are walking down the corridor to meet Tim. They are tired – it's 6.00 am in London right now and they are feeling the effects of jet lag.

'We think we'd like to head back to the apartment, Tim, if it's okay with you? Harry says. 'We'd like try to get a good night's rest. It seems like my father is comfortable, and there isn't much we can do just sitting here. Your father has prescribed us some sleeping tablets, so we should be able to drop off fairly quickly.'

The four head back to the apartment in relative silence, each lost in their thoughts about entirely different topics. On their arrival, Rachelle greets them in the lobby, while Janets waved her farewell and heads back to Mosman with Tim.

Rachelle and Janet have worked their magic in preparing the apartment for the Blooms. They drew the curtains and dimmed the lights so the candlelight creates a warm ambience in the bedrooms. The beds are turned down and fresh towels and toiletries are provided in the bathrooms, the refrigerator and cupboards are stocked with fresh produce, and on the breakfast bench they've placed a large bowl of fruit. The breakfast table is set, and the coffee table is laden with a selection of current magazines and books on fashion, food and travel in Sydney. There is also a computer available for use in the study.

The next morning Rachelle helps everyone to prepare breakfast and then travels with them on their first bus ride to the hospital. She leaves her phone number with Sandra and arranges to meet them again that afternoon after her lectures.

While there are still many uncertainties around his father's health and recovery, Harry is starting to feel a little more relaxed and less overwhelmed by everything that has occurred over the past few days. His mother seems to be coping well now and is happy that the family is together to support her and Robert through this traumatic experience.

He checks in with Frank Chi via text message, and it seems things are on back on target with the project in London. As he strolls around on the upper floor of a bookshop in the city, Harry notices a book called *Feedback (and other dirty words): Why we fear it, how to fix it* by Laura Dowling Grealish and M. Tamra Chandler. The title is familiar, and flicking through the pages he recalls that the facilitator of a training session he attended months earlier had recommended it. Coincidence or not, Harry was intrigued that he would come halfway around the world and be prompted for a second time to purchase this book. He remembers the training program and the discussion of how different situations present opportunities for seeking feedback and how to grow as a result of them.

As Harry queues up to buy the book his mind drifts back to a few days ago at the office. First, he learned about the project's setback then faced his boss's angry response, followed by the call advising him of his father's collapse. It's the second time he has caught himself thinking about a possible connection between these events. The last time was while he sat in his office after the phone call with Australia. Now, he motions to Sandra that he is going to sit down and have a drink while she continues to browse.

Seated there with his coffee, Harry continues to ponder the situation. He knows that he and his team are quite strong and open to receiving and delivering feedback, so it's not that. Then it hits him. The one person he has struggled with his whole life when it comes to receiving feedback is his father. His famous father, the economics legend, as Rachelle so aptly put it, is also Harry's strongest critic. Robert has always pushed his son, wanting him to stretch and excel in his life. But this only led Harry to shy away from challenges, especially when he was young, and he remembers how he avoided being alone with his father. Robert often used such opportunities to question Harry's thinking and goals.

It wasn't until Harry moved out of home and established some degree of freedom from his father's constant scrutiny, that he was able to find his own way in life. At university he excelled in problem-solving, and found his analytical, process-oriented mind well suited to solving mathematical equations even while others struggled. Over time, these skills evolved, and Harry began to utilise his talents and to thrive, first as a design engineer and then as an electronics manager. Harry discovered that he was a natural leader, a strategist and a futurist. It was what had attracted him to his current company, Snemeis, as the production manager of their factory in London. Still, at family gatherings he avoided discussing his achievements in the presence of his father. Now, halfway around the world, seated in a tiny corner of a Sydney bookshop, Harry realises he needs to address this issue with his father, if their relationship is ever going to grow.

Tim

On the day after Harry and Sandra's arrival in Sydney, Tim Henley drives all three Blooms to the hospital. While they visit Robert, he's taking the opportunity to catch up with his father. It's been some time since he their last catch-up, so he's looking forward to the opportunity to discuss a few things that have been on his mind recently.

For his part, James Henley has been puzzling over a couple of things he observed in Tim at their recent family lunch. It seemed to him then that Tim was grappling with something, so he is particularly pleased when Tim suggested that they catch up for coffee this afternoon.

After exchanging pleasantries, Tim starts the conversation, by sharing with this father some of the challenges facing him in his current project and the recent fire at the construction site. He also tells James that he has seized on an opportunity to be mentored through work, and that this has led him to ask one of their family friends, Justin Cagney, to be his financial mentor. Tim explains how Justin has agreed to a regular get together on alternate Wednesdays, and the difference that is making to the feeling he has had for a long time, of being the most financially inept member of the family, especially since Janet is a chartered accountant.

James listens without interrupting. He knows his son well and understands that Tim is building up to something important.

'This leads me to the two things I want to discuss with you, Dad. You're the first person I'm speaking to about this. Next month during the Christmas break I plan to ask Janet to marry me. We have a holiday planned, and I figure I'll pop the question once we're relaxed and away from our normal hectic lives here in the city. It's long overdue, and I know that Janet would love to settle down and start a family.'

This brings a broad smile to James's face, and with a firm handshake he responds enthusiastically.

'Congratulations, Son! Your mother and I have been wondering whether this would be coming anytime soon. I'm very proud of you, and happy, as I know your mother will be also. When do you plan on telling her?'

'Not immediately,' Tim responds. 'I want to get a few more things sorted out first, such as buying an engagement ring.'

James sits back a little in his chair, smiling and observing how mature his son appears at this moment.

Buoyed by his father's response, Tim works up the courage to raise the second topic.

'There is one more issue I want to discuss, Dad.'

After Tim outlines the background to his nightmares and feelings of helplessness, he turns to the current situation and actions that have led to him speaking with a university professor about it and his subsequent visits to a psychologist. Tim pauses and waits for his father to speak. It seems like an eternity before James Henley responds.

'Tim, we've known each other since your birth 25 years ago. Probably not as closely as I would have liked, largely due to the distractions with my career, and for that I'm truly sorry. I've observed from a distance that you have developed into an independent and intelligent young man. I think it's very courageous of you to seek help from experts when things happen that you can't explain. It doesn't mean there is anything wrong with you. More so, it's a realisation that you may not always be able to identify the answers to every problem that arises in your life. You may not be aware, but you are not alone in this feeling, and our society today is triggering more and more insecurity in people who now feel a similar way. The key I've found is to surround yourself with people you can share your life with – all the highs and the lows. People who don't judge you, who enjoy being in your presence and simply love you for who you are. To that extent, you have four people in your immediate life who you can count on for support, regardless of what arises. I am pleased that you have found your way to sharing this with me, and I can assure you that your mother and I will always be there when you need us. Be it with your career or your personal life. Just know that life is too short to spend any moment of it alone or isolated.'

When they have concluded their discussion, Tim thanks his father and James returns to his rounds in the cardiac ward. Tim remains in the coffee shop for a while, reflecting on his father's comments and advice. A long time has passed since he last sat on his father's lap and asked questions about life. He remembers feeling the warmth and love of his father's embrace. Tim had forgotten how he would hang onto every word his father spoke during those formative years, and realises he now longs for those times again. His father's gift was his ability to save people's lives and, as a result, Tim often found himself competing for his father's attention with strangers who put their lives in James Henley's hands. It was a vital profession, and the greater world seemed to need Dr Henley as much as Tim did, so he has learned to settle for those private moments they could find together. Today has been one such moment.

Tim and Harry

Rachelle is delayed at uni and asks if Tim can pop over to meet their guests in the city. As he steps off the escalator to the upper floor, he spots Harry with his head buried in a book. Tim is surprised that Harry is able to focus so intently on a book at a time when his father is in hospital under sedation, following major surgery.

Tim surprises Harry by sitting in the chair opposite him. 'Find something interesting?' he asks with a grin as Harry looks up, momentarily startled. Harry is happy to see Tim.

'Do you mind if I ask you a personal question? You seem to be an intelligent guy. You have a highly successful and influential father. Your mother is a successful fashion designer and your sister is studying law and economics and will most likely move into some high-paying career very soon. Yet, you have chosen your path, working as a project manager for an elevator company. I'm curious as to what led you down this path.'

Tim studies Harry's face for signs that he is making fun of him, but Harry's interest seems to be genuine. He pauses for a moment and wonders if Harry is a gifted mind reader or body language specialist. Has he picked up on the fact that Tim is not comfortable around his family's success and their expectations of him? He decides to answer the question with a question.

'Would it surprise you to learn that I am running from the pressures and expectations of following in the footsteps of my father?'

'Not at all,' replies Harry. 'I only ask because that's what I've been doing all my life! I've just now had an epiphany. I need to stop and confront it if I ever want to be truly happy and fulfilled. The source, in my case, is also my father, and it's a long story. But this book has been pushing me for several months now, towards that realisation and my next actions.'

'If I can offer you any advice,' Harry continues, 'it is for you to do the same, sooner rather than later, if you truly want to understand success in your own right and not live in the shadow of those who have come before you.'

Tim smiles. 'Thanks, Harry! Just yesterday I had the first conversation in that direction and I know there will be more to follow.'

Chapter 6: Maddie learns to invite feedback

Trying to find one word that adequately sums up Maddie's life and career right now is almost impossible. 'Successful,' yes, but that's too hollow. 'Inspiring,' perhaps but that better describes her character. 'Pioneering' comes some way, but again paints only a portion of the whole. 'Abundant, triumphant, fulfilling, joyous, hmm…' that's more like it.

'AMAZING' is the word Maddie uses when she calls her husband during a lunch break, to share the news of her appointment as the Melbourne branch's field operations manager.

A few months ago, Maddie and Terry discussed the possibility of Maddie taking on the role as New Installation Operations Manager. She raised the idea and left it with Terry to think through, which he did. Aside from the service operation, which Maddie was responsible for, Terry wasn't happy with the performance of his other two field managers in New Installation Sales and New Installation Operations. It led to him rethink how to drive change and improvement at a time when the city of Melbourne was experiencing a minor construction boom. TYSO's market share had been sliding for almost 12 months, and his managers were becoming increasingly frustrated. Most recently, during the budgeting process, when the requirements for releasing a new customer-centric program and expectations for a financial turnaround were made abundantly clear.

Terry decided, therefore, that change was needed, and that meant a shift towards a more customer-focused structure. One of his first moves was to say goodbye to the New Installation Operations Manager.

In Terry's mind, Barry Wolanski was not the right person to implement the required changes to support such a program, nor was he capable of proceeding with the necessary speed. Instead, Terry had intended to shift the New Installation Sales Manager, Tom Brady, to the role of the New Installation Operations Manager and get Maddie to turn around their failing new-installation sales business. The service business, which was in great shape, could do with some fresh ideas, and Maddie would be able to support it until the new service manager was settled into that role. However, Maddie's surprise suggestion of taking on the new-installation operations role had caused Terry to pause and rethink his strategy. Shortly after that meeting, and during a session with his mentor, Alan Wright, Terry created a plan to address several immediate concerns. He would appoint Maddie as the Melbourne head of field operations, responsible for overseeing all four functions of new-installation sales, installation, modernisation and service. At the time, modernisation was part of the New Installation department. Terry planned to make this a separate profit and loss function, giving modernisation greater focus and the ability to be driven more aggressively.

Tom Brady will still be moved to run the new-installation operation, but in this role he will only be responsible for installation. Terry has already commenced a search for a specialist new-installation sales professional, and is considering recruiting from outside the industry. His plan is for one of Maddie's team to take over the role of service manager and for Maddie to assume responsibility for growing the modernisation business in addition to the overall improvement in field operations. The genius in this plan is that while it will give Terry an opportunity to groom Maddie to take over his role, it will also enable him to focus on introducing the company's required customer-centric program immediately. He also needs to look at developing the three smaller outlying offices for which he is responsible. If all goes according to plan, Terry himself will be able to seek new career opportunities that aren't possible with the current results under his management.

There is no time to be wasted, so Terry sets about bringing his plan to reality. It is a calculated gamble, based on putting one new person into the sales role and ensuring Maddie has his support. And with this, fortune seems to be on his side, as negotiations are now well underway with a leading sales candidate who seems to be ticking all the boxes in Terry's plan. It looks like they may be able to secure a customer-centric, highly engaging and successful professional with little effect on the salary cap. The candidate is very confident in her ability to secure orders and reclaim market share, and is even willing to stake a portion of her bonus on achieving incredible results in her first and subsequent years.

Maddie has been grooming her successor for some time now, so this part is an easy decision. Immediately after returning from parental leave three years ago, Maddie had assessed the talents within her group and identified the gaps she needed to fill. One was a replacement for the service sales manager role and the other was a new position of deputy service manager. The latter would be responsible for turning around the ailing maintenance business and getting the equipment repairs backlog under control. For service sales, Maddie brought in a colleague she had known and worked with years earlier in the hospitality industry. As for the deputy manager, she chose a technical supervisor from within the team. The supervisor's talents had particularly impressed Maddie and seemed rare for someone with his background. He had managed to establish a reputation for being an excellent trouble shooter as well as a highly empathetic people manager, with good business acumen.

The three have formed a strong team over this time and have been largely responsible for successfully delivering year on year with their strategy and results. The outcome has been an incredibly stable and profitable business, with happy employees and happy customers. 'Utopia', was a term Terry once used.

Fast forward six weeks from that conversation, and Maddie is now being advised of the pending changes, including her new role. Naturally, she is thrilled by the opportunity and promises Terry that he won't regret the trust he is bestowing on her. They met for the entire morning to discuss the other roles, people and structural changes, which would be announced later in the afternoon.

Now, as Maddie hangs up the phone from her husband, she sits back and glances around the office, wondering if anyone overheard the conversation or noticed her excitement. Seems not, but she decides to avoid showing any outward signs of the news for now. Regaining her composure, she leans forward and make a second call, this time to her mentor.

'Hello Alan, it's Maddie. I'm wondering if you might have time for a meeting within the next week? I have some topics that I would truly value your opinion and guidance on.'

Alan confirms his availability next Friday and they agree to meet at the usual coffee shop. This will be their third face-to-face meeting since the start of the mentoring relationship, and the most recent meeting was only two weeks ago. Maddie's a little surprised that Alan was not more curious about the urgency in her request or about the topics she wants to discuss.

As she hangs up, Terry appears at her office door, knocks and walks in. Closing the door but making no attempt to sit down, he says, 'By the way, I neglected to mention this morning that I'm planning to call a branch meeting with all of the office staff and outside office managers next Friday afternoon. For sure, there will be ,people with many questions after my announcement this afternoon, so I'm planning a series of meetings for us to discuss the changes with staff and answer any questions they have.'

Terry continues: 'I'll include these meeting times and locations in today's announcement, so people can plan to be there if they have questions. It will be a good opportunity for you to answer them and weave your magic.' Pausing, he adds, 'I hope that's ok with you?'

Maddie nods. She's hesitant but also excited that this is more than just a dream. The gravity of the new role is starting to sink in. As Terry leaves the room, she feels the smile spreading once again across her face.

On the morning of the scheduled 'Meet and Greet your New Branch Management Team,' as Terry called it in his announcement last week, it seems to Maddie that her world hasn't stopped spinning in those seven days. Congratulatory messages have poured in from her customers and her service colleagues. Things are now a little stretched, which she did anticipate, but Paul has been doing everything possible to hold down the fort during this transition. Maddie's mother and sister have also been more than willing to provide support when and where needed.

Maddie arrives at the coffee shop five minutes early, as usual, for her meeting with Alan. She has reserved the usual table in the corner. At their last meeting Alan had commented on how much he enjoys the ambience in this location, with the view overlooking the Yarra River. She is surprised to find Alan already enjoying his coffee and the view. He seems deep in thought but looks expectantly in Maddie's direction as she approaches. He stands to greet her, and the smile on his face immediately sets her at ease.

'Congratulations!' he says as they shake hands. The fact that Alan has already heard the news hadn't occurred to her, and the surprise on her face was enough for Alan to explain.

'Surely you didn't think this information would escape us in headquarters?' He smiles, 'Terry is in close contact with the executive team and had already run his plans past the board for approval before proceeding with any of the branch staffing changes, including the most critical of course, your appointment.' He pauses, and a strange nervousness suddenly overcomes Maddie.

She really has not stopped to think thoroughly about the extent of this restructure. Terry had explained to her that the state and national teams weren't satisfied with the branch's performance and had demanded action. Still, the full extent of these expectations are only now beginning to sink in. Alan senses her uneasiness and interrupts her thoughts.

'It's okay, Maddie. We all have the utmost confidence in your ability and are 100 per cent in support of your appointment. You have been on our radar for some time. Therefore, news of this opportunity was warmly received by the Board. Terry highlighted your potential a couple of years back, and you were on our mentoring shortlist for the next wave, so even if you hadn't made the first move, we would have been speaking within the next six months anyway. We were happy to hear of your request as it confirmed Terry's confidence, and the Board was pleased to receive the news that I was already in contact with you. The fact that I'm here today reflects the Board's support. The state manager and I will attend your meeting with the office staff today to show everyone that we are aligned and happy with these changes.'

'Really? The National Board is aware and supportive?' Maddie manages to ask.

'Yes, of course. Not only do we need to know about all our promising talent in-house, but we have a keen interest in seeing that they have every opportunity to grow and succeed. The Melbourne branch is a significant contributor to the overall results of the business and, therefore, we need to ensure its continued success.'

Maddie draws in a deep breath and regains her composure. She removes a large folder from her bag and opens it on the table. Alan can see the wealth of notes from Maddie's preparation since their first meeting. It does seem that the size of that folder has grown considerably since the previous session, however! Maddie begins to outline her thoughts on the new role, the direction that she and Terry are planning to take the business and her views on how they might succeed. Alan can't help but wonder why they haven't acted on this solution earlier – Maddie being the solution.

Maddie pauses and looked up at Alan enquiringly. It appears that Alan is impressed by the detail in her strategy. Given that there are only a few hours before the meeting, he suggests that they discuss first the broader 12-month projection and then specific targets for the next three months.

Thirty minutes later, Alan sits back in his chair and asks Maddie how she is feeling. Then he asks, 'So what do you want to achieve from today's team meeting with Terry?'

Maddie considers his question for a moment. 'I would like people to see that we have a clear strategy, that we, as a management team, are focused and united and that above all, I am confident and ready to lead.'

'I'm impressed, Alan says,' smiling. 'Can I offer one suggestion? This could also help in the months ahead. Today and after the next few team meetings, I recommend that you conduct a very brief survey so you can get feedback from branch employees and evidence to validate that your strategy will get the support it needs to work. In the survey, you ask three simple questions and ask everyone to complete the survey right then and there:

1. What is going well in their area at present?
2. What should we stop doing?
3. What can we start doing?'

'After collecting feedback from the survey and consolidating the responses, share those responses at the scheduled team meetings next week and then post them for everyone to read. Prioritise the suggestions into a list of future projects and discuss them at follow-up meetings. At the follow-up meetings, call for volunteers to work in project teams on those suggestions that can be actioned immediately.'

Maddie can't stop herself from smiling at this idea, and can hardly write fast enough to capture each point. Looking at the time, she knows she needs to get moving if she is going to find time to get this prepared and added into her presentation. Thanking Alan for what sounds like the hundredth time, Maddie says a quick farewell and heads back to the office to get started.

The afternoon turns into a milestone in Maddie's career. There is great interest from staff in the changes, and Terry does an excellent job in illustrating the significant results of the company, the state and the branch, highlighting how the branch's performance affects the company's results overall. He then describes the reasons behind the restructuring and details each of the new roles, being careful to emphasise the importance of the department teams in realising the desired turnaround. Maddie watches and listens as he speaks and addresses their questions. Finally, it is her turn, and Maddie does not disappoint.

In the week since the announcement, most staff have already agreed that Maddie's appointment is an intelligent decision on the company's part and well deserved. Employees outside the service business are happy and looking forward to the opportunity to support her in turning around their area's performance.

After outlining her high-level strategy, Maddie closes with the three-question survey, asking the managers to hand out the questionnaire and pens while explaining her intention and the next steps. Maddie also takes matters two steps further than Alan suggested this morning.

First, she has prepared a large suggestion box and copies of the same three-question survey, positioning it at the entrance to the office. She hopes that all employees and customers will be encouraged to contribute freely and discretely whenever they wish.

Second, during the presentation, Maddie tells those assembled that she wants to establish a culture in which everyone, including herself and Terry, regularly seek feedback, formally and informally. It means that feedback should have no boundaries, with management soliciting team feedback and vice versa. This is an invitation she plans to extend to their customers. Maddie says that only with absolute openness and transparency, can they hope to understand whether the performance of every staff member in the business is at the level necessary to ensure they reach their objectives and become the 'Employer of Choice' and most customer-centric organisation in the industry.

These ideas seem to resonate with many of the staff, and the chatter immediately grows louder and more exited as they complete the surveys. At the end of Maddie's presentation, all employees stand and applaud.

News from this first meeting spreads quickly to the remainder of the branch's employees, and the two subsequent team meetings are greeted positively and with enthusiastic support offered to Terry and Maddie. Responses to the survey are encouraging, with a healthy number of comments on all three questions. Terry is particularly pleased to read through many of the congratulatory comments added to the bottom of the survey sheet, especially given the history of negative feedback from field employees towards anything remotely similar in the past.

As a first pass, three core project teams, including employees from all departments – professional, administrative and trades – are established, with Terry, Maddie and other managers participating as sponsors or members of the teams.

Project 1: Explore ways to enhance employee engagement.

Project 2: Explore ways to enhance customer engagement.

Project 3: Explore ways to enhance engagement with other key stakeholders.

Over the next six months, Maddie meets daily with her immediate reports, being careful to coach and guide rather than micro-manage. She and Terry meet weekly for formal discussions, and she meets with Alan monthly for a mentoring session. She finds that the push for open communication and feedback is starting to take hold, and notices that people, in general, seem to be smiling more; the number of internal complaints has dropped and customer feedback is starting to show a positive upward trend. All three direct reports have taken on their new responsibilities with vigour. There are almost immediate results, with strong order intake at healthy margins. The sales team seems to have a clear direction and purpose for the first time in Terry's memory, and are producing positive results. The existing installation projects, which previously have had numerous issues on a daily basis, have started to settle, to the point at which Terry wonders why he has so much free time and isn't attending customer site meetings to support his project managers. And the newly commenced projects seem to have more rigorous preparation. Noticeably, the site crews are starting on time, design approvals and factory orders have stabilised, while deliveries are occurring as scheduled. The service business has continued seamlessly, thanks to Maddie's development work with her deputy over the past three years and his competence continued to grow in the new role.

Even the new modernisation division is showing early signs of success, with a couple of large orders received and several others at the negotiation stage.

For the first time in 12 months, Terry sits in his office and allows himself to smile and relax. He had been feeling so drained and as though he were operating on autopilot for far too long. It had become a lonely existence and had it not been for the support and guidance from Alan, Terry probably would have left the role many months earlier. Now, as he reflects on the changes, he challenges himself to look for any weaknesses in the current structure that they might be overlooking. To his relief, just about every operational and financial question can be answered as stable, improving or very healthy. It is a stark contrast to just six months ago.

At the same time, Maddie is sitting across from Alan at their regular corner table, in the same coffee shop overlooking the river as they have done since the beginning of their mentoring relationship. This time, however, Maddie listens in silence as she receives unexpected and disheartening news from her mentor. The one person who has been more instrumental in her career development than anyone else, has just shared the news that he has accepted an offer to move into a new role with a competitor in the Asia–Pacific region and, therefore, can no longer continue their mentoring relationship. Alan will be moving Hong Kong. However, as Alan describes it, her development and mentoring program are being reassigned to a more experienced and much more capable executive on the Board. Apparently, through pressure from Alan, the Australian CEO has agreed to take over the program and continue to support Maddie towards more extraordinary things in the year ahead.

As flattered as Maddie is that the company's CEO is taking a personal interest in her career, she is disappointed at the thought of losing this relationship. Alan is, however, quick to point out that his change of role and location doesn't mean that they can not remain in contact, provided it is purely on a social basis and doesn't breach any professional or compliance boundaries.

While Terry heads home feeling happy, Maddie seeks the comfort of her husband and son, hoping to be distracted from the disappointment of the news from Alan. Before saying farewell to Maddie, Alan shared with her some thoughts and observations he had compiled in preparation for their meeting. Alan was candid and painted a positive picture with a balance of reality. He suggested that if Maddie wanted to continue growing her career, she should stay in the position just long enough to demonstrate that the improvements and results were sustainable. By his estimate, that would be two to three years from now. He said she needed to consider whether career progress would be possible from the same branch or state. Alternatively, based on her ambitions, she may need to consider moving interstate or abroad.

Maddie had half-listened at the time, but as she reflects later, it is a message she indeed has internalised and now she beings to contemplate his advice. If she has to nominate one key lesson from her mentoring by Alan, she will say without hesitation, 'The need to be open to feedback throughout your career'. This one lesson will remain with Maddie throughout her professional career and personal life.

Transformational Strategy 2: Feedback

The topic of feedback – or *advice* – has seen a resurgence in recent years. Countless academic studies in the fields of online gaming, education, medicine, business, leadership, sport, even religion, illustrate a similar desire for giving and receiving feedback. As Sheila Heen, Harvard Law Professor and co-author of *Thanks for the Feedback* (2014), suggests, we are just not very good at it. We need to learn how to receive feedback first.

But *feedback* comes in many forms. We can offer, receive and solicit feedback, in both our private and professional lives. And we can find ways to make it less personal or not so directly related to us. For instance, we can ask team members to provide feedback on the business overall, or a project or a product. It has become quite common to provide feedback through surveys related to a company, or product or service.

If we manage the process well, feedback or advice can be an invaluable source of information that enables a situation to be analysed and improved. Hence, in this second strategy, **soliciting feedback and advice**, the message is that a leader needs to find ways to incorporate feedback successfully into their toolkit.

The first step in a business context is to look for ways to engage customers and employees, by seeking their advice.

Here are five simple ideas to get you started.

1. Remember the old suggestion box? Dust it off and bring it back to life. Turn it into a competition by rewarding the best suggestions each month. Obviously, this means the suggestions cannot be provided anonymously.
2. During your meetings, open the floor to feedback on topics, projects, strategies or the main reason for the meeting. Persist with this approach until it becomes embedded as the norm. It helps to build a culture of giving and receiving feedback.
3. Conduct surveys and solicit feedback – remember Maddie's three questions?

   What is working well? (Keep)

   What should we stop? (Stop)

   What could we start? (Start)

   You can apply any version of these three simple questions to suit the purpose of the survey. It works equally with internal staff and with customers.

4. Make a point of seeking feedback and advice from your customers, team members, colleagues and boss about your own performance. You might be surprised by what you learn. Don't disregard the comments but take them as a means of improving how you operate.
5. Hold 'world café' exercises where several small groups of employees (3–4 per group), spend up to five minutes brainstorming a topic before rotating to the next topic, where they review and add to the previous groups input. Continue the rotation until all topics have been covered by each group. Keep it lively and friendly, sincere and structured, making use of the feedback received.

Powerful questions to support Strategy 2

Let's look at some powerful questions you might ask when requesting feedback, and some questions you may ask when offering feedback.

The quality of the questions you ask determines the quality of the response you receive. Therefore, when you seek or give feedback, make the most of the exercise by asking well thought-out questions.

If feedback is not something already practised in your organisation, here are a few helpful tips to consider.

1. As a first step, educating people on the value of giving and receiving feedback will help everyone prepare for and better understand the importance of the process. As humans it can be difficult for us to believe we could be wrong, and even more so when the comments come from others. Our brains have evolved separate, more sensitive circuits to handle negative information and events, and they process these negative things more thoroughly than the positive things. That means receiving criticism will always have a more significant effect than receiving praise.
2. Trust must exist between both parties. A handy tool is the 'Johari Window model'. This tool helps you work with and share information between yourself and team members team. Just be aware that you may need to practise the exercise several times before all members of the team are comfortable enough to offer honest feedback, but it is well worth the effort. Check-out the short Mindtools video on YouTube, titled *The Johari Window*.
3. To support that trust, here are five ways to respond when receiving feedback:
    - Be open.
    - Don't take it personally.
    - Don't argue.
    - Consider receiving feedback as a skill and practise it.
    - Thank the person providing the feedback.

The primary focus of this strategy is for you to learn to solicit feedback. However, be aware of the need for you to be educated and skilled in delivering feedback. Just as you may ask for feedback, in a perfect world other people may ask you to provide feedback as well. Refer to page 115 for a few tools to guide you in that process.

When asking your team for feedback about your performance

- Set up the environment or location to provide a relaxed atmosphere, one in which everyone participating can feel at ease. This could be a coffee shop, workshop, or while taking a walk. Wherever you choose, ensure that it isn't in your office, sitting on each side of your desk.
- An excellent opening to the discussion is to explain the reason you are asking for feedback. Describe why you need for you to understand whether people are aligned or feeling overwhelmed by your strategy or approach, whether they are engaged or resistant to your ideas, and why. Having this knowledge will enable you to make corrections and change direction when needed, so that your group can work together towards the shared vision.
- Two questions that tend to get the discussion going:
  - How can I make your job easier?
  - What support can I offer to help you perform your job better?

Follow-up questions:

- Could you please provide feedback on my skills? – or other topics you require feedback on.
- Should I have … sooner during our meeting?

When asking your customers for feedback

If you search the internet for 'feedback questions to ask your customers', you'll find an extensive array of sites to guide you.

One standard tool widely used across many industries is called the **Net Promoter Score (NPS)**. This tool enables you to gauge the likelihood of the customer recommending your product or service to a friend or colleague. Through the response you can determine the strength of their loyalty to your brand, clustering them in one of three categories:

1. **Promoters** score 9–10 out of 10. This is your target for customer satisfaction.
2. **Passives** score 7–8 out of 10. They tend to be sitting on the fence.
3. **Detractors** score 0–6 out of 10. The lower half of this scale is referred to as the 'red alerts', as these are the customers you will likely lose.

Multiple customer surveys are needed to calculate your NPS. The higher the positive number the better. (It's possible to have a negative score.) As a strategy, a business may initially identify its score close to zero but by working hard on addressing the issues that score can be improved upon incrementally year on year.

When asking a team or group for feedback

The 'Keep, Stop, Start' questions listed earlier provide a helpful start.

Regardless of which of these questions you are addressing, the real skill you must be able to ensure is the follow-up action and feedback. Nothing destroys trust faster than asking for and receiving feedback and then neglecting to do anything about it. There are five steps in this feedback request and follow-through process:

1.Prepare yourself and the questions ahead of time (whenever possible).

2. Ask intelligent questions that will help gather the feedback you require.

3. Analyse the feedback and determine the necessary actions.

4. Implement the changes.

5. Report on your progress to the party who offered feedback.

When asking for feedback via assessment platforms

Whether you and your company use the traditional 360-degree feedback method or a HR platform that enables instant employee feedback, the same rules apply. *The quality of the question will determine the quality of the output.*

360-degree feedback is a process that involves asking your boss/line manager, your peers, direct reports and sometimes even customers/ suppliers to evaluate your performance. You also complete the same series of questions about yourself. An analysis of the result offers an insight into how you perceive yourself versus how others perceive you.

With the increasing availability of feedback platforms, the 360-degree feedback process or a shortened version of it is more instantaneous and less formal but no less powerful. Studies indicate that contributors are open to developing a more transparent and honest response once they are assured of the anonymity of their feedback.

As mentioned above, the key to successful feedback is what is done with it once received. Platform or no platform, feedback requires that acknowledgement and action follow.

It's necessary at this point to acknowledge the need for leaders to become equally as skilled in delivering feedback as they are in seeking it. Below are several tools that you could research further to practise in this regard.

- **Informal feedback**: The FAST model, as the name suggests, is the type of feedback you may provide at the water cooler or in passing –

  F – frequent

  A – actionable

  S – specific

  T – timely

More formal feedback: Ensure that you have a private location where both parties can feel relaxed and that they are not on display. It's also preferable to be a neutral environment if possible.

Remember that even constructive feedback can promote growth in individuals and relationships if handled appropriately. Here are several behaviours to keepin mind during the feedback exercise:

– Enter the situation with the desire for dialogue; be tactful, show empathy, and use active listening skills.

– Understand why you are offering criticism – is it appropriate and constructive?

– Engage in perspective-taking or role reversal.

– Offer criticism of the person's *behaviour*, not the person.

– Focus criticism on behaviours that the other person can change.

– Focus on a particular situation rather than a general or abstract behaviour.

– Direct your criticism to the present rather than the past.

– Avoid 'critical overload' – if the recipient has a lot of areas where improvement would be beneficial, prioritise those that will create the most value first. Follow-up with additional suggestions after progress has been made on these.

- Two models you can research to use as a further guide are:

  – **BOOST** (Balanced, Observed, Objective, Specific & Timely)

  – **SBI** (Situation, Behaviour, Impact).

  Both are widely used and provide a nice structure for you to follow.

Transformational Strategy 3: Strengthening collaboration

© S4E Publishing

In our rapidly changing world, we need leaders who seek solutions through collaboration. Building partnerships through your network and establishing joint projects with potential influencers and groups from within and outside of your industry provides an agile, diverse and scalable approach.

Chapter 7: Maddie learns about the value of collaboration and partnering

'Regardless of your religious beliefs, the December to January festive season is a truly joyous time of year. It's a time when everyone across Australia receives a free pass to reset their lives – personal and business. As we come together into a united family, we place our troubles on hold and forgive each other for hurts and transgressions over the past year. It's a time when we acknowledge those around us who have contributed to our growth through their humility, integrity, generosity and sharing.'

'As we launch our annual festivities this year, I would like us to take a moment to pause and reflect on those around us; whether it was a neighbour, a friend, a relative or, especially, someone from within our working teams who has gone that extra mile to make our lives a little easier. Think of them now and send a thought of gratitude into the universe to find its way to them.'

Maddie pauses for a moment to allow people to reflect on those words, then continues.

'This year, we are going to embrace the spirit of giving a little differently than in the past few years. We are spending today working with a group of children who are less fortunate than our own or than we were at that time of life. Many of these children have been born into this world with a debilitating condition. Their childhood has been robbed of the joys and experiences as we know them. I'm sure you will quickly notice, however, that even with these limitations, they manage to give unconditional love and warmth to everyone they interact with,' Maddie concludes her briefing as the bus pulls into the parking spot at the hospice.

The Melbourne branch staff are about to disembark and experience something exceptional. As she looks into the faces of those on the bus, Maddie notices that many appear to be in self-reflection, and she can't help but wonder whether they heard much of what she had said. Terry is travelling with those on the second bus and will be delivering a similar briefing.

This outing was selected several months earlier from ideas provided anonymously to the suggestion box, which sits in the foyer of their office. An employee engagement committee, which was formed shortly after Maddie's appointment, meets every second week to discuss different ideas, and voted for this activity as their end-of-year event. After the committee did their groundwork and chose this children's hospice, they brought Terry and Maddie to visit the team responsible for caring for the children and managing the centre.

The immediate impact of the hospice and the children they met was so overwhelming that Terry had tears welling in his eyes. Together, they agreed on the venue and type of event they would organise. The tour was so moving that Terry put in a special call to the committee and pledged a considerable sum of money to ensure that these children got to experience just a small slice of joy this year.

As news of the event spread among the employees, offers of support flooded in. Gifts of all shapes and sizes were sent to the committee. Large gift bags were purchased and carefully packed with an assortment of goodies, ranging from books, games, clothes and toys to sweets and chocolate. They hired three clowns to perform, including Maddie's favourite, a balloon folding artist. A large outdoor marquee was donated for the event, together with tables and chairs. The Christmas tree was purchased, delivered and set up inside the tent ahead of their arrival. Bags and bags of decorations, cooking equipment, utensils and food were also delivered earlier this morning. One office employee volunteered to make a unique Santa costume, lined with stuffing and a full white beard. At Terry's insistence, the suit has been tailored to fit him and will be his outfit for the event.

The committee received so many offers of assistance from staff that they had no trouble assigning people to various roles and activities. Everyone set about performing their tasks, with some decorating the Christmas tree and fitting it with lights, while others wrapped presents and some set up games. Others decorated the tables before laying out an abundance of hot and cold snacks, salads, meats, fruit cakes and, of course, a wide variety of sweets.

Christmas carols echo inside and out of the tent, and everyone is wearing their elf outfit. The atmosphere is electric and the sense of camaraderie between staff working side-by-side has seldom been higher. They have found a worthy common cause and purpose.

The months of planning, endless preparations, countless calls to local businesses in the area to seek support and sponsorship was all worth it. The children now burst through the main hospice doors and head across to the large white tent in the car park. 'Not a dry eye in the house,' is what they will all remember. It is a very emotional time for staff to witness the excitement of the children and watch the expressions on their faces.

Every employee stays until the very end of the party. By now even the most resilient of the children are exhausted and carried off to bed by parents and staff. Before leaving, Maddie and Terry's team ensure the place is left spotless and the last items are cleared away. Any presents that have not found their way to the child's rooms have name tags attached and are placed neatly under the tree. There is also a pile of presents under the tree as a surprise for the hospice team, which does such a wonderful job day-to-day. The tent will be dismantled after New Year's so that the Christmas tree has a home and the hospice staff, parents and visitors can utilise the venue as much as they like. The cooking equipment used for the event is also gifted to the hospice, along with a host of other donations and sponsorships collected by the committee from local businesses. It is an event that no one will ever forget, and one that sets a new direction for all involved.

After the event, Terry and Maddie make it their short-term mission to visit and personally thank each one of the dozens of local businesses for their contribution, regardless of the value or size of the donation. Maddie has never experienced this level of collaboration before in her career, and it is a memory and lesson she will carry with her forever.

It is now 18 months since Maddie's move to head of field operations and, while things aren't always plain sailing, the branch has indeed managed to turn around its performance. Most importantly, they have established loyal fans, both internal and external. Through a series of social events, meetings and promotions, Maddie and Terry have worked tirelessly to re-establish the customer connection, building relationships previously damaged through poor performance or management. Additionally, Maddie's team of three senior managers have risen to the occasion, developing each line of business to a level that now surpasses the initial restructuring hopes and, in the process, bringing the branch's employees along with them on the journey.

From the outset, Maddie's vision was to bridge the divide between departments. 'Silos' had developed over the years, and relationships between sales and installation, and installation and service had become very strained. Maddie set about breaking down those invisible yet rigid barriers and it helped that she has a new management team to work with. It was clear from the immediate feedback they collected during the three-question surveys in those opening meetings that staff wanted to work in a more harmonious and enjoyable environment. Hence, her brief to the team was that they needed to find ways to bring the branch's departments closer together in a collaborative manner. There was zero tolerance for any silo mentality from that point forward. The message was received and acted upon, with regular cross-functional activities and meetings. Changes to procedures ensured that departments had to interact and cooperate with each other. As a result, internal collaboration is now alive and well, and this has translated into performance improvements.

One example, a by-product from this way of working is the removal of challenges staff faced in getting their jobs completed, meaning that productivity improved almost immediately. Staff began to display their happiness at work and this was evident to the customers. Comments filtering through the random customer NPS calls now show that people are noticing the turnaround in attitude and efficiency improvements in dealing with the branch in general.

One crucial barometer of the branch's success is that the sales manager is well on target to receive her bonus for the second year running, which means that the order intake is flourishing. This healthy pipeline is having a ripple effect through the operations of the company. It means that the installation business has a consistent backlog, where they can get smarter with their work processes and retain the right teams. These stable crews are ensuring a higher likelihood of the project's completion on time, on budget and to a high standard. That, in turn, has resulted in less re-work and a reduced drain on the resources of the service department during the warranty phase. At the very end of this food chain is a happy customer who experiences a reduction in breakdowns and the improvement loop is completed by receiving fewer complaints.

What previously has been an excellent service department under Maddie's direct management has turned into a highly successful and profitable stand-alone business. A result that the service manager eagerly highlights during each one-on-one review with his manager. Service sales are now a significant contributor to revenue and, of course, the bottom line, with 50 per cent gross margins now the norm.

The reliable financial results are even enabling the repairs team to tackle the replacement of some of the more troublesome equipment on the large sites, which is assisting in a reduction of the callout rate. This lower callout rate is freeing up time for the service technicians to complete their maintenance as required and to ensure the breakdown level remains at an all-time low – fluctuating between 0.2 and 0.22 stoppages per unit per month across a portfolio of more than 7000 units. It is a healthy environment and one that has not gone unnoticed in the organisation.

The national field operation is again preparing to spend time in the branch office. They want to develop a case study on the factors needed to achieve this dramatic transformation. The country CEO and Maddie's mentor, James Blake, already has a good idea of the reasons behind the successful turnaround. After the strong recommendation of Alan Wright before his departure, James agreed to take a personal interest in Maddie. From the outset, he witnessed why Alan had been so insistent. Maddie is a breath of fresh air with her diligence, thought-provoking questions and curious mind. James knows she is destined for great things if she continues in this vein. His biggest concern is the ability to retain her within the company, long enough to cascade her skills to other leaders throughout the organisation.

The location of face-to-face mentoring sessions has now shifted from the coffee shop to a meeting room in the Victorian state headquarters. Maddie knows the building's management team very well as it is one of their elite flagship contracts, where they showcase TYSO's elevators and escalators. Naturally, whenever she is onsite she takes the opportunity to invite the building managers to coffee, together with her service manager. Sometimes she asks James to stay for a few minutes longer to demonstrate the importance of this client to their business.

Only a few months ago, Terry, Maddie, their management team and senior branch staff hosted a workshop with a gathering of their premier customers in one of the large meeting halls in the building. In all, there were more than 100 guests, and Maddie was instrumental in making sure that all the Victorian senior management, together with a few of the Australian vice presidents, were in attendance.

The outcome from the workshop was client confirmation that TYSO Elevators is heading in the right direction. At Maddie's request the customers came prepared and ready to contribute ideas. Together they identified the customer's journey and expectations, the touch points that needed improvement and ways to enhance what they were doing now and into the future. It was a masterstroke that ensured the branch could remove the guesswork from its future actions and focus on those critical requests at hand.

Within a week, all participants received a professional summary of the existing challenges, future requirements and, most importantly, the action steps that will realise many of their suggestions. On the inside cover of the summary document was a full-page picture of the participants, together with a link to the email addresses of everyone for networking purposes. Back in the office, the project teams sent invitations to a few customers who wished to continue their involvement as members of the project steering committees, to evaluate progress as the group reaches its nominated milestones.

Maddie set her target of attending at least one formal gathering, client meeting, social event, or company promotion every other week. And the results are speaking for themselves. Starting from the base she had created during her time as service manager, Maddie built on this through meetings arranged by her sales manager with architects, consultants, developers and construction company senior executives.

She is impressed by the skills of her sales manager, particularly her ability to extract commitments for the next step if it becomes clear that the client isn't ready to close. Her endearing personality is leading to many invitations to company functions held by those clients, thereby strengthening the relationships.

A select target group the service manager and Maddie have worked on tirelessly are the large body-corporate organisations. These businesses manage the growing number of apartment buildings and commercial properties across the Melbourne skyline. Actively sponsoring and supporting them, and being visible at every opportunity, has the dual benefit of strengthening the service contract base and enabling Maddie to develop a considerably long list of potential modernisation prospects.

While the modernisation pipeline often has a longer gestation period than that of new installation sales, she has been able to obtain a handful of fruitful leads already and has managed to convert several into orders. Terry is very pleased, as these orders come at the expense of their competitors and grow their service revenue significantly.

Maddie has even ventured into the male-dominated domain of project job sites, to sit with Tom, the New-Installation Operations Manager, and their project managers and faced clients' abuse when things haven't gone as promised. Maddie enjoys watching the faces of the construction managers when they see her enter their office. They aren't used to situations in which it isn't appropriate for every second or third word to be punctuated with an obscenity. Over time, however, everyone has become more relaxed, and they often slip back into their typical dialogue. Maddie uses her mirroring skills, which she perfected during her hospitality training, combined with her experience in the use of colourful language, during some equally heated responses when the occasion calls for it. For the most part, however, she maintains her dignity and takes the high ground in seeking a solution to the challenge. A couple of the project managers have reported back through Tom that the construction managers truly enjoy the exchanges with her and look forward to the next opportunity to meet. They even joke that they might need to find problems with the TYSO installation to bring her back onto the site sooner.

It is no surprise to Terry, therefore, when he starts to receive requests from the Victorian and country executives for Maddie to accompany him to their meetings. Terry welcomes this, as it helps with his own broader plans of parading his nominated successor and, in turn, enabling talks about his career and the next move.

Naturally, he is aware that James Blake is mentoring Maddie and has heard through his network that James sees great potential in Terry's understudy. So long as the branch continues to perform and grow, Terry is comfortable that Maddie doesn't pose any threat to his role. He plans to capitalise on the situation when the right opportunity presents itself. Alan Wright's departure from the company meant Terry lost a spokesperson as well as a mentor and friend. Unlike Maddie, the company had decided against finding Terry a replacement mentor, which he interpreted as a negative statement about his future. Gradually, over the months that Maddie has been joining him on the trip to Sydney HQ, they began to tag-team their presentations, with Terry providing Maddie the opportunity at each subsequent visit to play a more significant role. The branch is fast becoming the number one performing operation in the country, which places them squarely in the spotlight at each meeting. Everyone wants to understand more about their strategy and actions. Terry uses this for his internal networking and to sniff out potential opportunities for his next career step.

Maddie, who is her usual diligent and confident self, is building her following of admirers. The executive colleagues who gather around the boardroom table each month are starting to know her well enough to joke about who is really running the show in Melbourne. The NSW State Manager has already begun to consider her as a potential replacement for his role. Still, unbeknown to anyone other than the country CEO, CFO and CHRO (Chief Human Resource Officer) however, Maddie is being groomed for something considerably bigger – a shot at the big league and at least a first for the country.

The announcement of Maddie's nomination as a participant in the holding companies 'Top 50 Global Talents Program' means she is the first-ever participant to come from the Australian operation. It typically suggests that a participant's career is being fast- tracked and the nomination is seen as a launching pad to much more prominent and broader roles in the short term. The TYSO world headquarters needs to identify with the Asia Pacific regional team – a suitable promotion for Maddie within the next 12 months.

Back home, word of Maddie's talents is starting to spread to the competition as well. In the past six months, TYSO has managed to capture some of the leading technical experts in the industry from major competitors. One rumour emanating from a recent hire suggests that even the hardcore union officials have nominated TYSO as the employer of choice in Victoria – high praise indeed for what Terry and Maddie have been able to achieve together. They have undoubtedly become a force to reckon with, and Terry only hopes this doesn't become a restraint on his efforts to move on, should the company feel that disrupting the winning formula was bad for business.

The months following the announcement of Maddie's nomination were like a whirlwind for her. It started with a trip to New York, where she, together with the other 49 employees in the program, received trophies for 'Outstanding Achievements and Performance'. The corporation's head and the CEO of each division greeted those attending and briefly introduced the talent program. It is a two-year-long event, combining leadership studies with several core assignments. An evaluation occurs every six months before a selection panel, which monitors progress and delivers feedback. It has meant a significant increase in Maddie's workload in the office and at home; it was akin to completing a fast-track MBA. There is one aspect of this opportunity she is a little more concerned about, however, and that is the mention of a position change, which most likely will require her to relocate. According to her mentor, the most likely scenario is a relocation to Hong Kong. James Blake can't hide his enthusiasm for her to grab the chance while it is on offer, but he also understands that it isn't an easy decision. Maddie has already highlighted the family challenges that might exist should that be the case – her ageing mother, her husband and his career, plus her son, who was about to commence primary school. In the past 12 months, the family has regularly reflected on how fortunate they have been. Their financial debt, which once was a significant burden, has virtually been eliminated. Additionally, Paul has become a leading authority in his university and in the field of political science, and Maddie herself is enjoying the new role and challenges it offers. To risk upsetting that now, in the pursuit of a new career opportunity, which still isn't clear, seems a little scary and premature. She and Paul have decided to delay focusing on the topic until Maddie knows more about the opportunity.

Each year Maddie likes to take time out to reflect on the past 12 months and examine what has worked well and the areas that have not gone as hoped. She has done this regularly over the previous four years, since returning to work after the birth of her son. This time, the fifth year, there is certainly plenty to consider. So far, she has been able to summarise her approach under the following broad statements.

> *Approach everything you commence with genuine curiosity and seek to learn about it thoroughly; otherwise, don't waste your time starting.*

Maddie has proved this to herself numerous times during her life, and it has become part of her inner-belief system.

> *While you may have a clear view about a situation and study the topic in detail, there is a high chance that others will have a different, even opposing perspective and be equally as sure about it. Therefore, you always need to consider the situation from multiple angles and try to listen for various viewpoints.*

> *Leverage from the learned knowledge of others (so-called) experts who have experienced more on a specific area or subject. Whether with work or in private matters, they can offer invaluable insights that may otherwise have taken you a long time to realise.*

Maddie recalls the mentoring program she has been fortunateenough to be part of and the benefits of working with Alan Wright and James Blake. Additionally, many industry experts and business influencers Maddie follows online confirmed her limited depth of experience in many fields.

As importantly, Maddie has come to realise the need to seek input and feedback onideas related to performance. One precious lesson she learned from Alan's suggestion was the three- question survey. Another was that no matter how clear you are about the future, youare never able to read the minds of those around you.

One of the safest ways to ensure buy-in and commitment is to seek input about what people would like to see and about how your performance may help or hinder their efforts. In the past 12 months, the learning has been more of a continuation of the above. There is a need to build a broad network and to seek collaboration across that network. Finding common goals that mightbenefit many rather than just one, will galvanise the group and result in exceptional performance. The unexpected should become almost an expectation, where making one connection leads to multiple relationships, somerelated and some from left field. The impact of such a network can open the door to surprising outcomes.

Maddie leans back on the comfortable high-back desk chair in their family study and smiles to herself. She is happy to have learned these lessons, and remembers examples where those lessons have played out throughout her life. She recalls a saying that her father wouldoften repeat to her and her sister in his heavy Greek accent:

> *υπάρχει μικρή χρησιμότητα να μεγαλώνει αν την ίδια στιγμή αποτυγχάνετε να γίνετε σοφότεροι.*

Loosely translated, this means, 'There's little use growing older if at the same time you fail to become wiser'. Maddie's memories of her father momentarily distracts her from the lessons. When her thoughts return, they arrive at a different place.

This time she is visualising the future and possible scenarios that she knows will soon present themselves. If Hong Kong is indeed the next leg of this journey, would she continue with the scheduled train ride or let it depart from the station without her?

Chapter 8: Tim capitalises on his relationships and seeks a promotion

The past two years have been a tumultuous phase in Tim's life. He has managed to grow on several fronts – personally, financially and professionally – despite significant challenges. Around the start of this period, Tim met Harry Bloom and his wife, Sandra. They were visiting Sydney to care for Harry's father, who had suffered a severe heart attack. Even though Harry returned to London six weeks later, they have remained close. One of the reasons being that Harry is now mentoring Tim in the area of technology developments and future trends.

During Harry's time in Sydney, Tim met two of Harry's colleagues who shared his interests. Together, this group decided to work on developing an app to solve a common pain point in the construction industry; the ability to provide accurate, visual, real-time data that tracked the construction progress on job sites. Once released, the group plans to pitch it to all major construction and subcontractor companies. After signing a licence- based agreement, each site will have access to run the technology, which can integrate seamlessly into any internal legacy platform. The app provides the ability to upload live data whenever an internet connection is available. With the timing of their release aligned with the introduction of 5G technology globally, it means that there is little restriction in securing high-transfer speeds for data streaming.

The three-person project team has been working considerable hours on the backend coding of the app. At the same time, Tim has enlisted his sister to engage, under confidentiality agreements, specialists at her university to map out a strategic marketing campaign, complete with promotional material.

The app is currently at the beta-testing phase with the first prototype and early indications are even more positive than expected. Their platform is functioning smoothly, and the interfacing with other platforms appears to be stable. The front-end user experience is also sure to please; the high-end look, feel and effortless interfaces make it intuitive for all levels of users who need to gather data and send instant updates.

Whether on a smartphone or tablet, the user will be able to capture images, enter information or select pre-written responses from a series of dropdown options. Everything can then be uploaded within minutes of arriving at a location and capturing the information. Once received on the company's platform, the data is automatically cross-referenced and overlaid with the last upload from the same area and a projection for completion generated. This helps to flag slippage in schedules and assists with the verification of progress claims. Issues can be immediately addressed without the need for meetings and wasted time arguing about the accuracy of the claims or necessary solutions. The system then dispatches an automated email to the related subcontractor and project supervisor, with a screen capture of the analysis.

The second prototype version is already in the planning phase, with improved safety and quality management features. It is an exciting but draining time for Tim, whose lack of previous exposure to anything comparable is causing him to work extra hard most evenings. His day job was the inspiration behind the idea for the app, and his site role enables him to liaise with the main contractor and other subcontractor teams to understand some of their most significant challenges.

From the other side of the world, Harry is able to support the project by leveraging his own project team's expertise with software development and to help answer any questions that arise from the coding team in Sydney. With a 10–11-hour time difference, this is invaluable. It means that the team can send through their queries before retiring late at night and, in most instances, can have a series of suggested solutions waiting for them on their return the next morning. It also has a tremendous advantage of keeping their development on schedule. While their research did not identify even a remotely similar project, they also know enough of the industry to realise that time is always of the essence in these situations. Their field research places even more urgency on getting this product to market as it confirms keen customer interest for such a product. Based on their entry-level price, the projected sales forecasts suggest a break-even on the initial investment – for R&D, current material and a 12- month marketing provision inclusive of sales team salaries – at a brief six-month timeframe. Even better news from their marketing model, which is unable to find a usage saturation level. It deems the market as infinite if the product is regularly updated with minor modifications and open to different lines of business.

All in all, Tim feels quietly confident that he will soon be making a significant contribution to the future financial health and wellbeing of his new and growing family. He proposed to Janet 18 months ago and, after a short engagement, they were married over the following Christmas period. Shortly afterwards, Janet announced her pregnancy and just last month delivered them a son. Naturally, the new grandparents on both sides are delighted. For Janet, it is the perfect conclusion to what seemed, at times, just a dream. Inside 18 months, she got engaged and married her long-time love, and then gave birth to a healthy younger version of her husband.

Being a financial adviser, Janet is aware of Tim's struggles with managing his money and anything remotely related. He usually avoids the topic and she senses that he feels intimidated by her knowledge. As a result, Tim meekly concedes to ideas and planning based on the guidelines she prepares and manages. Now, with the birth of Andrew Timothy Henley, Janet knows it was time for her and Tim to have a serious conversation about their financial future.

Tim is particularly proud that he and Janet are open within their relationship and can share their thoughts and discuss most things. He has observed many times how Janet is particularly skilled in getting him to feel comfortable enough to speak on any topic, whether sexual, health-related or professional. There is one area, however, he knows they both avoided talking openly about: money. Tim understands that he is the main reason for that, and two years ago he took the bold step, following a meeting with his boss, of finding himself a financial mentor. Until now, Tim has kept this arrangement a secret from Janet, hoping one day to have the opportunity to surprise and impress her.

His mentor is a family friend, so it is quite easy for Tim to speak honestly about his concerns and lack of knowledge on the subject. Tim's initial goal was to develop his abilities in the areas of financial planning and management. He hopes to reach a level of competence that allows for a meaningful conversation with his wife about money.

Over the past 12 months, Tim has been meeting his mentor every two weeks over lunch, to discuss and learn about financial matters. He has been surprised by how much they have covered in that period, both from the teaching and his research. He has even taken to listening to podcasts by two social media influencers on the topic of money matters.

Half-way into the mentoring period, Tim had saved the minimum required to open a private share trading account and, with the assistance of his mentor, analysed several blue-chip stocks and completed the purchase. The share account isn't so much for investing as it is to learn about the stock market and the different products it offers. He has learned to read company portfolios and to invest for the long term while trading short term. The lessons have been precious, as his involvement has increased with the development of the app. Tim has often sat with his mentor for two hours at a time, working through projections, looking at expenses and generally digesting everything he can.

It has been a great introduction into the financial world, and at the end of that 12 months, they agreed on a plan to meet once a quarter for the next year. At each quarterly meeting, Tim would detail his current financial plan and areas of focus. During that meeting, his mentor will give additional insights and guidance, helping Tim to tweak his understanding and approach. Tomorrow will be their final session, and Tim is eagerly awaiting the opportunity to share the news about his latest family addition. He wants to seek his mentor's guidance on the best strategy for securing his son's financial future. Tim knows the time has arrived for a heart-to-heart talk with Janet about their finances. Following the discussion, he also wants to lift some of the burden from his wife's shoulders.

Several mentor meetings earlier, Tim had floated the idea of using an external financial adviser, and together he and his mentor had canvased potential candidates, eventually narrowing down the list to three. Tim planned to suggest to Janet, very carefully, that they might meet and interview those candidates together. He is hoping that Janet will feel comfortable placing a large portion of their investments with one of the institutions and allow them to start managing their portfolio on their behalf.

Saying his farewells to his mentor for the last time, Tim replays the meeting in his mind and the critique he has received about his new plan. Overall, the feedback was quite positive, and he thinks to himself, 'it's now or never'. Removing his phone from his pocket, Tim calls his mother to secure her babysitting services for tomorrow night. Then he calls one of Janet's favourite restaurants and makes a booking for two.

Finally, he calls Janet.

It is their first evening away from Andrew and, naturally, there is a mountain of preparation that Janet insists on before she takes a final glance at her son, on the way out to dinner. It is also the first night in a long time that Tim won't be doing any work with his app team. He has been purposely vague about the occasion and the reason they are dining out. Janet wonders if she may have been too occupied with their son and has forgotten their anniversary or a birthday. Tim seems extremely coy and aloof as he sits back in his chair, staring at his wife and dodging her questions. Finally, he breaks the silence and confesses all to her about his financial mentoring, the trading account, the future considerations and even the search for a financial adviser.

Janet is amazed and impressed, although inwardly she wonders how much Tim understands given the complexity of her industry. As they talk over dinner, it becomes clear that he has indeed been learning quite a lot. They are able to have an intelligent conversation about derivatives, about the pros and cons of self-managed superannuation and the advantages of running a company versus operating a partnership or as a sole trader. Tim shows off his knowledge by chatting through the idea of investing for the long term in low-fee funds and a host of other topics. Once Tim feels he has earned enough credibility with Janet, he removes a folder from his bag. The first page contains a summary that Tim has prepared of their current financial plan. This is followed by several other pages showing options for additional divestment from several of their existing funds in order to establish a trust for Andrew.

Janet stares at the pages, feeling a little overwhelmed and not exactly sure what to say. Finally, she smiles and says, 'Well, it seems that we will have a new topic for debate at the dinner table in the future!' Without realising it, Tim releases a huge sigh of relief as Janet's eyes sparkle with admiration for her husband, who it seems has conquered his fear and addressed one of the most unspoken yet stressful barriers in their relationship.

Before finishing up and paying the bill, Tim hands Janet the final page from the folder. He explains that he and his mentor have screened over a dozen advisers, based on criteria that Janet had introduced earlier when preparing the guidelines for their family's financial strategy. Tim is quick to add that Janet has done a great job in managing their finances single-handedly until now. He hopes that they can free up some of her valuable time and allow her to focus on their son and her career without the burden of overseeing their investments single handedly.

It is a memorable evening and two years in the making – by theend of the dinner both leave the restaurant feeling elated and fulfilled.

Over these past two years, Tim's relationship with his father has improved considerably. Tim recalls the day in the hospital when he confided in his father about seeing a psychiatrist and his father's positive response, saying that both his parents would always be there if Tim needed support. That day, Tim also told his father about his plans to ask Janet to marry him and was happy to receive his father's blessing. Since that day, their relationship has grown deeper and closer than it has been since his childhood. Tim has met many of James Henley's colleagues, and it has surprised him to learn just how many of them knew little of the outside world beyond their field of expertise. The real value from this, as James would have realised, is not the direct contact but more so the opportunity to connect with people outside their professional network. Tim shared with his father his interest in developing his leadership skills and how he wished to take on a more senior role in business. He explained to his father that he is laying the groundwork now, trying to understand people better and to understand himself much more by being present and aware of how he deals with the daily challenges of project management. Tim confided in his father his goal of seeking financial mentoring from a family friend, mostly to feel adequate at home, but also as part of his professional development.

Tim's engagement in the creation of the app is something James finds very interesting and has encouraged Tim to pursue. While James doesn't fully understand the concept and its potential in the construction business, his view is that it presents an excellent opportunity for Tim's personal and professional growth. He has even offered to support the project financially if Tim thinks it a sound investment.

Through one of James's colleagues, Tim recently met Jonathan Yanks, a venture capitalist specialising in supporting start-ups. While Tim is far from an expert in this field, he knows enough to be careful as he introduced the concept. Jonathan offered Tim his card and expressed an interest in learning more once they got close to launching. Tim thanked him politely and said he would certainly keep it in mind. As he left that meeting, he made a mental note to do some research on the workings of venture capitalists and to call his financial mentor for a chat about it.

That meeting with Jonathan came to mind as Tim and Janet drove home from the restaurant. With his new confidence following the favourable reaction from his wife, Tim feels no hesitation in asking Janet what she know s on the topic of venture capital.

This time her reaction is less reserved as she swings quickly in her seat to face him. Janet immediately interrupts Tim's question to ask if he is thinking about investment capital for some bizarre scheme towards building their wealth. After a pause, Tim explains the reason behind the question. He has been wondering about how they might start to scale up the release of the app if it proves successful at the local level. The line of questioning from Janet makes Tim realise that he needs to move slowly and tread carefully around financial matters for some time to come. Janet is close enough to the project to understand Tim's thinking. Early in the group's formation, Tim convinced the other members of the group of the value of having someone with Janet's financial expertise to act as the pragmatist for the team. Her task, as Tim explained it, will be to oversee the marketing research and subsequent sales projections, bringing a rationale and logic into the equation if the group becomes too ambitious about changing the world.

Tim's research on the topic has led him to understand that the risks from venture capitalist investment vary depending on the timing of their financial injection into the project. The earlier they inject money, the higher the risk and, therefore, the higher the proportion of return expected. At the same time, the earlier they invest, the more control they will be able to exert over how the money is spent, particularly on things such as marketing. Hence, if they seem eager to come on board early, it is likely that they have a good sense of the size and scale of opportunity presented.

Once he understood this, Tim was immediately excited by the fact that Jonathan had been interested enough to want to learn more. He had spoken in private with Harry about it afterwards, but they both agreed that they didn't understand the pros and cons sufficiently to make a judgement at that time. So Tim set aside the idea until tonight. Now, however, he is a little unclear about whether he has done the right thing, raising it with Janet without giving it further thought.

To his relief, Janet's tone and body language immediately change as she begins to understand why he is asking the question. Then she proceeds to outline the thinking process and subsequent actions required before considering this direction. It becomes clear to Tim that now isn't the right time to seek venture capital, as there is little need for additional capital at the moment. Based on Janet's conservative calculations, they are likely to be operating with a net positive cash flow well inside 12 months after launch. Only after that will they need to consider scaling their business outside of the state or even the country.

Over the past couple of years, Tim has continued to place a heavy focus on managing his project site and ensuring he doesn't drop the ball in his performance. After all, this is still his primary source of income, and with a young family he can't afford to lose that. Perhaps more significant, however, is the fact that this job is his intended catalyst towards a leadership career. Indeed, he has matured considerably in this current role, and his knowledge about business through this app project and his activities has improved significantly.

According to Tim's project schedule, they should be close to handing over the last elevator units within six months, leaving another few months to tidy up loose ends and finalise contractual and payment issues. Therefore, within nine months, Tim is likely to be looking for a new project or a different role. His hope is to secure a new position, but he hasn't heard any rumours suggesting that his boss is planning to leave. Besides, who would recommend Tim as an obvious first choice for his replacement? This realisation sparks immediate concern for Tim, and he starts to think about increasing his visibility and presence in the office. If his activities in the past 12 months have taught him anything, its that he needs to have a strong support network lobbying for him in the background. Changing from the role of Project Manager to a manager sitting in an office requires different tactics to those played out in other field roles. Relying purely on his ability to shine through isn't one of them.

To Tim's surprise, his arrival at the office coincides with the cutting of a birthday cake for one of the office staff. He didn't even know that this type of thing occurred! A look of concern must be visible on his face because a colleague from the service team nudges him and makes some quirky comments about the need to keep the players fed and friendly. Tim decides not to stand around too long as he doesn't want to attract attention for the wrong reasons. Instead, he makes himself a coffee and scans the office for a conversation partner. Looking around, he spots a notice board that seems to be overflowing with information.

Standing there and reading the various notices, Tim sees a bulletin about the company's career opportunities. There is an employee website for open positions across the entire global operation! Tim quickly takes a photo, hoping nobody sees him. An exciting discovery, he thinks to himself and then wonders what else he might find during this visit. Remembering the purpose of the visit is to build his network, he starts mingling and looks for those who could offer some value – first stop is the head of sales.

Tim is curious to understand what projects are likely to be secured in the coming months. From the discussion with the head of sales he learns that the order backlog is very healthy and that the company is tendering on several large projects at present as well as negotiating on others. It occurs to him to participate and learn about this process in some way, so he enquires about whether there would be any possibility of supporting. To his surprise, the head of sales mentions that they are in discussion on an attractive project with the same developer from Tim's current project. The sales manager is interested to know whether Tim has a working relationship with the client, and what other people he has met over the course of the project. In short, is there anything that might be useful for the sales team to know as they put their tender together and prepare for negotiations? Tim offers up what information he can but finishes the conversation with a promise to do some investigating and report back by the end of the week.

That was a fruitful conversation, Tim thinks to himself as he walks towards the CFO. He notices himself smiling as he approaches and wonders if it's because of his new-found financial confidence or the value of this visit to the office. Tim introduces himself and starts a discussion about the general health of their business. It seems they are having a good year and the bottom-line results are above budget. Tim mentions the importance of closing projects as quickly as possible to avoid profit slide. His statement generates an immediate response from the CFO, who confirms that profit 'fade' is always his fear. In particular, he elaborates on the need for project managers to forecast accurately and leave adequate provision for those last remaining tasks to be completed. Identifying ways to protect their company against slippage due to the antics of the main contractors, whom the CFO believes are always on the lookout for ways to minimise their own slippage.

Tim speaks proudly about his project and their approach towards securing variations.

'Variations,' he says, 'are the project manager's best friend. They have saved us on many of my projects over the years.' Tim wonders out loud if the company might hold a workshop so the project teams could come together. Perhaps even invite manufacturing, sales, installation, service and finance teams to sit down together with the project teams and discuss the challenges encountered during a typical project. 'Most project managers are well versed in contract risk management and various onsite issues but are mostly oblivious to the workings of other departments. What I feel is missing is a more collaborative understanding between departments about the challenges experienced at each stage of the product life cycle.'

'What do you think is the solution?' the CFO asks.

'Developing a better understanding and strengthening collaboration might resolve many of the repeated mistakes,' Tim responds confidently.

The CFO is immediately interested and agrees to pursue the idea of hosting a joint workshop or meeting.

Tim spots the branch HR manager, excuses himself from the CFO and makes a beeline for her. He introduces himself and enquires about the company's policy on providing workers with incentives as recognition for performance. He explains that his team has done a fantastic job throughout the project and he hopes to reward them in some way. The HR manager replies that usually Tim would need to speak with his department manager and get approval from the MD, but there is nothing in the policies that say it isn't permitted.

'What do you have in mind?' she asks Tim.

After tossing around several ideas, they agree that financial recognition isn't always the best option, and that there are usually many more intrinsic motivators available at lower cost and have a more lasting effect. Tim is happy to learn this and thanks her before moving off to chat with the MD, whom he has just spotted walking out of his office. The last time Tim spoke with him was after the site fire, and the world has changed significantly since then. Tim is eager to have a one-on-one with his branch boss to see whether he remembers Tim. More so, however, Tim wants to demonstrate that he has matured and is now leadership material. While walking over to talk to him, Tim tries to read the MD's body language. Does he look happy, is he smiling or, worst case, looking stressed?

The MD has a reputation for being a fair but a no-nonsense guy. Tim smiles and extended his hand. He explains that he has popped in to see Nathan but is taking the opportunity to speak with many of the staff that he would usually only see at the Christmas party.

The MD congratulates Tim on his marriage and birth of their child, which makes Tim pause for a moment. The MD smiles and says 'Even I read the papers, you know! Having high-profile parents means that these events don't escape the local news.'

Tim recalls the articles, which Janet dutifully cut out and pasted into her journal at the time. Recovering, Tim thanks the MD and quickly shifts the conversation back to business. He confirms that it looks like his project will be closing in the next six months and they are on budget thanks to multiple variations they have been able to secure. The MD smiles while waving to a colleague, who gestures for him to join them. As he starts to move away, the MD pauses and said, 'Then we had better start looking for a new and bigger challenge to keep you busy, Mr Henley. Make sure you speak with Nathan about the options.'

It turns out that Nathan isn't in the office today. Tim figures he has covered about as many people as he cares to meet in one afternoon and heads home. On the way, he recalls his conversations and makes mental notes about follow-up actions. One of the most significant lessons for him is the need for him to network more frequently. He believes he has now given himself the excuses needed to make that happen. One thought that keeps replaying in his mind is the MD's parting comment – was it just a throwaway line, or is he serious about something bigger and better? It was a topic he intends to pursue with Nathan at the earliest opportunity.

Chapter 9: Harry's collaboration helps him evolve in a different direction

Harry returns to London, pumped and recharged after the unexpected journey to the 'land down under'. The combination of his father's recovery and the hospitality received from the Henley family during their stay has raised Harry's spirits and helped him to reflect on his life.

Two heart-to-heart conversations have also boosted Harry's spirits. The first, a discussion with his mother during those early days after arriving in Sydney. The love and loyalty demonstrated by Claire, who insisted on remaining by her husband's side every day and long into each night, led Harry to sit her down and talk about her plans should the unthinkable happen.

Initially, Claire brushed him off, saying that everything will be fine and the doctors are giving Robert a very high chance of making a full recovery. Even so, Harry insisted on talking through arrangements. They were, after all, in a foreign country. If the recovery goes as well as expected, they still need to consider the complications associated with transporting Robert safely back to London at some point.

Harry was surprised to learn that Robert and Claire had spoken about moving to Australia some years back. However, Robert had not retired as planned, due to the demand for his guest lectures. Perhaps, she said, this was a sign that they should think more seriously about the plan.

Gradually, Harry works through a list of formal procedures they will follow if required in the future. Critical topics to be covered include the location of his parents' wills, estate documents, funeral requirements, future home care and execution of their wills, including Power of Attorney. Claire's profession as a librarian instilled in her an eye for detail. Therefore, the organisation of their family's affairs, such as the location of private documents and personal arrangements are mostly in order. Harry has wanted to have this discussion with his parents for many years but just never found the courage or right moment to touch on what he saw as a somewhat morbid subject. His mother's grief over the loss of her parents when he was a child has remained in his mind, and the last thing he wants is to risk triggering those memories for his mother.

One thing that he hasn't spoken about with Claire is his concern for her health and a worst-case scenario that plays out sometimes when he closes his eyes. The potential for having both parents hospitalised in Sydney seemed very real. His mother's mind is sharp, but her body hasn't been as fortunate, and seeing her sit there in the hospital made her look frail and vulnerable.

The Henley's generosity and friendship during that period has been one of the most blessed and unexpected acts Harry has experienced in his 50 years. He can't determine if the support for their family was borne from the severity of the situation or the global importance of the individual. Maybe Dr Henley appreciated the spirit and trust Claire Bloom had shown him and his staff. Whatever the reality, it was a gift from above that Harry will happily work the remainder of his life to repay.

As each week passed in Sydney and Robert Bloom's health improved, the family became more relaxed, which had been most noticeable in Claire's mood and body language. The sparkle returned to her eyes, and she started joking with the hospital staff. Even Robert was out of bed and moving around by the end of the first month. Slowly at first and supported by the aid of a walker. His progress was encouraging and allowed Harry to contemplate heading back to work. During that first month, Harry connected with some of his colleagues in the Sydney office. They met several times in global workshops and formed a good relationship, and his contact with them seemed welcome. With their support, Harry accepted the use of a temporary desk, which enabled him easier access to the company's servers and his project files than using his laptop.

When not at the hospital during the day, Harry worked on the mountainous backlog of paperwork, which seemed to have exploded in his absence and, despite the time difference, he organised regular late-night calls from the apartment with his team to discuss open issues. It felt good to have this distraction and to be connected to the project once again. His deputy, Frank Chi, was extremely grateful for this support and excited by the prospect that Harry may soon be able to rejoin them. Frank enjoyed the opportunity to stand in, but this type of spotlight wasn't his thing, and he would be more than happy to resume his original position on Harry's return.

According to the latest project schedule, they were tracking okay and close to the original projection for completion. Harry wondered how accurate this was, given the issues they had been facing at the time of his departure. Another surprise was Harry's boss, who was also happy to hear from him and learn that he was back on the project remotely as an interim step. Over the phone, it sounded to Harry as though his boss had softened in his absence and was quite considerate regarding his father's condition, even expressing that Harry's priority was to ensure his personal life was in order. After hanging up from the call, Harry wasn't sure what to read into that conversation. Did it signal that his boss appreciated Harry after all, or was his boss saying they could manage without him? The uncertainty made him feel uneasy.

Around the same time, Harry's wife, Sandra, headed back to London to get things in order on the home front. She also had a full-time job and, though her company was understanding, they were anxious for her to return. As much as she wanted to stay and support her husband and parents-in-law, Sandra knew it would be easier for everyone, including their beautiful hosts. To her surprise, there was a small press gathering at Heathrow, wanting to learn firsthand what they could about the recovery of one of the country's most renowned academics.

'Seems that events from recent weeks would alter their once obscure and relatively peaceful life, at least for the short term,' Sandra recounted to her mother.

Harry remained a further three weeks in Sydney until his father was strong enough to leave the hospital and take up temporary residence in the Henley's apartment. Once Harry was confident that everyone was comfortable, the three of them agreed that Harry should go home to be with his family and get his work affairs sorted out. Under advice from the medical teams in Sydney and London, Robert and Claire planned to remain in Sydney for a further three to six months, to ensure Robert's full recovery under the supervision of Dr Henley and his team. Harry would return around that time to escort his parents back home, accompanied by their family doctor, who would join them in Sydney for the return flight. Before departing, Harry observed that his father's mood had improved and sought the opportunity to speak about the various matters that had plagued him for some time. Some of these issues were quite old and others relatively new, such as the arrangements his mother and he had made in the early days shortly after arriving in Sydney. His father was still quite heavily sedated, and Harry was cautious about structuring the conversation in a non-confrontational way. The discussion went well. Harry came away feeling that he had received a fair hearing and even some positive acknowledgment from his father.

On the flight back to London, Harry's mind drifts to his future. He wonders whether he might be content to commence another project as this one moves to a close. He considers whether he could ever get a senior leadership role, and even whether this is something that interests him in the long term. He suspects that the desire is driven more by the fact that he hasn't had the chance previously, rather than a genuine longing to spend the rest of his life working long hours for a corporation.

He reviews his options. Financially his family is comfortable; even though they aren't rich by any means, they have managed their money well for many years and havea sizeable nest egg put away. His adult children are mostly self-sufficient, and with both he and Sandra working and no mortgage to repay, they are able to save a significant portion of their salaries each month. A persistent thought surfaces once more – what if he did start building his own business while still employed? It could give him a chance to minimise the risk and think through different strategies, without the pressure of having to make money immediately to survive.

He has already brainstormed this notion multiple times in the past, and the result was always similar. There is a considerable upside and an unlimited number of options available. The challenge he is struggling with is which idea is right to pursue. However, on this return flight, things are beginning to become clearer. For many years, Harry enjoyed being able to contribute to the growth of people. In more recent years, this desire has grown into a desire to shift from mentoring to the professional coaching of others. His passion for triathlons has spurred a secret desire to look in that direction, becoming a sports coach for elite athletes. One obstacle is that his academic background is in engineering rather than in social and human psychology. If he does pursue anything in the sports or life coaching arena, he will need to look at studying again and possibly on several fronts before offering his services with confidence and adequate credentials. Even so, the idea is appealing, and the encounter with Rachelle and Tim Henley made him realise that there might indeed be a niche market. He can provide a service for those fitness fanatics who love the concept of the triathlon but are unlikely to reach that professional level due to their personal and financial limitations. On the positive side, their passion ensures that they are almost as dedicated and loyal to the cause as their professional counterparts, and eager to seek personal improvement.

Harry is keen to provide a mixed coaching package. Not purely for sports enthusiasts, but also for those who have a dual interest in sport and personal development. Harry recognises that triathletes are a special breed, and that the commitment to their sport echoes a broader commitment to the way they live their whole lives.

As Harry ponders the idea more seriously, many unanswered questions arise that he will need to explore deeper before this direction could even be a topic for discussion with his wife. The one action he does commit to during the flight home is to investigate the matter further in the weeks and months ahead. He has already identified two people he could speak to for initial guidance. The first is a close friend from his early university days at Imperial College and who is now one of the track-and-field athletic coaches for the United Kingdom squad. The other is a fellow triathlete who recently gave up her career to turn professional. Between them, he hopes to confirm the areas of expertise and steps required to move away from his current career into this field of sports and life coaching.

Almost one month since his return, and Harry has settled back into his project. In his absence his team managed to pull back that lost time. His boss has continued to treat him favourably, and reports of his father's continuing improvement are all very welcome developments. Plus, it seems his mother has become close friends with the Henleys and has taken to accompanying Rachelle to the university, spending countless hours mingling with the library staff. Rachelle's standing with the university has grown considerably after becoming friends with one of the world's most acclaimed economists and for introducing his wife to campus faculty. Claire loves the chance to spend time with those sharing similar interests. She is taking every opportunity to re-live stories of times when royalty or prime ministers had visited her library. The famous family story of the scheduled trip to Sydney, cancelled at the request of the Prime Minister, has become a favourite to share with all newcomers to the discussion table.

It seems that Harry is now able to relax a little and continue to grow his understanding of a potential career change and to direct his focus to researching the coaching world. At the same time, he is speaking with Tim and the team in Sydney at least twice a week to support their app project. It has become a fun activity to present his London team with a coding challenge and see who is the first to find a solution for a small reward. The regular exercise is providing a welcome distraction for his team, and Harry notices their engagement and performance tends to peak for that day after each challenge. Sometimes Harry joins in and is able to resolve the occasional coding problem himself. Other times he presents an immense challenge to the team, knowing that it will benefit both camps. The solutions his team provides are forwarded to the Sydney group. It's a win–win situation and has been tremendously helpful in keeping the app development on target.

Today Harry arrives at his office early, to finish preparations for a morning team meeting. He reads through a message from Tim, thanking him for his continuing support and chatting about their collective ideas around the app development. Before Harry left Sydney they agreed that he would mentor Tim. It's one small way to return the friendship and hospitality that the Henleys showed to his family. The app is something that he and Tim discussed several times before his departure and is partially the reason behind introducing Tim to his company colleagues. Still, it is very pleasing to see Tim's eagerness and drive continuing, and Harry is starting to wonder how big this idea might become as they move to make it a reality.

App development isn't anything new for Harry; he has worked on similar projects before. However, the potential market for this idea seems quite considerable, and he imagines the application being useful even within his organisation. This realisation has piqued his interest, and having an expert project team at his disposal in London gives him further reason to feel a little excited by what may be possible.

The coaching guidance he has received from his two friends on his return from Sydney has been beneficial. The athletics coach has provided a picture of the qualifications he will require. So it is possible to develop a clear study path and a list of likely expectations any sportsperson might have of him as a coach. His triathlete friend has spoken openly about her mindset shift, together with the financial and family preparations she needed ahead of the transition. Harry's research is building on this advice, and he is now gaining the necessary clarity to start mapping out a timeline of events and activities that may one day lead to realising his dream.

Harry is a skilled electronics engineer and has headed up many business departments over the course of his career. He found his calling in developing teams and individuals, so he is comfortable with the idea of interacting and working with strangers. Running his own business, however, will require different knowledge and skills, so he begins to turn his attention to the specifics he needs to understand and learn.

There are countless internet sites offering advice on everything from starting a gardening business to building an empire, plus a broad range of sites about the world of coaching. Harry is a little surprised by the sheer number of coaching sites and wonders if this market might already be saturated. He decides that he needed more face-to-face communication with business experts, whom he can ask questions and perhaps even sound out his ideas. The most prominent person to turn to is his father, but Harry isn't quite at the point, yet, of wanting to share this possible mid-life career change with anyone, most notably his parents. As he fumbles around the idea of whom he might know, he encounters a Small Business and Freelancers Convention being hosted in London this week. He can't believe it. After reading the program carefully, he quickly registers and makes plans to be there tomorrow. It seems like a tremendous opportunity and will surely provide some of the answers he needs.

The next day is an eye-opening experience for Harry as he starts to develop a feeling for just how many independent small business areas exist. The convention is invaluable for several reasons. First, he finds multiple coaching booths, where he spends considerable time asking questions and trying to get a feeling for the industry. Indeed, it seems the world of personal coaching has exploded in recent years. Harry is heartened to find no one is offering the same combination as he is considering. Filling his backpack with brochures and business cards, he sits back to listen to some of the keynote speakers. Looking at the day's program, there are four speakers who interest him the most. One will be speaking on the topic of business systems and processes for sole traders and small business owners. The remaining three will be covering issues related to business legalities, building your brand and lastly, tips on growing a client base. Harry hopes to connect with as many like-minded people as possible so that he can build a network after the euphoria of the convention has passed.

He arrives home in the evening feeling exhausted but hugely satisfied by his achievements and what he has learned. The day turned out to be everything he'd hoped for, and his backpack is bursting with the information he plans to explore in depth in the weeks ahead. He feels that he now has a basis from which to build his ideas and is anxious to get started tomorrow.

Until this point, Harry hasn't spoken about his coaching ideas with his wife, other than a few passing comments implying that he wouldn't mind pursuing the idea at some stage. He decides that tonight he will break the news. Since their experience in Sydney, Sandra and Harry's relationship has been strengthened, and he knows her happiness had improved. The connection she made with Cynthia Henley, mother of Rachelle and Tim, and one of the leading fashion designers in Australia, was incredible. Amidst the sadness and uncertainty surrounding Robert Bloom's future, Sandra and Cynthia have struck up a friendship through their shared interests in fashion. Sandra runs one of the clothing departments in a leading British establishment and has made a point on her return to connect Cynthia with the store's head of fashion. It seems that Cynthia's brand may be expanding to London, and they are now negotiating an exclusive agreement to promote Cynthia's winter line.

After dinner, Sandra and Harry sit together in their living room and share their days' events. Sandra is brimming with the news about helping Cynthia, and Harry seems genuinely happy to hear the story. He plans to have a second coaching call with Tim in a few days and both are eager to help their newest friends. Although neither has said it aloud, they have both wondered whether one day they may find an opportunity to move to Sydney themselves.

It is Harry's turn to introduce his day and his activities, which have occupied his spare time since that long flight back home. He starts by asking Sandra to think of the feeling she was experiencing from being able to assist Cynthia. To visualise the joy and happiness, the exposure and financial benefits her actions are sure to have for the Henley's business.

'That is the same feeling I am experiencing,' Harry explains, 'in being able to give back a little with Tim. In fact, through my career, I've known that this character trait, being able to support others, to help them develop and grow as individuals, has brought me the most satisfaction. More so than any successful projects or promotion. On the flight home, I had the opportunity to gain considerable clarity around what I would like to do with the remainder of my life and, for the past few weeks, I've been investigating and learning about different elements of that to make sure it is indeed the direction I want. It turns out that it is.'

Harry describes the steps he has taken so far and what he has understood from his research. He shows Sandra the rough timeline he has created, to give her some idea about how quickly all of this might happen. Sandra is pleased to see that Harry is planning to continue working for at least another two to three years while he undertakes some study and learns more about the business side of coaching. Harry pauses and looks at Sandra.

'Do you think I'm crazy to want this and walk away from my corporate lifestyle?'

Sandra takes Harry's hand, looks into his eyes and says, 'I believe you would make an incredible coach and I wholeheartedly support your ideas.'

As they speak more about the idea, they also talk about how Sandra could lend her support. What are her superpowers that could contribute to the success of Harry's venture? By the time they retire to bed, they are both mentally exhausted from their brainstorming, but very firmly aligned and clear on the direction and next actions both will take to help convert Harry's dream into reality.

One thing Harry has learned from recent events is that networking and collaboration with others are essential throughout life, in both personal and professional matters. He recalls the medical connections that were immediately mobilised with news of his father's heart attack – the offers of support from family and friends that flooded in for Sandra and Harry. And how his own company and the project team had rallied to remove any burden from him while he dealt with the family emergency. If the need for a reliable and robust network hadn't been evident to him before, it most certainly is now.

The next day, Harry is in a particularly good mood and arrives at work early, noticing how much less traffic there is at this time of the day, compared to his regular commute. Setting his day in motion, he plans the mornings' sprint meeting. By the time the entire team has arrived, he feels like he has already completed as much as he usually does on an average day. Even the meeting seems to flow better than usual.

Frank has run the meeting very effectively over the past few weeks, and Harry is comfortable letting that continue. Harry participates more as the project sponsor rather than as the project leader. He introduces the progress reports and next sprint package – a two-week build-out of a critical software function, which ties together several of the platform's core applications.

On the same day, without discussing it with Harry, Sandra enlists her children to support their father's new venture. Their youngest daughter, Peg, is studying at the London College of Fashion and has an eye for the creative. She is assigned the task of engaging with her graphic design friends to come up with a contemporary yet professional design for the coaching business and Harry's brand. Travis, who is studying civil engineering at Imperial College, agrees to the task of building a website and landing pages once the design is ready – ensuring that he leverages off his colleagues and introduces the latest technologies. Their eldest daughter, Charlotte, who is now working on her master's in economics, takes on the business's development. Her tasks involve researching the core requirements for setting up a small business, including automated platforms and systems that can be scaled as the company grows. They decide to include the potential to develop and offer online coaching, plus coaching courses, all linked via the website.

Each person's brief is simple, make your dad proud and bring to the table a range of professional, integrated working elements that will help kickstart his business. The timeframe is five months from now: Harry's birthday. Sandra will do her part by seeking out details on establishing a company, sourcing insurance and selecting suitable uniform apparel such as clothing and footwear. Everyone is tasked with seeking out and securing from their network anyone remotely related with or connected to sports who may be a potential coaching candidate.

In the meantime, Harry begins by categorising the people he met at the convention and identifying how each might be useful in his network, applying simple criteria he'd found on a site during his research about building a business:

- Continually expand your business network and develop new leads.
- Learn about your industry and create business development opportunities.

- Explore ideas, services and products for new innovative approaches.
- And simply look for ways to keep yourself inspired and energised!

On this journey, Harry reviews each company's website from the convention as well as affiliated site links. He is looking at the products and services they offer as a means of getting further information or even as a potential competitor. With each company he reviews, he matches the business cards from his collection of more than 50. Then, scanning each card with his phone, he makes notes related to the products, services and initial discussion. If the site has a newsletter, he subscribes to this as well. Harry also sends thank-you emails to those who had shared their time and information with him.

He takes to the search engines, looking for coaching-related sites and finding the various certifying bodies that existed inside the United Kingdom and globally. He researches different social media business and coaching influencers, shortlisting those he thinks sound interesting to follow. Logging into his podcasting and social media, accounts, Harry spends almost the remainder of the day clawing through the endless content, listening and subscribing.

Towards the end of the day, he looks at the list he has created and from which he has downloaded several episodes and posts. Once he is in the routine of daily listening, he plans to search back over older shows to see if there are specific topics of interest he can listen to on his daily commute. Finally, before shutting his computer and heading home, he starts a new spreadsheet titled 'My Network'. Tomorrow, he plans to begin populating this document by brainstorming a list of everyone he knows personally. Once he has finished this, he will ask Sandra to perform a similar exercise. The list should include everyone the family knows. Regardless of their interest or connection to coaching, Harry wants to understand the extent of the gap he has in his network. The people listed may provide an opportunity to connect with and learn or leverage from later.

Transformational Strategy 3: Collaboration

© S4E Publishing

There are many stories in our history about people who have joined forces to overcome their mutual adversaries. We have seen joint action against corporations and on sports fields where teams face off against each other – club against club, nation against nation. All demonstrating that the power of 'we' is greater than the power of 'I'.

Collaboration is a common practice between companies across numerous industries, bringing together contracted groups to perform in specialty areas as one part of building the whole. Mergers are another form of collaboration in which companies join as one, leveraging their expertise for more significant gains.

Our industry is one of those that has benefitted from collaboration, working as a specialist partner in construction and infrastructure. Closer to home, within our tribe of the elevator and escalator industry, we have a so-called 'product life cycle' whereby our products originate from customer demand and then evolve internally through R&D, manufacturing, installation and servicing, before being modernised or decommissioned. Throughout that life cycle, the different departments must collaborate to produce the product and maintain it.

In the past 50+ years, we have seen an acceleration in collaboration between competing companies within the same industry. Very often, this occurs in significant acquisitions and major projects, where consortiums are formed for the sole purpose of pooling resources to achieve the desired outcome.

Recently, companies from different industries have begun leveraging off each other's strengths to tackle significant development projects. In our industry, this has traditionally occurred in R&D, with collaboration with other research entities such as universities and developers of machinery and electronics. Today, the rapid development in technology allows us to witness new cooperation with large IT groups leveraging their expertise in information gathering and data analytics and shifting from a heavy reliance on high-skill labour resources. The industry has progressively become automated and now is on the verge of utilising artificial intelligence (AI) to replace much of the skilled labour force.

As collaboration accelerates in this field, in parallel with technological advances, we begin to witness a transformation of our industry towards the supply of commodity products and spare parts. Possible mergers between the larger companies will likely result in the safest way to remain viable in business.

For you, as a leader within any industry, this means that it's crucial you understand the need for and look towards building stronger relationships, by partnering internally and externally with suppliers, customers, influencers and other industries to leverage those relationships across sectors and to remain abreast of the rapid developments ahead.

It's no longer enough to have a network of colleagues or like-minded individuals with similar interests. You need to broaden your perspectives and imagine a different future. From that perspective, you can determine which parties will serve you best in collaboration.

Strategy 5 focuses on team coaching, which is fast developing as the leading form of coaching in organisations, outpacing executive and leadership coaching. Companies are beginning to realise how essential strong collaboration between their functions and immediate external groups has become. So, for the remainder of this strategy review, we look at how you might start to enhance your collaboration skills and build those all-important partnerships for the future.

Strengthening collaboration with your team and colleagues

You might wonder why I am starting this section with a discussion of the importance of team collaboration, rather than focusing first on the customer. In my experience, getting your team sorted needs to be the priority if you are to have a fighting chance of creating a successful collaborative partnership with the customer, or even with suppliers. The shift towards a more harmonious and cooperative existence requires both team and customer collaboration to occur, and in the purest sense. However, reality dictates that resources and focus need to be prioritised. Therefore, I advise you to start with your team. It helps if your internal business process can sustain the relationships with external partners before going out to grow them.

From the outset, you need to ensure the team, and any colleagues you involve (individual and collectively), understand your expectations and the requirements for their successful participation in the project or strategy. Within this collaborative environment, each member becomes responsible and accountable for the outcome. Therefore, everyone has a certain duty or power to oversee the actions of others as well as themselves to ensure the desired results.

Whichever method you use for setting your objectives (SMART or otherwise), make sure everyone understands the approach, by being concise and providing measurable, time-bound targets that enable them to see when they have reached the desired result. Hold regular reviews and discuss progress.

At the beginning of the exercise, invite questions and conduct brainstorming workshops to promote a more profound understanding and to explore potential and alternative approaches. During each review, conduct a similar process to foster creativity and continued progress. Challenge the group to solve problems together and look for unseen obstacles. The outcome should be greater unity among members of the group and a more successful outcome for the project or strategy.

Make it compulsory for all group members to attend progress reviews and to contribute to the discussion and activities. Establish workflows and assign responsibility for these. If you are adopting an agile project approach and have split the project into specific sprints, then you may even need to hold daily 'huddles' to review the previous day's achievements, challenge progress and redirect as needed, before defining the day's activities.

Assigning people to subgroups requires that you consider the different dynamics of the individuals. Numerous tools are available to help you build these profiles. Consider using a variety of tools when thinking about the best combination of project teams and help them to function well. Here are a few you might investigate further:

- Skill / Will matrix to determine ability versus attitude
- SCARF social model to identify personal motivation
- DISC, Myers Briggs, Hermann Brain Dominance Instrument (HBDI), Enneagram and Hogan assessments test for personality profiles
- Clifton Strengths for insights into core working strengths
- Values in Action (VIA) for insights into personal strengths
- Johari Window for building transparency, relationships and trust
- World Café for dynamic group work

- Tuckman's Four Stages to learn about improving team development
- Belbin Team roles to define who plays what role in the team
- The 6 Hats model for thorough discussion and decision-making processes
- 8D for problem-solving (or a version of it), together with critical thinking andcreative thinking exercises to address roadblocks in the project
- And a personal favourite – 'Draw Toast' by Tom Wujec, to make processes graphic and visual.

All of these tools mentioned are useful, but the list is by no means exhaustive and a quick search online will provide ample alternatives. Be aware of two elements that can hamper collaboration:

- **Risky shift or group polarisation** – the tendency of workgroups to make extreme decisions.
- **Groupthink** – exhibited by group members who try to minimise conflict and reach consensus without critically testing, analysing or evaluating ideas during a group decision-making process.

Whichever tools you select and implement, be sure to make the findings visible so the knowledge doesn't only rest with you.

Finally, celebrate the successful conclusion of the project or strategy. Conduct a 'Lessons learned Q&A' with the group and document it. With each subsequent project, this list should grow. Open this file at the start of every new project and discuss how to minimise risks and avoid repeating past mistakes. In addition to the above suggestions, you would be well served to consider Team Coaching and change management theories and applications, of which there are too many to list here.

Strengthening collaboration with your suppliers and customers

Ensure you have a plan for moving from a focus on the team to a focus on the customer at the earliest opportunity. Avoid putting yourself in a position where you establish the perfect internal operation but have no customers to service.

When you do take those first customer steps – which is all about the other party and not about you – employ the following actions:

Action 1 is to establish 'situational fluency' – meaning you need to understand your customer/supplier business. What are the challenges they face and the areas of concern? That is, understand their pain, if you will. It doesn't need to be related to your business but so much the better if you can identify issues where there are common interests.

Action 2 is to ensure you understand that pain and whether they already have their ideas about resolving it before you go charging in with your solution, which may be entirely off target. If they do have ideas for a solution, then consider whether you can further support it. If not, turn your focus to look for something else.

Action 3 is to consider options for a solution to the problem and what value each brings to the customer/supplier business. How can this be quantified? Think of ways in which you can provide value to them and address at least a portion of the challenge.

Action 4 is where you offer your support in working through the problem, utilising the selected solution or enabling the other party to choose from the options available. Naturally, if there is a cost element, this would need to be discussed before proceeding. However, if you are creative, you will likely come up with ideas that may not resolve the entire issue but address part of it.

Taking this approach shows your willingness and empathy towards the other party and is an excellent way to establish trust. Remember, if you want a healthy and long partnership, then being committed upfront, in terms of time, is usually handsomely rewarded manytimes over as different opportunities arise.

Strengthening collaboration with other external partners

The scope here depends on the direction you wish to pursue. Are you wanting to establish yourself as an expert within a group and aiming for later collaboration on one of their projects? You'll first need to identify what it is you want to achieve. Once you're clear, ask yourself what resources you require for assistance.

The following questions may be useful in pointing you in the right direction to get started:

- Who are the influencers in your industry or in the chosen industry of interest?
- Are they active on social media and do they have a following?
- Can you participate in the group discussions and contribute to the betterment of the group and support the influencer?
- What organisations exist in this field that you could follow?
- Can you become a member and attend meetings, workshops etc.?
- Do you know anyone else who can provide you with an introduction?
- Do you need to learn more about the group or individuals?

Use the above as prompts to identify additional questions that will take you towards the next steps to establishing a relationship and potential for future collaboration.

Transformational Strategy 4: A lifetime of continuous learning

© S4E Publishing

Business requirements are constantly changing through advances in technology. It means skills that once served you well will most likely become insufficient to keep you employed.

The only solution is to embark on a lifelong quest to remain current with your knowledge and skills.

Chapter 10: Harry returns to study

London is cold and quickly turning white. Roads and homes are burdened under the weight of heavy snow. In the relatively short time since Harry's return to London, winter has arrived across England. Harry feels like a new man. And just like the cold, clean, crisp air that hits him as he steps outside, Harry has a fresh zeal. He is delighted with the turn his life has taken. Harry credits a series of unplanned events with enabling this to occur. It all started with his parents' surprise trip to Sydney, Robert's heart attack and the challenges that presented. Then there was the chance friendship that developed with the Henley family and Harry's decision to embark on a coaching career, with his wife's support.

'Sometimes, things happen that are beyond our comprehension,' Harry thinks and, as if to scold himself, he pauses, realising that this was why he wanted to get into the coaching business in the first place. Miracles exist all around us, but it's when we are open to them that we attract them.

Over the past two weeks, Harry has been researching the types of study programs he will need to complete in his preparation for certification as a life and sports coach. When he started his research, Harry was unprepared for what he found. He had anticipated 12–24 months of focused effort to gain the necessary knowledge and acquire the skills requisite to the role. Being a thorough kind of person, Harry also wants to get enough experience in the field before launching his career in earnest. But the more he researches, the longer the list of possible study programs becomes.

Following the advice of his sports coach friend, Harry found that taking a psychology program on a part-time basis would take him a minimum of four and a half years. Maybe longer if he added a couple of sports modules as electives.

Based on his current age, that means he would turn 56 before graduating. The three-year full-time option would mean he'd have to give up his job, and he wasn't willing or able to do that. This was the first reality check for Harry. Feeling a little deflated, he discusses it with Sandra.

'Harry,' she says 'what is it that excites you about becoming a coach? And what would it mean if you realised that result, now that you understand this to be your life's purpose?'

Harry smiles and reaches out to hold her hand.

'Thank you,' is all he offers in return.

The next day, Harry enrols in a bachelor of health science program at the London South Bank University, hoping to major in sports psychology.

Now that he is committed, Harry has mixed feelings. He is happy to have taken his first concrete step towards becoming a coach but still, he is feeling the pressure. As the morning wears on, Harry feels more comfortable about it. He sends Sandra a text message: 'Hope you don't want to do too much for the next five years, as I've just assigned myself to long nights and many weekends of study. And you'll need all the patience you can muster. I promise to try hard and make us proud!'

With several months before the course commences, Harry begins to prepare himself by reading up on the topics he will be covering. Then he revisits his initial list of studies – which he had shortlisted from almost two pages. He decides to take a just-in-time approach to make the workload bearable and breaks it down into the following steps.

Online study

- How to build a coaching business – 8 modules
- Neuro-linguistic programming (NLP) practitioner course: 2 online modules
- Life coaching practitioner course: 2 online modules

Coaching and business podcasts

- The Team Coaching Zone
- Gallup's Call to Coach
- SMART Passive Income
- Ask Pat

Books

- *Becoming a coach: The essential ICF guide* (202) by Jonathan Passmore and Tracy Sinclair
- *Co-active coaching: The proven framework for transformative conversations at work and in life* 4th edition (2018) by Henry Kimsey-House, Karen Kimsey-House, Phillip Sandhal and Laura Whitworth
- *Positive psychology coaching in practice* (2018) edited by Suzi Palmer and Stephen Palmer
- *Getting things done: The art of stress-free productivity* (2001) by David Allen
- *Superfans: The easy way to stand out, grow your tribe and build a successful business* (2019) by Pat Flynn

And, most importantly, the need to start working towards acquiring his International Coaching Federation (ICF) Associate Certified Coach credentials, which requires:

- a minimum of 60 hours of accredited training
- 100 hours of coaching experience (75% paid)
- 10 hours of coaching by a mentor
- performance evaluation (audio recording and written transcript)
- coach knowledge assessment.

On the weekend, during a family lunch, Harry asks each of his three children what they think the future workplace will be like. He is curious about how their generation views the changes that are to come and how they are preparing for them. After they have shared their thoughts, Harry confesses his misgivings in this area during the past decade, and that until now he has not taken additional studies to keep current. As a result, he is now paying the price with a very steep learning curve to prepare for his career change. He lays out his rough plans for bridging that gap and jokes with the family that he may need some study partners around the time of the examinations.

Everyone agrees that his diligence and logical problem-solving traits will be more than enough to help him work through any challenges. Still, they also offer to assist him whenever needed. But all three siblings admit that that they are happy that he isn't attending their universities as they didn't want to have to answer questions about whether the old guy in class was related to them!

Later, Harry and Sandra receive a text message from their eldest daughter, Charlotte: 'Proud of you both, and you have our support.'

The next day, Harry and Tim Henley connect for their monthly coaching session. Tim seems particularly upbeat, and Harry notices how Tim's mood has an uplifting effect on him at the same time. It is their fourth call and they have been working towards Tim developing his knowledge and capabilities with technology. Tim wants to update his skills in programming languages. He had studied PHP years earlier and touched on C language when completing his electronics certificate but he hasn't practised it much in recent times, and he realised there are new languages he should be learning if he wants to stay in touch. It seems even more critical for their start-up business.

Harry is more of a mentor than coach to Tim, offering his own experience and knowledge on the industry and it's future direction. He believes that older computing languages will eventually become obsolete.

Harry advises Tim that 5G, the internet of things (IoT), quantum computing, cloud-based technologies and videocasting and podcasting will fast track much of that evolution. He has been following the most popular programming languages for some time and often discusses them with his own team, encouraging everyone interested to learn and share new coding skills. Following their first session, Harry provided Tim with a list of his top 10 languages in terms of their associated role and field of technology. He encourages Tim to think about how he will use the coding knowledge and skills he plans to develop. Harry cautions that whichever direction Tim pursues, it is likely to change considerably within five years. Therefore, unless he genuinely wishes to include programming and software development into his career, then this desire might result in considerable wasted effort.

Tim has pondered this advice carefully and has discussed it with Janet and others in the app group. Tim wants to move into leadership, but he sees the future of businesses as much more agile and lean, so that coding knowledge is an advantage rather than a burden. Tim hasn't settled on any single idea for growing his company. He knows that sooner or later this will be his direction and, therefore, he concludes that growing what is a genuine interest into something that gives him multiple options is worth the effort. He had reported this to Harry during their second call, and Harry has agreed to support Tim in whatever way he can. Their partnership within the app group means that their level of knowledge with C++ language, the base language used in the development of their software, is essential.

By now, Harry realises that mentoring is very different from coaching. The former is very much about offering advice and giving guidance, while the latter is about co-creation on the journey to finding solutions, with the coach responsible for powerful questioning that enables the coaching counterpart to explore and reflect. Harry briefs Tim about this new approach, explaining that, in the long run, it will be more beneficial for Tim to discover the answers himself rather than having someone else provide solutions that may not always be best suited to him. Harry uses the analogy of teaching him to fish rather than handing him the fish.

After the call, Harry reflects on his ability to coach. He knows that there is most likely much he doesn't understand at this point – the conscious incompetence stage he read about recently. Still, the feeling of satisfaction after each call with Tim is unmistakable. He feels tremendously happy in the knowledge that he is helping others, and each time it reaffirms that this is his calling.

A surprise meeting with the country CEO during a promotional event leads to a conversation about Harry moving uptown to the country headquarters. There is an opportunity for Harry to lead a new division the company wants to establish there. He would be responsible for a team of innovators whose focus will be to come up with ideas for development – to continue disrupting their industry and maintain the company's new dominance over their competitors. The concept is attractive and the timing is perfect, but he is still trying the understand aspects of the role and how success might be measured. Harry knows that coming up with ideas isn't so challenging but bringing those ideas to realisation is an entirely different matter. Developing 'use cases' that provide substantial business outcomes and return on investment is why some companies flourish and others fail.

It will most certainly mean an increase in salary and a contract for several more years, which is appealing as this could fit perfectly with the development of his coaching career. He discusses the idea with Sandra over several weeks, and they are both leaning towards accepting the opportunity, provided Harry can get clarity on a few more open questions. They feel that someone must be looking after them. The experience Harry could gain from running this new division offers him a much broader business perspective and exposure to a network that until now has only been visible on paper. If he accepts the position, the transition will start almost immediately, with a target of becoming permanent on the conclusion of his current project.

It also provides Harry with the opportunity to explore an avenue of study through the company's academy, which he is keen to utilise. This includes soft skills modules that focus on leadership, business, communications and change management – to name a few. Plus there is the allure of a vast digital library, which will give him free access to several external platforms with thousands of short-course modules.

As Harry thinks through this situation, he is amused by how his mindset has changed regarding personal development, ever since deciding to develop his own business. Today's technology, of which his career has been an integral part, has made learning so much more accessible. While academics still debate whether education via online self-study offers the same benefits as classroom and face-to-face sessions, what they do agree that the digital medium is critical to it. Like everything else in commerce, this industry is on the verge of seeing technology reshape how people will learn in the future.

Harry's own form of convergence occurs in February 2020. When his project is finalised, his full-time role as head of the newly created 'Disruptors Lab' commences. At the same time, his first semester of study commenced towards his sports psychology degree. Each proves to be a significant event and somewhat of a test of Harry's ability to juggle responsibilities. He is extremely pleased to find that several of his team members want to follow him across into the new department and so he has had the opportunity to handpick the balance of the six-strong team. Even so, there is a lot of planning, endless meetings, strategic and critical thinking workshops, equipment purchases, brainstorming sessions, as well as procedures and system development. All need to be worked through, deciphered, consolidated and implemented, and require considerable effort on everyone's part. Thankfully, it's largely a one-time setup.

Still, Harry toils late into the evening, six days each week for the three months prior to his transition. He reminds everyone from the outset what to expect. He also commits to having one day a week that is work and study free. Typically a Sunday, these days are reserved for recharging and family time.

Harry's birthday is approaching and Sandra, together with their children, have been working hard behind the scenes to prepare a significant surprise for him. As per Sandra's initial briefing, they have each embarked on a separate project to give Harry's new business a considerable boost. Once a week, while Harry is away at night school, they connect by videocall and review their progress. Now, with only three weeks before the unveiling, Sandra is getting a little concerned that she might be lagging with her contribution. Her self-appointed tasks are quite simple – research company set up, insurance, uniforms and building a network.

The first two tasks are comfortable enough. Sandra finds a website to guide her through the company establishment steps, and she speaks with a solicitor about supporting them once they are ready. Similarly, a local insurance company is happy to cover professional coaching, and the charges seem reasonable. It will take only a phone call to trigger the first annual policy once Harry reviews the coverage and agrees.

Identifying the latest sports fabrics is the most enjoyable activity, and Sandra has spoken with many suppliers, who have been extremely helpful. All vendors have pointed her in a similar direction, to a company that is heavily involved in researching the performance of different sporting apparel. In the end, she selects a range of colours and tests these with Peg's logos and other brand designs. This same vendor is able to provide advice on accessories and footwear. Sandra lays out the samples on the bed and examines the range to ensure she is still happy with her selection. 'All good,' she thinks. She is especially pleased with the outcome. Together with Peg, they have designed a series of uniforms for Harry, covering winter, mid-seasons and summer. Everything is ready to produce on Harry's sign-off.

The final task hasn't been as easy, however. In trying to identify potential life and sports coaching clients, Sandra realises the challenge this presents. What determines a prospective client? Thinking about the task seems simple enough and straight forward. Putting that into practice, however, is proving more difficult. While almost everyone is a potential client, when adding interest, cost and time into the equation, the matter becomes much more complicated. Sandra has canvased some people she believes could benefit from Harry's coaching but while they appear to be interested and listen politely to Sandra's pitch, she has only been successful in identifying one person so far who is willing to meet with Harry and learn more about the process. So she decides to change her strategy.

In the week leading up to Harry's surprise birthday reveal, the team speaks almost daily and the excitement is building as everyone applies the finishing touches to their efforts. Each person will present and demonstrate their handy work, giving due credit to those outside of the circle who have contributed, and will then provide Harry with the opportunity to ask questions and request modifications.

On Sunday morning, Harry wakes up early and lies in bed with his eyes closed, reflecting on his life. At 51 years old, his life is undoubtedly hectic. Before beginning his morning routine, Harry casts his mind back over the past 12 months. It certainly has been one filled with twists and turns, unlike any other year he can recall.

In the afternoon, following lunch, everyone gathers in the lounge room. The door has been kept closed to prevent Harry from seeing the suspended sheet dividing the room in half. Now, with the door open, the sheet was visible and he is naturally curious, making a beeline to see what is behind it. Fortunately, Travis and Peg manage to intercepted him, ushering him to a seat and telling him to prepare for his birthday surprise.

As the curtain falls, the surprise still is not readily apparent. Carefully packaged in four boxes are the team's projects. Sandra takes the lead in explaining to the audience that Harry is a man of great empathy, a loving husband and father, who holds the highest standards for commitment and determination. Many months ago, he confided in her that he wished to embark on a new chapter in his life. One that will require considerable preparation and effort, but for which he feels a strong calling. Once she saw the sparkle in his eyes and heard the conviction in his voice, she knew it was her role to support him and help realise his purpose. History will show that like everything Harry Bloom set his mind to in the past, this journey will also be successful.

Harry is feeling flattered but still very unsure about where this unexpected turn of events is heading.

Sandra speaks directly to Harry now. 'After that night, when you told me your thoughts and what you had been working on, I knew that I needed to help, but I wasn't sure how best to support you. The next morning, an idea came to me, which we'll now introduce to you. We hope you like what we have done, but we also welcome your questions and suggestions for modification.'

Peg starts by giving Harry a black leather-bound folder. Inside is a logo printed in colour on quality paper and opposite is an embroidered fabric version. She introduces multiple options, which form a range of potential designs for branding the business. Each cleverly focuses on weaving together the two aspects of Harry's desired coaching – sports and lifestyle. Peg explains that her friends at university have helped her to captured a contemporary look of professionalism and vibrance in these themes. Harry is stunned. He loves what he is looking at and seems unable to speak.

Without further ado, Travis opens his package to reveal a shiny new laptop displaying the branding Harry had seen in Peg's folder. The home page flips between the designs and a variety of site themes. After displaying all the ideas several times, Travis moves the page down to reveal the structure of the website. It looks spectacular. Travis proudly clicks on a link that takes them into a sales funnel, where he and his friends have established and tested landing, order and confirmation pages. Each is designed to accommodate future campaigns as Harry's business grows. Harry stares at Travis, fully aware of the amount of work that would have gone into generating something as professional as this.

Travis hands the laptop to Charlotte, who navigates her way back to the top of the screen and keys in a password, gaining access to a backend platform. From the platform menu, Harry quickly realises the beauty of the design. The website he had first observed is much more. It doubles as his window into his business systems. As Charlotte explains, this is an automated array of programs that are interlinked to eliminate redundant effort and minimise data entry duplication. Furthermore, each program is from a leading business institution and confirmed by her university as scalable and suitable for small to medium-sized businesses. It includes everything conceivable, from customer relationship management (CRM) software through to administration, accounting and invoice generation. What makes this even more impressive is that each of the branding options Peg presented earlier can also be seen here. The whole package works seamlessly and will enable Harry to experience the visual impact this would have on his future clients.

Harry is astonished. But there is more to come. Sandra opens the final carton and removes a series of fabrics, laying them neatly on the floor in front of Harry. She continues to extract patterns to illustrate seasonal outfits. She positions two pairs of sports shoes and several baseball caps, alongside the fabrics, asking Harry to feel each one and look through the designs to see if there is anything that he thinks could be right for him. After he has chosen several options for fabric and patterns, Sandra explains the scientific research behind each choice. Harry can only sit there in amazement.

As a final part of her package, Sandra asks Charlotte to open two documents sitting in a folder on the backend of Harry's new website. The first is the company registration form, which has been prepared by the solicitor and simply requires Harry's decision on the company name and his signature. The second is the insurance company policy for his review and approval.

It is the longest the family can remember Harry being so quiet. He is genuinely speechless and overwhelmed. They all embrace, and Peg hands him an envelope. This is a birthday card and, after reading the message inside, he takes the laptop and follows the instructions. Logging into his new platform, Harry opens the Salesforce CRM software to find six coaching clients already entered, awaiting his immediate contact. He can hardly believe his eyes. He is in business and although he has only been studying for a short period he also recognises the need to have coachees that enable him to practise and apply his new knowledge and skills.

Chapter 11: Tim learns the importance of continuing professional development

'Okay, Boss, I'll head over immediately. Is there anything I need to bring with me? Great.'

Tim puts his phone back into his pocket and prepares his backpack. Since his unannounced and very fruitful visit to the office some months ago, he has made a point of maintaining contact with anyone he has spoken with, either by popping into the office more regularly or by calling when the opportunity presents itself. This call is one such example. Tim met with the sales manager two days ago and is now headed to a client meeting with that same manager to discuss installation requirements on a potential new project. By learning to identify the 'pain' of those he wishes to influence, Tim is now able to provide support and options for a solution.

Just as he did with the CFO following their initial discussion, Tim has taken action to obtain feedback from his project peers about the challenges they are facing in the financial management of their projects. He has now consolidated that feedback and, with the aid of Janet, put together a program proposal for management to consider. For the first time he feels that he has something of value to bring to the table for discussion outside of his project management skills. Also, he has pitched the idea of holding regular inter-department meetings to share information and create awareness of how the work of the different departments affects the work of colleagues in other departments. These are small steps, but for someone in Tim's position but they are unusual. It has undoubtedly raised his profile in the eyes of branch management.

In parallel, Tim has been lobbying for his next assignment and has been rewarded with an appointment as the project manager of the most significant contract the company has secured to date. While he is pleased with the acknowledgment of his ability to perform on these mega projects, this one means a commitment for at least the next three years. To avoid being isolated on a job site and forgotten for that period, Tim has expressed his concern to his manager, Nathan, and opened a discussion about his career prospects. He has explained that he wants to develop beyond project management into a more general leadership role and wants to explore the options available to him.

Nathans's response has been positive, and he has promised to speak with his senior management about this. That was several weeks ago, however, and Tim has heard nothing since. He realises that the longer it drags on, the less likely it will be that anyone will remember the conversation or request. So he decides to find a way to contact the HR manager himself.

At their last meeting, Tim and the HR manager spoke about team incentives and now he plans to lead with that, by thanking the HR manager for her advice and giving an update on the outcome. Hopefully this discussion will provide the opportunity to enquire on his topic as well.

As Tim steps into the reception area of the branch office, he is surprised to see the client that he and the sales manager met with yesterday, sitting there reading a magazine. He walks over and greets the man, who smiles and says, 'You convinced me yesterday, and I'm just here to finalise a few of the terms before proceeding with the contract. I hope we can count on your continued support during the project.'

Pleased, Tim confirms the request, saying that they have a great team of project managers, and whoever is assigned will be capable and competent, but he will certainly be an active party. Quickly checking with the receptionist, Tim learns that the sales manager is on a call and that they will be meeting the client in the boardroom, so he offers to escort him through the office and to the meeting room. As they walk there together, talking amiably, Tim notices staff watching him, including the sales manager, who waves from his office and gestures that he will be there soon.

Once in the room, Tim offers the client a coffee and they continue discussing the project, exploring challenges the client is anticipating. Tim learns that this is his first major project in Sydney. The client comments on the noticeable difference in the construction business between states and is surprised to find this within the elevator industry as well. He confides in Tim that at the end of the day, all he wants is to work with professionals who know their job and can deliver.

'Internal politics have become such an obstacle to getting the job done correctly. The company that can sort that out first will surely be greater in demand and, as a result, more successful.'

At that moment, the sales manager enters with the MD and warmly greets the client. Tim takes this as his cue to depart and bids farewell to the client, confirming that he will keep in contact with the project.

Later that morning, the MD comes in to speak with Tim and Nathan while they are conducting their regular monthly project reviews.

'Good morning, gentlemen. Tim, the sales manager has briefed me on how helpful you have been in securing new contracts recently. Thank you. I didn't realise that you have an interest outside of the project field.'

Tim smiles, but before he can respond, Nathan chimes in that he and Tim have recently discussed a career change and that he has spoken with the HR manager about the possibility.

'Well, that presents a dilemma,' the MD replies. 'We risk losing one of our best project managers! But even worse, if we do nothing, we could lose him to a competitor,' he says with a smile.

He continues, 'Let's give this some further thought then and see what options might exist for us. Until then, Tim, keep up the great work, and we'll be back in touch within the month.'

Tim feels like jumping to his feet and shaking the MD's hand but thinks better of it, thanking him and saying he is looking forward to the opportunity to develop further. As the MD leaves, Tim looks over to Nathan, who is smiling in approval.

Within two weeks, Tim is back in the office, this time for a meeting with the HR manager. She greets him warmly and he feels as though they have become close friends. The HR manager starts by saying how happy she is to be able to have this conversation with him as she feels they have developed a good relationship in recent months. She can sense that he is someone with a bright future. To this end, the HR manager says that the company would like to develop Tim's expertise further by bringing him into their talents program. She explains that the company only offers this opportunity to those they consider have high potential for future leadership. They would like to bring Tim into this program and, over the next two years, groom him to take on the role of a branch manager at one of their smaller operations. The plan requires that he participate in various leadership development workshops and complete a considerable number of short modules in that period, in addition to his current daily routine. Tim listens intently and feels sense of gratitude to those who have made this possible. It seems there was no time to waste, with the talent onboarding workshop commencing within the next two weeks. He accepts an embossed black leather folder with details about the program and what to expect. The HR manager tells Tim he should expect a workshop invitation via email in the next 24 hours, and if he has any questions he can contact her directly. If they don't speak before the workshop, they can talk then.

Before leaving the office, Tim stops in to see Nathan and thanks him for his support in this career step. Nathan smiles and says he is happy to help. 'You deserved the chance, Tim! I went through the talents program some years back, and that led to my current position. The company honours its commitments in this regard, provided you work hard to fulfil the required study and continue to perform.'

On his way back to the site, Tim decides to take a detour and surprise his wife by taking her to lunch. Over lunch, they discuss what this opportunity means and how it can be a great stepping stone into his future career. Having the company educate you in leadership, with the potential to practice what you have learned by running a small branch will undoubtedly fit their five-year goal of starting their own business. It means that by the time Tim turns 30, he will be managing a branch himself. It's something he has wanted but has doubted he would achieve so quickly. As they look through the folder's contents together, they find a document setting out the two-year education plan. In total, Tim will need to complete 12 blended – face-to-face and online – modules, six per year. In the first year the modules include 'The first 365 days', 'Stakeholder engagement', 'Safety leadership', 'Sales success', 'The installation game plan' and 'Servicing customers' – 15 days in total, occurring every two months. The second year goes deeper into 'Servant leadership', 'Business problem-solving', 'Change', 'Collaboration' and 'Finance and digitalisation'. Spaced at six-month intervals are four workshops in which the group will come together and plot their way through a series of computer- based business simulations, applying what they have learned in each module. As part of this program, the group will be split into small teams, and each team will be coached on its performance after the workshop. Plus, there is an online self-study platform to support them during each module. It is a comprehensive program, and they can both see how much this would help Tim in his professional development. It's more than they have ever dreamed of or even knew was possible.

There is another surprise waiting for Tim on his return to the site office: two messages from the HR manager. That was quick, Tim thinks as he begins to read through the first one, which provides information about the onboarding workshop. Tim accepts the invitation and it loads into his calendar. The second email is copied to the MD, Nathan and someone called Alan Wright, with the subject line 'Company Mentor'. It informs Tim that he has been assigned a mentor from the company's mentorship program; his mentor is the head of Field Operations based out of Hong Kong, Mr Alan Wright.

The HR manager suggests that the two of them find time for an introductory call. Tim is thrilled to have been given these opportunities. He realises that he needs to capitalise on these as much as possible.

Speaking to his wife for a second time today, Tim fills her her in on this latest development. Janet suggests that he immediately start to look at his weekly and monthly work plans to ensure that he is able to fit in everything around his already busy schedule. Usually workday is under control, unless something unforeseen arises. The new education program will mostly occur during the working week and, therefore, apart from travel time, it shouldn't create too much of a challenge. He anticipates that there will be homework, but again, this should be manageable. However, they do have a young son and he needs to ensure he has time to spend with him after work and on weekends. Tim loves their time together and doesn't want that interaction to suffer. Now, on top of this, he needs to add the monthly mentoring sessions with Alan Wright.

That leaves his mentoring sessions with Harry and the night classes on C++ software programming he has committed to. He is already three months into this six-month course, which requires two evenings a week – his intention to commence a second module immediately on completion might need to be reconsidered. The final ingredient is his work on the software app. Both he and Janet have become increasingly involved in the program development as the project nears the launch date. They are responsible for the marketing campaign locally and have had multiple discussions with firms that can handle what they need. Their vetting process is now complete, and all they need now, before the engagement, is to get the approval from the other group members. Janet has been working on registering the app business as a company and establishing a proper set of accounts. Tim and Janet knows that when the marketing campaign starts it means a significant increase to both their workloads as they will be responsible for responding to inquiries. They have tentatively enlisted support from Tim's sister Rachelle, who is eager to be a part of the action.

After looking at his revised schedule, it seems tight, and Tim wonders if he is overcommitting. Is there anything that he could avoid or stop doing? A worst-case scenario will be if he has to push back taking the second software programming module by a year or so. The flow-on effect will be that he won't be able to handle many of the coding issues himself, which is probably not a bad thing. He could leave that to his Sydney-based colleagues and Harry's team in London.

Later, in bed with their son, Tim and Janet continue talking about these new developments. They review Tim's schedule and agree that it could work and then realise that maybe they could find an extra hour in the morning, before their son awakes, for Tim to do his exercise program and, on occasion, even some study. Tim also commits to keeping the mentoring and talent program confined to daytime activities as much as possible.

Alan Wright

Alan's first face-to-face mentoring session with Tim is scheduled during Alan's visit to his company's Sydney office. They have spoken over the phone, and Alan introduced Tim to the overall process and what to expect. The two to three-hour time difference between Hong Kong and Sydney seems to be working in both their favours, as immediately after lunch is Alan's preferred time and late afternoon suits Tim best.

It is Alan's first trip back to Sydney since changing employers, and he feels a degree of nostalgia as the taxi transports him to his hotel from the airport. He hasn't stayed at this hotel before but has read about its magnificent views across to the Bridge, Harbour and Opera House. Based on the success of the mentoring program at his previous company, Alan has been instrumental in convincing his CEO about the value for those participating, both mentors and mentees, describing as an example the success story of Maddie Agnes, the first female elevator executive selected from Australia in the top 50 global talent program run by their competitor.

During his years of mentoring Alan has witnessed numerous positive outcomes and, therefore, he wholeheartedly supports the company's foray in this direction. Tim's name has come up unexpectedly from the Sydney office and his placement into the talent program drew Alan's attention as one of the program's sponsors. After that first call, he is keen to meet with Tim but cautions himself not to place an undue expectation on him based on Maddie's success.

Tim meets Alan

Tim sits in the hotel lobby, watching child-sized robots roaming the floor and greeting guests, providing guidance on popular tourist destinations and hotel services. It seems that the robots are able to answer almost any question the guests ask. Tim's mind wanders to his app group's potential next project. They have already been brainstorming, but no one has mentioned the concept of an office robot. He suspects that there are already companies exploring the idea but the office is just one example – there must be many other applications to appeal to the market.

Alan has been standing and observing Tim's facial expressions from a few metres away for the past couple of minutes. It looks like Tim has plenty on his mind, with his expression shifting from puzzlement to excitement, as if he has just solved a problem he has been working on for some time. He approaches Tim, introduces himself and they shake hands.

On the way to finding a coffee house, Alan mentions his observations of Tim and asks if he has had a breakthrough on a problem. Tim is a little unsure at first but decides to share a portion of the story with Alan, confirming that he has been sitting in the lobby for 10 minutes, watching the hotel robots. His naturally curious mind wandered to other functions for similar robotic applications, particularly inside their industry as an interface between the elevators or escalators and facilities such as hotels, offices, metro stations and airports. The list seems endless and now Tim is wondering how he might find out if anyone is working on anything similar.

'That must have been when you observed me,' Tim says.

Alan smiles and starts talking about cloud-based analytics, which is used to enable predictive maintenance based on the number of component cycles.

'Similar to what we had back in the 1980s with run counters installed on control systems?' Tim interrupts.

'Yes,' Alan continues. 'But much more sophisticated thanks to advances in technology. We are now able to monitor many more functions and predict the life expectancy of individual parts. The system is even able to transmit notifications to our operations before the part fails.'

'Wow!' Tim exclaims. He has heard about this development, but the penny has just dropped about how it could influence the industry in the future.

'All of the major companies are working on their secret projects at the moment. You may have read about "Multi" the first ropeless elevator, which uses linear motors to propel the cabin. Through a turnstile coupling they can move horizontally as well as vertically. While this doesn't directly relate to the topic you mention, think of it as having a similar effect to Roger Bannister breaking the four-minute mile. It's liberated the thinking of architects and developers and our industry as well. Everyone is now working on what they hope will be that next major quantum leap. Many companies are working on interfaces between the elevator and building services as well. Our company led the way with a system interface into the building security system, and we already use robots to communicate remotely with the elevator control, registering landing calls and car calls. It means the robots can travel effortlessly with room service and laundry requests, right to the door of the guest. We're even using robots to assist with the plumbing of our shafts, as I'm sure you are aware. As technology continues to develop, for sure, all these technologies will continue to be improved. Many IT companies are investing heavily in AR technology. We envisage a time in the near future, when learning can be conducted across the world between different countries, using different languages. And through simultaneous translation and the use of holograms, people will be able to attend technical workshops. The expert will be speaking in their preferred language, and participants anywhere in the world will be able to receive the message in their own language. It will also be possible to interact with and explore the projected hologram regardless of where the trainer is in the world – rotating and manipulating the hologram as they work through the lecture together. It will save companies millions of dollars in travel and training expenses.'

This first meeting between Tim and Alan is undoubtedly an eye-opener for Tim, and he quickly discovers that Alan has a wealth of knowledge about their business and the future of the industry. This is going to be an invaluable side benefit for Tim over the coming years. The conversation lasts well past the scheduled hour, and at the end, Alan asks Tim to complete several questionnaires to provide details of his interests and desired career direction. Alan assures Tim that these documents are purely for his understanding and will remain completely confidential between them. Alan also suggests that Tim identifies industry and interest related influencers on social media channels whom he would like to follow so that next time they can discuss the role of influencers.

Later, Tim sits in the living room at home, where he has sat on countless nights over the past years, staring across the harbour to the former construction site that is now home to a new building complex. The complex was once his daytime home, and tonight, as Tim gazes at the hotel tower and the lights dotted across it, he ponders the discussion he had earlier with Alan. Tim casts his mind over his life journey, recalling key milestones. Has he been an active participant or merely a passenger along for the ride? He decides he is going to take steps to ensure he remains an active participant from now on.

Beside him, Janet is nestled into his arm. It's Tim's scheduled night to explore the online platform that will enable his journey over the next two years and the 12 modules he will complete through the talent program. Tim tells Janet about his discussion with Alan and the thoughts that have been running through his mind. Looking at the sophisticated learning platform in front of them, they both realise just how disconnected and passive their lives have become and together they vow to make changes to take control of their future. They now have an opportunity that most people never get – to squander this would not only be foolish but to the detriment of themselves and their son.

After shutting the online learning platform, Tim decides to explore what other educational platforms are available. To his astonishment, he finds hundreds of sites. Then he finds blogs listing the top 10 and 20 websites, which he explores in some depth. The major sites include Udemy, Coursera, LinkedIn Learning, Cross Knowledge and Skillsoft, to name just a handful, and all offered an array of topics, from general knowledge to specialist courses.

Beside him, Janet is also on her laptop, scanning the university sites and exploring their curriculums. Many universities today offer a range of online short modules and provide recognition of them as a part of their degree programs. Over the past six months she's started her thinking about the need to continue her education. She is a chartered accountant, and this is always going to provide a sound basis in her career but still, her involvement with their app development company and the requirement to be their finance and business sounding board, plus 'go-to person' for marketing advice, has given her cause to consider whether she could benefit from gaining other skills. On top of this, Tim's invitation to his company's talent program makes her feel like she might be getting left behind, so she starts researching study options she might be able to fit into her hectic world of mother, wife, employee and businesswoman. She knows now isn't the time to embark on anything major, but she also doesn't want to sit idle while opportunities bypass her.

One thing has become much clearer: their five-year plan is looking more certain given Tim's recent promotion. Janet looks at the skills Tim will acquire, together with the skills they still lacked to successfully launch their app and running their entrepreneurial start-up. Based on this, she concludes that taking some form of commerce degree would best serve their future needs. She identifies courses offered by the University of Sydney with majors in international business and marketing with minors in business law, industrial relations and human resource management. They also recognise modules from her accounting degree, meaning she could fast track the program a little. Plus, Tim will soon acquire the necessary leadership, operational and technology skills to complement those.

Janet feels confident, therefore, that their shared financial expertise, together with these new areas of study, could provide a solid basis for their success in future ventures and their ambitions for their shared life.

Chapter 12: Maddie blossoms with new knowledge

A large package arrives at the Agnes home from Maddie's company's corporate headquarters in the United States. Judging by the weight of the box, Paul thinks it must be laden with books or documents. Sitting it on Maddie's desk where she can't miss it, he knows that this is most likely another piece of the puzzle she has been eagerly awaiting.

In the month since Maddie's nomination into the Top 50 Global Talents Program, there has been talk of a new position for her, which means the family may need to relocate. It is a tremendous opportunity and recognition of Maddie's talent. The issue, however, was the effect on the family. Her mother is ageing and if they leave her sister will be left to look after her on her own. Their son will soon turn six and start primary school. As a professor of political science Paul is in high demand but hasn't admitted to Maddie, however, that he would welcome a change of scene and a new direction for his own work.

Paul sends Maddie a text message: 'Box arrived and sitting on the desk, no sound coming from inside, so guess it needs you to open it for full disclosure.'

Maddie is in the middle of her afternoon meeting when the message comes through, and there's still 90 minutes before she is due to pick up her son from kindergarten on the way home. The message from Paul is fun but at this moment, she would prefer to know what is in that box. Excusing herself, she makes her way to the bathroom and replies. 'Open it. Just watch out for snakes as they don't make a noise until they are about to bite.' Within a minute, Paul sends photos.

It looks like an impressive official welcome pack from the program director including:

- a leather embossed folder with the words 'TOP 50 GLOBAL TALENTS PROGRAM – the picture doesn't show details of the contents, but she can tell by the thickness of the spine that it contains a lot of potentially valuable information
- three books by Harvard business professors

  Forged in crisis: The power of courageous leadership in turbulent times (2017) by Nancy Koehn

  The language of global success: How a common tongue transforms multinational organizations (2017) by Tsedal Neeley

  Extreme teaming: Lessons in complex, cross-sector leadership (2017) by Amy C. Edmondson and Jean-Francois Harvey
- two workbooks – a 'Learners Diary' and a 'Master reference and toolkit'
- a USB stick with the company's name and logo.

As Maddie walks back to the meeting, Terry intercepts and ushers her to the state manager's office, where the MD and HR manager are seated. It looks like they are on a conference call. Both stand to shake hands with Maddie as she walks towards the table. She glances at Terry a little nervously, and he smiles his reassurance. All four people take a seat around the conferencing device.

'Are we good to go?' someone asks from the other end of the conference line. Maddie immediately recognises the voice as that of James Blake, the Australian CEO and her mentor. He addresses her directly.

'Good afternoon Maddie. I guess you're wondering about the secrecy surrounding this call?' James doesn't wait for a reply. 'I'm here in Hong Kong at our headquarters, with a colleague, Ms Lamport, our corporate board member and head of human relations. We have spent considerable time in recent weeks communicating via email and phone to discuss your future with the company. Today we sat together with the HR team and finalised an offer that you'll receive by close of business. Just one moment while we try again to connect this call to video so we can see everyone.'

James and Ms Lamport appear on the video screen, with the Hong Kong skyline visible in their background. 'Now that's better,' he beams. 'I thought it was an excellent opportunity and most appropriate for Ms Lamport to speak with you during her trip and to share more about the program in person and what we are proposing. It will also allow you to ask questions. Please be aware that we understand you have a young family that will need consultation regarding this offer, so we're not looking for your answer today.'

Maddie nods, thanks her mentor and says hello to Ms Lamport.

The discussion continues for the 30 minutes. In part of it feels like an interview for which she is underprepared and in part as if they are all best friends sharing stories and jokes across the virtual airwaves. Ms Lamport concludes by saying that she is looking forward to welcoming Maddie to the onboarding workshop next month in Boston.

And that is it. As quickly as it started, the meeting was over. The others offer their congratulations to Maddie, and express how deserving she is to have this life-changing opportunity. Thanking everyone for their support and well wishes, she excuses herself and goes back into her own meeting, apologising for the unexpected absence.

Maddie politely listens to the concluding comments before wrapping up the discussion and heading to pack up her things and head home via the kindergarten. As she drives there, she tries to put everything into context and thinks about how she might commence the discussion with Paul.

Gathering her son she wonders how he would adjust if they decide to move. That thought triggers memories of her childhood and the transition from Athens to Melbourne. It had been an emotional time as she said goodbye to her friends and family members but she also remembers how quickly she fell in love with her new home and settled into life as a Greek-Australian.

Paul is waiting for them at the door, smiling and happy to see them both. As his son races from the car and up the stairs to meet him, Paul's eyes remain on Maddie, trying to read her face for signs of new information. He senses that there has been a new development but does his best to hide his anxiety. They have been married for a long time and have both learned early to read each other's signals. This time the message is quite clear; something is troubling her, so he braces for the news and tried to remain as supportive as possible. He has already called ahead and reserved a table at their favourite local Greek restaurant in case they decide they need a night out and a break from the tradition of only dining out on weekends. As it turns out, his intuition was accurate, and Maddie looks pleased when Paul suggests the plan.

For the second time that day, Maddie finds herself being ushered into a room, this time by Paul, as he suggests she takes the time to have a nice warm bath to refresh and when she is ready, they will head out to the restaurant. It is a welcome suggestion and gives Maddie some much needed time alone to collect her thoughts and regain her usual composure. She emerges to find her husband and son playing quietly in the lounge room, having already completed the evening's homework and cleaned up the mess of toys.

In the car, the adults make small talk and joke about the contents of the box, which Maddie still hasn't seen. Maddie works up the courage and tells Paul about the afternoon meeting and proposal, saying that there will likely be an email outlining the offer by the time they return home from dinner. Paul listens intently and asks questions, being careful not to sound judgemental in any way. He tries to gauge whether she feels good about it or not. Maddie says that they should wait a little longer to read the email, which promises to contain the details about the proposed package and the role.

The one conclusion she can draw at this moment is that there seemed to be a degree of envy in the room during the call, particularly from her boss, Terry. She is feeling uncomfortable about the recent attention directed towards her and has communicated it many times to anyone who cared to listen. Maddie believes she is only one part of the reason for the business's success. Turning the branch around in such an astonishing manner was as much Terry's doing as it was hers. Besides, the three other managers reporting to Maddie have proven to be highly competent, and their contribution should be equally acknowledged. Still, she is the person who seems to be receiving the accolades from the senior executive teams. Maddie has spoken at length about this with Terry, and each time he shrugs it off and says she is a deserving recipient of the recognition and whatever the company throws her way, she should accept gladly and run with it.

'Life doesn't offer us career opportunities like this very often, so don't waste it,' he had told her. Still, it doesn't do much to change how she feels or how she thinks the others might be feeling. Perhaps the most natural way out of this situation is to accept the new posting. That way, they won't need to work together face to face. A worse outcome might be if she doesn't take the role, and the others see it as weakness or a wasted opportunity. She realises that these thoughts are leading her towards a decision without even looking at the offer, so she stops herself.

Paul is listening and concurring where appropriate. He senses the inner struggles his wife is grappling with and has decided that if the package is reasonable and the change offers them both the opportunity for growth, then he will share with Maddie his feelings. The more he listens, the more he feels that relocating and starting afresh might be the best thing for them both. As they enter the restaurant, the owner spots them and greets them as part of his family. Maddie and Paul instantly share the same thought – this decision is not going to be easy.

Dinner is consumed in relative silence and seems more rushed than usual, with Paul and Maddie playing out the different scenarios in their heads. Perhaps it is the anticipation of reading the offer when they get home, but they are both relieved to walk in the front door and prepare their son for bed. While Paul reads his bedtime story, Maddie looks through the package sitting on her desk. It is as thorough as Ms Lamport suggested it would be, and Maddie is impressed by the high quality of the contents. She hasn't noticed this at the local level and can only recall seeing something slightly similar before when she was working in the hotel industry. Perhaps this is a signal about how much learning and growth are lying ahead for her. She is aware that this next move will be only one step in her career and that the real value at this time was the level of connection to a network that might never have been possible otherwise. Maddie thinks about her former mentor, Alan Wright, and what he would be saying to her at this moment. She has an urge to call him but remembers that he is most likely travelling. Instead, Maddie sends him a text message, asking for a chance to connect. She needs to decide on something important and would love to hear his thoughts as a friend.

Finally, the moment arrives. Maddie stares at the computer screen with a finger on the mouse, paused and ready to open the email. Paul is equally nervous and as he leans over her shoulder.

They both scan through the message quickly focusing on the most critical details:

- A three-year contract with the option for a two-year extension
- Approximately 80 per cent base salary increase
- Annual bonus @ 40 per cent of her base salary
- Continuing contributions of 10 per cent to her Australian superannuation fund
- A generous relocation package, inclusive of an establishment provision
- Four weeks' rental while searching for living quarters
- Significant monthly housing allowance

- Fully maintained vehicle
- Education allowance for their son to attend an international school
- Annual travel home for the family
- Medical and life insurance coverage for the family
- Access to the company-wide share distribution program.

They look at each other in stunned silence. It seems too generous to be true. They look again, reading more carefully this time and looking for the 'catch'. Instead, they find more to celebrate, reading this time through the description of the role. The position is 'graded', meaning Maddie would associate with the upper level of senior executives, comprising one per cent of the worldwide company. It entitles her to participate in the company's university programs. She would attend the annual leadership conference, held in a different global city each year, where she would have the opportunity to network with more than 500 other leaders. She would also be required to travel regularly to countries inside the Asia–Pacific region. And part of her engagement in the talent program, she would need to visit the United States regularly as well as other locations, depending on the facilitators' requirements.

Maddie leans back in her chair and Paul collapses onto a footstool nearby. They sit there, staring at nothing in particular as they take it all in. Eventually, Paul's face breaks into a broad smile.

'We're going to Hong Kong, baby!' he exclaims. 'No wonder everyone seemed so confident that you would accept the offer,' he adds. Maddie is relieved to hear these words coming from Paul's lips. Of all her concerns, she has been most nervous about her husband having to leave his job.

'Are you sure?' she asks. 'What about your job? I can't ask you to leave it.'

Paul confesses that he hasn't wanted to say anything too soon. He is looking forward to a change, and he has already had preliminary discussions with several of the Hong Kong universities. While there is no official offer as yet, he feels that is because he hasn't pursued it as a definite possibility. A couple of the universities are well-established, with highly regarded business and economics faculties. They seemed interested in the strength Paul would bring to their political sciences division. Hong Kong is experiencing some political unrest, and his reputation and insights would bring some much-needed credibility and stability to their shores.

'So that's it, then?' Maddie asks. 'We're agreed?' Paul gestures to Maddie to wait there and returns with two glasses and a bottle of champagne.

News spreads quickly within the company, and within a month, Maddie has wrapped up her activities and is ready for her replacement and their handover. Unfortunately, the transition isn't possible yet as they haven't found someone Terry believes would be a suitable substitute. It means that Maddie has to make several journeys to Hong Kong to start her new role and then back to her current position in the Melbourne office to ensure the wheels don't stop turning in either location. The trips to Hong Kong, however, prove useful as Paul is able to accompany her on two occasions, taking the time to visit the Hong Kong universities and look for their new housing. The long flight between the two cities offers Maddie an excellent opportunity to commence her studies, which she is very aware are falling behind.

The following week Maddie makes the journey to Boston, home to arguably two of the most elite universities in the world – MIT and Harvard. Growing up, it had always been a dream of Paul to one day lecture in this north-eastern city, and today his wife is attending the Harvard Business School as a corporate executive student. She knows that Paul wishes he could swap places with her, and therefore she vows to make him proud through her efforts and grades. As is her nature, Maddie prepares meticulously, studying the names and backgrounds of her program professors, reading up on the history between her corporation and Harvard University. She looks up which professors are most notable on the topics she will be studying so that she can watch out for opportunities to meet with them or attend their lectures.

By the time Maddie takes her seat in the lecture room of Esteves Hall, she is fully prepared and ready to engage. She is determined to leave a lasting impression on her colleagues and professors alike. Earlier she had noticed Ms Lamport and made a point of greeting her, restating how pleased she was to have such a fantastic opportunity. Ms Lamport is now standing at the front of the room with a gathering around her. As the rest of the students make their way to their allocated seating, Maddie studies their body language, making mental notes to herself. She has always found this part of the experience fascinating and later will check back on her first impressions to see how accurate they have been. This practice has enabled Maddie to trust her gut instinct on more than one occasion in the past.

As the days pass, Maddie has opportunities to meet with her colleagues and, like many of them, she sizes up her competition. On day one she made appointments to meet privately with each of the professors. The aim was to learn more about the modules they would be delivering, to ask if there were additional resources or research and to ask questions related to the topic. By the end of her third day, she is feeling satisfied that her mission has been successful and she is ready to return home triumphant. She is, however, surprised by the extent of additional material those meetings have opened to her. During the evenings, she spends long hours in the library, researching the information shared. She ensures that she follows up the next day by email or in person with those professors, confirming her progress and findings.

On the last evening before her departure, the faculty hosts a graduation ceremony with participants from a different global corporation. There, Maddie meets with as many of the graduating students as she can, looking for any tips they might share about the likes or dislikes of the professors, ways to ensure she focuses on the right things and what to do if she finds herself in trouble or overwhelmed. She also runs into several of her professors. Instead of speaking more about her modules, she purposely talks about current affairs, books she is reading and generally tries to understand them at a more personal level.

Before retiring for the evening, she decides on one last chat, this time with her marketing professor. 'Professor, if you could give me just one piece of advice as I begin my two-year learning journey, what would it be?' The woman looks first at Maddie's name tag and then deeply into her eyes.

'My advice to you, Ms Agnes, would be to stop faking it and let your true self shine through. You run the risk of getting caught up in the politics and forgetting to take in the real purpose for being here – to learn and grow as a person for the betterment of those you lead. It matters less what others think of you right now than it does for you to acknowledge your self-worth. Doing that will, in turn, be noticed by those around you.'

She continues, 'Look around this room. Do you see the people out there acting just like you have been since arriving here this week? They are eagerly trying to make that lasting impression. Eager to show everyone how important and successful they are. Do you think when they return home and sit with their families that any of this will matter? Of course not!'

'Now look around this room and tell me who you think is the richest person in our presence tonight or the most celebrated academic, or the greatest leader among us?' Maddie looks across the room and spots many potential candidates, motioning to several. The professor smiles and says, 'My dear, you should not let appearances deceive you. Come with me. There is someone I want you to meet. Please ask him to tell you about his career and then come back and tell me what you have learned.'

Maddie follows the professor, feeling quite foolish and awkwardly transparent by her behaviour during the evening and in recent days. The professor introduces her to a man she describes as one of the world's most successful and influential entrepreneurs in the past two decades. At first, Maddie thinks she must be joking and that this probably is a close friend that she likes to use to play pranks on her new students. Maddie has never seen this man's picture in any of the social media outlets, nor does his appearance give any suggestion that he could be worth large sums of money.

He does seem approachable and pleasant to speak with, however, showing genuine interest. He has an accent that Maddie guesses is European. She concludes, based on his demeanour, that he was likely from the field of IT.

Following her marketing professor's instructions, Maddie introduces herself to the man and repeats what her professor had suggested. She apologises if now isn't the right time, and says she would fully understand if he isn't inclined to share this information. However, to her surprise, he introduces himself as Sergey Truin, co-founder of one of the leading software companies in the world. Maddie is sure that she is turning red from the embarrassment of not recognising this man and for her conceited misgivings over the entire past week. Maggie listens intently as Mr Truin tells his story of having escaped his homeland with his family to avoid persecution, eventually studying computer science and being fortunate to meet his co-founder at Stanford University. Maddie thanks him for his openness and for sharing his story, again apologising for taking up his time. She excuses herself to search for the marketing professor. She has left, and Maddie decides to close her night as well.

Lying in bed, she reflects on the most important lesson she has learned since her arrival in Boston. What was she thinking, and how has she allowed herself to deviate so far from her true self? It is a timely lesson and one she hopes to remember for the remainder of her career.

The next morning, she sets off for the airport, bound for Melbourne via a short stopover in Hong Kong, where she has agreed to meet Paul and finalise the contract on their new house. The long flight gives Maddie ample time to review her notes and make modifications based on her reflections. Maddie also pens a thank you note to the marketing professor for seeing the real person in her and helping her find that lost soul.

Paul meets Maddie at the airport in Hong Kong and is bubbling with excitement, wanting to share the news that he has secured a position and will be able to continue lecturing on his favourite topic of political science. With Maddie's office based in Kowloon Bay and her frequent travel abroad, they have already decided it will be most convenient for them to live in Kowloon. They have found an ex-pat community in the area called Kowloon Tong. In addition to the lifestyle and housing available in the area, it is also the home of the Australian International School. They hope it will help make the smoothest transition for their son and have enrolled him to start in the coming weeks. It means Paul will need to commute every day, but he has already done a test run and believes that with the convenience of the Hong Kong transport system, it won't be a big ordeal. The flexible working hours of a professor will also work in his favour as most of his lectures occur around midday.

To quote from the title of a book by one business influencer Maddie follows, Robert Iger, 'It has been the ride of a lifetime', and at the age of 37 Maddie can honestly look back and say that she could never have imagined the way her life would turn out. Growing up with hardworking parents in Athens and then emigrating to Melbourne as a teenager seemed like a lifetime ago. Graduating from college aged 17 and then majoring in hospitality in her arts degree led to a full-time role as customer service manager at a 5-star hotel chain, until she was enticed into the elevator industry for a different challenge and career direction. At one point, even leaving her career to start their family, she'd had no idea of what lay ahead. In the most recent five-year period after returning to work, several fortunate turns of events have gone her way. Initial success with the service business, showing her willingness and initiative to progress, the assignment of a mentor and learning from business and market influencers, expanding her professional network, and her impressive results in a new and very challenging role. These actions combined and created a path that saw her sitting in the Asia–Pacific headquarters as an understudy to the Vice President of the region's field operations. Now she is presented with the opportunity to study and grow through one of the best business schools in the world. It isn't a dream, but it does feel surreal.

Transformational Strategy 4: Continuous learning

This book speaks of strategies for reducing isolation, anxiety and fatigue as a leader. Through the processes identified, we are also positioning the reader for greater success. The two underlying messages we refer to are connection and coping with and prospering from change. Change in our role, change in the people and their functions, change in business demands and expectations, changes in technology, changes concerning just about every conceivable issue we encounter in our lives.

It seems logical, therefore, that we should include a strategy related to the need for continuous learning, which enables us to manage these constant changes and even grow personally and professionally as a result.

This need for continuous learning is not new. Still, as we have presented so far, the urgency for accelerating the practice is increasing due to new technology driving the changes in business. The following reflections, therefore, focus on the study methods you might consider together with an array of subjects we believe will be critical as part of your knowledge and skill set.

Traditional and conventional methods for learning into the future

By traditional I mean the typical school and classroom arrangement that is common in places like Australia and the United Kingdom. These institutions are unlikely to disappear in the short to medium term. Instead, we are witnessing their divergence towards a more liberal, free-form approach. That means we can expect to continue having the opportunity to attend colleges, business schools and universities in the foreseeable future. In parallel, however, we are seeing the development of multiple alternatives.

- Correspondence courses were popular between the 1970s to 1990s. As these began to fade out, we observed the early versions of eLearning, which later evolved into the full-blown online approach, mainly through the development of the MOOC (massive open online course) concept.
- cMOOC (more ad hoc and less structured) and xMOOC (more formal and often linked to universities) – have been around for the past decade and are steadily increasing their content and popularity. They offer an extensive range of content in the form of 'micro nuggets' and multi-week programs, and typically consist of recorded sessions, online assessments and forums.
- Social media influencers and many educational companies and academic groups offer blog posts, podcasts, videos, webinars and live streaming opportunities – most often free.
- Corporations have developed in-house academies or universities. These facilities offer product and services with specific, business-relevant modules often supported by one or more of the commercial online platforms. Some of them also partner with universities through their R&D and leadership programs.

- Virtual reality (VR) has entered the learning space in the past decade, and in recent years this has expanded to augmented and mixed reality (AR and MR). However, it is more the domain of large corporations and commercial enterprises due to the prohibitive costs involved.

Joining the above methods recently is one of the most critical developments in the learning space. It's a technology referred to as 'individual adaptive learning', which utilises algorithms similar to the major search engines to monitor the learner's knowledge retention and the depth of that retention. Often incorporating gamification, the advantage this technology brings for corporations is the ability to measure their employees' knowledge and confidence in applying this knowledge to targeted subject matter – such as safety and quality.

Online, digital learning provides the convenience of being able to participate from virtually anywhere but this medium suffers from a low completion rate, something developers are continually striving to reverse through increased engagement and interactive methods. We can expect to see further progress in the short term, with new tools introduced all the time.

The excellent news for students is that they now have a choice of learning methods, modes and platforms.

It's easy to be overwhelmed with the vast range of options available. If you're looking to obtain a recognised qualification, you still need to study a program certified by a college or university. However, if you are like a growing number of students, the lure of MOOC platforms and social media can also bring the confusion of what to tackle first. Here are some suggestions on how to create clarity around the process.

Step 1: Before you start searching for subjects to study, decide on the purpose of your learning. Is it for personal or professional development? Are you focused on increasing specific business or technical knowledge, or is this more a general interest?

Step 2: If the former, are you wanting to complete a short course or a full program with qualification or certification? If you need a certification, it is best to start with a college or university program. However, be sure to check some of the MOOC platforms as they also offer courses that issue credits in university programs.

Step 3: If the latter, how serious are you about studying it? There are short MOOCs available, and you can select from a wide variety of platforms. You can choose to obtain a certificate of completion or pay for an assessment that will count as a credit towards a diploma or degree. You could also take a self-directed approach, which won't cost as much (or may be free) and research places where subject matter experts (SMEs) offer free video content and podcasts.

Once you have the first module finished, don't hesitate to move straight on to the next one! Look to build momentum and avoid letting learning paralysis set in and become the reason for never using the new knowledge.

Subjects to consider for a future-led career

Subject selection is very much a personal preference. However, I believe that all leaders need to be educating themselves on current and emerging technologies. Here are five topics to whet your appetite:

1. artificial intelligence and machine learning
2. information and digital transformation
3. data analytics
4. robotics and automation
5. 5G, the internet of things (IoT) and connectedness.

Add Blockchain to this list if you have an interest in financial or related responsibilities. Apart from the the above, for more a general leadership, soft skills continue to be important:

- employee engagement
- emotional intelligence

- strategic and critical thinking
- problem-solving and creative thinking
- change practices and agile leadership.

If these subjects have got you thinking, then I have achieved my goal in this chapter. Remember, this is a marathon, not a sprint. Pace yourself and, most importantly, get started and don't stop.

For additional support and to deepen your understanding on a subject, identify some related expert influencers and subscribe to their channels. Listening to podcasts, watching videos and reading blogs will only help you retain the knowledge and broaden your perspectives.

Transformational Strategy 5: Identifying the right coach

© S4E Publishing

There's a reason coaching has become so popular in recent times. Working with peopleto co-create solutions reduces stress, isolation and fatigue. Qualified coaches exist in almost every conceivable area of life and business these days. A coach can become an invaluable partner in advancing your career.

Chapter 13: Coach Harry

Following Robert's recovery from a heart attack and triple bypass surgery, Harry's parents decided that there was no great hurry to return home. Instead, they took the opportunity to travel as much of the Australian continent as possible. For the past 12 months, under strict supervision and guidance from his heart surgeon and now close friend, James Henley, Robert has delivered a few lectures at some leading universities along the Australian east coast. Each occasion has been preceded and followed by a relaxing holiday in a nearby township.

Harry and Sandra have returned to Sydney to visit, taking the opportunity to meet with the Henleys and catch up regarding their app development business. It has been a happy reunion. Robert and Claire Bloom are looking happy and refreshed, and the weather seems to agree with them. Robert Bloom is noticeably more relaxed and enjoying life, much more than Harry's memory of his father back in London. The heart attack gave him a scare and a timely reality check to enjoy more of his twilight years. Robert's transformation seems to be agreeing with Claire also, who is much more like her youthful self. She is singing around the house again and always smiling. Nothing appears to be a problem for her, and she is relishing the opportunities to pull out her camera or laptop to show off images of their travels.

The Henleys are as friendly as ever, and Harry is extremely impressed by the growth of their app company under Tim and Janet's guidance. It is a real business, with the two original programmers now working as full-time employees. This has enabled the group to continue working on coding enhancements to their first app as well as to develop the latest idea. The success of their first app has propelled their confidence in making something of this venture. Plus, the steady income, now being generated from it is enough to support all five of the partners, as well as to fund ongoing development. Now, their plans are to take the original app global, and they have engaged a marketing firm to conduct the necessary research in multiple major countries where construction is consistent. The feedback is encouraging, and if Janet's conservative, yet realistic projections are proven right, then finance will no longer be a concern for many years to come following this next phase.

The one thing that has surprised both Harry and Sandra the most, however, is how much Tim has developed professionally. He was always confident but now seems to have matured considerably since they first met. Perhaps it's due to becoming a father and managing this small business, or perhaps it's Tim new responsibilities at work. Harry hopes a little of it has occurred as a result of his mentoring and coaching. Most likely, it's a combination of all these factors. On his return home, Harry plans to write and submit to a psychology journal a paper titled 'Contributing factors to personal growth and development' based on his conclusions, after seeking Tim's input.

For Sandra, the return trip to Sydney is another occasion to meet with Cynthia Henley. A few months ago Cynthia had visited London with her exclusive winter collection, and both women had enjoyed a great week together, touring the city's fashion districts. This trip is another opportunity for the women to catch up and share stories of their lives since that last face-to-face encounter. Sandra can see that Cynthia is expanding her business and feels a little pride in knowing she has played some hand in making this possible. It was, after all, the least that she could do, having been treated like a sister by the Henleys during her own family's challenging time. Not forgetting Rachelle, who has befriended the entire clan and with her warm, friendly demeanour and has become like a daughter to them.

Over the past 12 months, Harry, Sandra and their children have placed every ounce of their spare time and energy into helping grow Harry's coaching business. It hasn't all been plain sailing. They quickly discovered that there was a great deal to learn about running their own business. The best part about their approach was that there was little risk and no real financial pressure to worry about. They had the benefit of time to learn as they grew. Mistakes became lessons they could study, understand and improve on. It was, by all accounts, a hugely satisfying period and one that bonded the family. The siblings were able to experience firsthand the requirements of becoming entrepreneurs and make a direct comparison to working for someone else, based on observing their parents' lives. The monthly family day had quickly turned into a day of reflection about what they had learned, thoughts and discussion about the future. Both Harry and Sandra concurred that this was one of their favourite times of the month.

Charlotte, as the eldest child and with university graduation looming, is fast approaching a time when she will need to decide on her working future, and this has become one of the regular discussion topics in past few months. Her brother and sister have encouraged her to start out on her own, while her parents have remained neutral, saying that it is her decision and they will support her whichever direction she chooses. One Sunday, to everyone's delight, Charlotte sits down at lunch and tells them her decision. She has been questioning her life purpose and is extremely grateful for the experience and lessons she has learned in working with the family to develop Harry's coaching business. Charlotte has realised that her perspective is likely to change over time, after gaining more experience from life and work. Therefore, she has mapped out short-term and medium-term strategies for the next five years.

During her university years she has has been working as an intern for different companies in different industries. This has led to her current interest in working in the law. She has applied to law firms of varying sizes and has interviewed with several of the more significant and leading legal corporations. Three companies are very interested in her research in economics. Naturally, they are also aware that she is the granddaughter of Robert Bloom and, having someone of her capabilities and connections could only be good for business. Each company has offered slightly different but attractive packages, and Charlotte has now decided to go with the largest of these corporations. The role will feed into her short-term strategy of learning and growing from the best in her early years. She is choosing this path rather than going with a smaller company which has made her a handsome offer, as she wants to learn what to do first rather than discover it by herself. There will be plenty of time for self-discovery later in her career. For now, she wants to bed down the basics, and as part of her employment she will be the understudy to one of the senior partners for the first 12 months, after which time she will need to start pulling her own weight.

In the longer-term, or at least the foreseeable future, she would like to move to a smaller, more aggressive company where she won't have to build a business herself immediately. While running her own business is her ultimate ambition, there is no rush; it could come after she is sure this was the area she wants to work in and she can see the potential for branching out. At this moment, that vision is just too far away and, therefore, the risks are too high. She concludes that this strategy is all about learning to swim before diving headlong into the deep end. Not unlike what her parents have done, but perhaps a little faster.

Harry and Sandra listen intently, impressed by the amount and quality of thought Charlotte has placed in her decision. They also like the fact that, at this moment, they don't need to worry about supporting their daughter financially, while they are growing the coaching and app businesses themselves. Harry asks if Charlotte has considered her immediate goals – both personal and business. Charlotte says she wants to wait until commencing her job to get an understanding of the company and the industry before setting any business targets or goals for additional study. However, she has considered her personal goals.

Charlotte proceeds to outline her short-term personal goals. The first is to open three savings accounts: one for cash (a safety net), into which she will commit to paying 10 per cent of her salary; one for investing, into which she will allocate 15 per cent of her salary; and the third to save for a deposit on a property with a further 15 per cent of her salary. Her second goal is to work on her health and fitness, and to complete her first marathon within the next 12 months, adding that maybe she could engage a reasonable coach. Finally, she plans to commence a search for a life partner.

Harry and Sandra are empathetic, nodding and offering small notes of praise as Charlotte outlines her first two goals. However, her announcement of the third makes everyone sit up and pay attention. Charlotte has had boyfriends in the past, but these relationships have not amounted to much while she was focused on her studies. Now she feels it's time to give relationships a higher priority in her life. Sandra is looking very happy and curious about how Charlotte plans to realise this goal.

After the children have left, Harry pours Sandra a glass of white wine as they sit down to relax. As a rule, they generally don't drink on the night before starting the workweek, but it is a special occasion. They drink a toast to the coming of age of their first child and the success of their parenting.

'If I can be anywhere nearly as successful with those I coach from here on, then I am going to live a happy life,' says Harry with a smile.

The next morning, Harry is in bed with his laptop. Sitting back, he thinks about his parents. He has been amazed that even though he is in his early 50s, his parents still have so much influence over his emotions. Harry loves them both dearly, of course, but wonders whether his parenting style has derived from his own upbringing. He hopes his children feel a greater sense freedom than he had as a child and in his teenage years. They certainly have privileges he had not. He hopes one day they may appreciate the opportunities they have in making decisions about their future. The ability to give unconditional love is something else that he and Sandra have worked hard to demonstrate and encourage.

For Sandra it is natural, but Harry has to make a conscious effort. Still, he has learnt. Fortunately, he successfully applied himself as a parent to his children from the beginning. Now, as he closes his laptop, the planned afternoon visit to his parents begins to play on his mind. He will be telling them about his decision to move into coaching full-time. Moving away from a successful career that pays well, at his age, is something he expects his parents may struggle to understand.

Pulling into the driveway, Harry is rehearsing his opening statement. He notices the weather for the first time. It's pleasant, he thinks, hoping the reception inside will be equally enjoyable. Stepping out of the car, he sees his father already at the front door, smiling and waving at him to come inside. Robert has come to prefer the indoors since his return from Sydney, often comparing the lifestyle and complaining about the lousy conditions 'we Brits have to endure'.

Harry senses his father is in good spirits and looks remarkably well for someone in his late 70s. Moving inside and hanging up his coat, Harry greets his mother, and it was immediately evident that she is still her naturally cheery self. Robert and Claire usher Harry into the living room, Robert handing him a drink he has prepared in advance.

'Son, it's great to see you. How is everything with Sandra and our grandchildren? We haven't seen or heard from anyone for a few weeks, so we guess you've been busy?' His voice sounds quite jovial, which is somewhat uncharacteristic for Robert, unless he is delivering a lecture on economics, of course. Harry smiles and nods, acknowledging that work is always hectic and his studies are keeping him quite busy. He adds that the number of people he is coaching has increased and that the app company is about to launch globally, meaning that the quiet times are very precious. He concludes by telling them that Sandra and he would love them to come over for lunch whenever they can manage it. 'We'll invite the children to join us as well and make a day of it.'

Claire smiles and replies that she would love to do that.

'We have some news Harry,' Robert chimed in. 'We have decided to emigrate to Sydney before next autumn. Our real estate agent in Sydney has just advised us that our offer on a beautiful old property on the North Shore has been accepted, and we hope to close in the next 30 days. We think this will give us enough time to get everything in order here, complete some needed renovations to the new property, and to make sure your new business is up and running.' Robert pauses, giving Harry time to comprehend what he has just heard.

'Wait, what?' is the best Harry can come up with. 'Move to Sydney, permanently, at your age, with no family? We know that you enjoyed your time there but leaving everything behind? It's been your entire life. Your friends and colleagues are all here in London.'

'Won't you be lonely?' he continues. 'What will you do to stay busy?'

Claire moves closer to Harry to console him, just as she has throughout his life. Harry remembers that even when they first arrived at the hospital in Sydney, Claire comforted Harry rather than the other way around.

Robert smiles and continues, 'It should give you some additional freedom to grow that coaching business you have been working so hard on and to make the career transition without worrying about what Claire and I think.'

'Wait, you know about my decision to coach full-time?' Harry asks, shocked. 'How do you know about that?'

'Let's just say we have our ears to the ground. Besides, you have never been good at hiding stuff from us,' Robert says.

'Remember that time we came home early, and you thought we wouldn't smell the horrendous odour from your little cannabis trial?' Claire adds.

Harry is stunned. All this time he has been worrying about how to approach the topic, and they already know! And this isn't even the critical piece of news. His parents are moving to Sydney permanently, meaning for the remainder of their lives!

'Does anyone else know about your decision?' Harry asked

'Yes, the university board and our family doctor,' Robert confirms. 'Plus, we've been in communication with Dr Henley. All involved have been sworn to secrecy until such time that the Sydney house contract is signed. Now, it's time for us to come clean as we have many formal documents and preparations to finalise. We're hoping you'll understand and support our decision, son. And we also hope that your family will come and visit us from time to time. Given the fact that you're now a company director in Australia, we think this shouldn't be too big of an issue?'

Harry is starting to think more clearly now, and he can understand his parents' desire for the relocation. It is a beautiful place to live, perhaps marginally remote. Still, in our technologically connected world today, the only real challenge is the actual journey for face-to-face interaction and barring another repeat of a heart attack emergency, that should be manageable. This development will shift considerable pressure off him as well, and worrying about whether his parents will be critical of his coaching practice.

Robert Bloom is not renowned for his empathy and social tolerance, which has caused Harry's reluctance to share his intentions with them.
In the end, he gave in to the likelihood that they probably wouldn't approve, but as he is determined to pursue this new chapter in his life, he feels they need to know sooner or later, whether they are happy for him or not.

'You know Harry, Australia has one or two sports professionals over there as well. Perhaps your mother and I can assist in finding some clients for you? We understand that it's possible to work virtually these days? Why don't you provide me with the details of your coaching practice, and we'll do our best to keep an eye out for prospects. I would expect our friends, the Henleys, will be a great networking resource for you.'

Harry has already been thinking about the Henley connection and his business, but he wants to wait until he has enough experience and qualifications behind him before playing that card. However, if Robert and Claire are willing to put their name behind their son, then that will change everything. Harry thanks his father and says he would be grateful for any assistance in these early times, as he works to establish his credentials and reputation.

As the weeks quickly turn to months, the Blooms departure date is close. Claire has already completed most tasks and is happily working her way through the 'to-do list' to prepare their property for letting. They have offered Harry some extra income if he wished to serve as their letting agent, but he has graciously declined the offer based on needing to stay focused. The real reason, however, is that he can't imagine life with Claire and Robert Bloom as his clients.

After the senior Blooms permanent departure for Sydney's northern shores, Harry's own life enters its next phase. He is surprised, on arriving at his lab, to find the entire department deserted. On his desk he finds a note that says, 'Harry, please come to the cafeteria when you arrive'.

As he walks towards the dining hall, he hopes that they have not prepared a surprise farewell for him. This fear quickly becomes a reality as exploding streamers and cheers greet him as he opens the door. The sound of corks popping and glasses clinking sets the scene for the next two hours. It is indeed a well-deserved celebration – three years on since the Disruptors Lab became a reality under Harry's guidance. The team has been responsible for multiple award-winning innovations. At the same time, it is the closing of an era for Harry. He has reached financial independence with the assistance of several app releases, which he, together with Tim and their company, has been able to launch globally.

Over the past 12 months Harry has grown a sizeable and consistent five-figure monthly income from his coaching practice. Six months earlier, however, he had reached a tipping point where he began to struggle in managing his workload. Holding down a full-time job, keeping up with his studies, supporting the app team in Sydney and adequately servicing 10–12 clients a month was starting to take its toll. Consequently, he discussed with his boss the idea of reducing his involvement in the Disruptors Lab to three or four days a week. He will step away fully by the end of spring, which will coincide with his 10th anniversary at the company. This change will enable everyone to transition. The company will find a suitable successor while Harry concentrates on building his coaching business. Harry is somewhat relieved to learn that the company is interested in maintaining a relationship with him as a part- time consultant and team coach, offering him a contract for one week a month indefinitely, with reviews annually.

And today, the time has arrived to close one chapter and commence another. It is a milestone that five years ago was merely a dream and now is becoming a reality. As he looks around the room at the many colleagues he now calls friends, Harry hopes that one day some might even become his clients. His successor, whom he has been working with for a couple of months, is a smart young man with a good head and a healthy appetite for this role. Harry is happy in the knowledge that his team and the lab are in capable hands.

Later, after finalising the company's paperwork and packing up his personal belongings, Harry takes one last stroll around to say goodbye to each team member, individually. Even though he is likely to work with many of the team as part of the consulting and coaching agreement, he feels it is proper for the new manager to be able to start afresh. The journey home is filled with emotion and reflection as he bids farewell to the landmarks he has passed daily for so many years.

In the evening Sandra and Harry have their own private celebration at their favourite local restaurant with an equally local bottle of red.

'It's the dawning of a new era' are the first words he hears as he awakes from his slumber the next morning. 'Hope you don't plan on sleeping the first day away,' his wife says with a smile.

Harry looks at her and then sends his pillow hurtling in her direction before sitting up and sniffing the air to see if there is any noticeable difference. After deciding it is safe to step from the comfort of the bed, which does feel much more enjoyable than usual, he makes his way to the bathroom to commence day one as a new man.

Now shaved, refreshed and dressed, Harry strolls around the house, confirming he is alone, with Sandra already on her way to work. A strange feeling of emptiness suddenly overcomes him. Is this what it's going to be like every day, he wonders, starting to feel a little isolated and underprepared. As he walks into the kitchen, he notices an envelope on the counter with his name on it. The handwriting is Sandra's and inside is a single sheet of paper with one side titled 'Things to do when you start feeling lonely' and on the other side she has written two lists: 'Your top 10 reasons for becoming a full-time coach' and 'Reasons your wife loves you'. Harry recognised the items on the first list as the ones he and Sandra had brainstormed the first night he had told her about the idea. She is terrific, Harry thought, smiling. Looking through the top 10, he is amazed at how accurate they still are, and it reminds him that he needs to action a couple of the points that have escaped his attention. By now Harry is already walking towards his study. The second list is equally exciting and provocative. Had any added incentive been required at this point, this list would certainly have achieved the desired intention. He picks up his phone and sends Sandra a text message, 'You know me too well, my love, thank you. It was just the inspiration I needed on day one, home alone.'

With that, he sits down at his desk, opens his computer and starts reading through his calendar, reflecting on the big-picture targets for the coming year and beyond. It isn't long before all spare time across the coming three months are fully accounted for – family, coaching sessions, study, university, app calls, consulting, networking events etc. Harry starts to work through his to-do lists, ensuring he has the coming week adequately addressed as well as some of the items spilling over into the following week. He then sets his sight on those day one action items and gets started.

Picking up his newly printed business cards, Harry leans back in his chair for just a moment, before sitting upright making his first official business call as Harry Bloom, Sports and Life Coach. At the age of 54, the dream is now a reality, and the next chapter of his life has commenced.

Epilogue

Harry and Sandra eventually follow his parents to live in Sydney, some six years later. Their children have all completed their studies and are living independent working lives. Charlotte and Travis are both married, while Peg is still enjoying her freedom. Sandra has gone into partnership with Cynthia Henley and is responsible for handling the retail side of the fashion business. Harry is continuing his coaching practice, which has expanded successfully across multiple countries. His parents have kept their promise of promoting his business and, with the aid of their dear friends, the Henleys, have successfully introduced many high-profile Australian athletes into Harry's practice.

Chapter 14: Maddie learns the value in delegating

Sitting in a coffee shop overlooking Victoria Harbour and chatting with Alan feels to Maddie just like old times. They could be sitting anywhere in the world, including in Melbourne. Looking across the harbour at the skyline on Hong Kong Island, watching the ferries traverse the waters and the endless procession of harbour traffic on and off the water, is something she could enjoy for hours on end if only she had the time. After Alan's first message suggesting they meet, it has become a regular monthly catch-up for them.

Alan, no longer her mentor, is now a friend with shared interests, working in the same industry. They meet as two ex-pat Aussies enjoying life in Hong Kong and discussing everything from their families, to the Rugby 7s match and unrest on the streets of the city.

Since Maddie's arrival, the time has flown by, and it seems she is seldom home. The past 12 months have included a further two visits to Boston, punctuated by trips to almost every country in the Asia–Pacific. She also attended her first leadership conference in Spain. The change has undoubtedly provided her with a very different and much broader perspective on their business. Alan's time is also stretched, following a similar travel schedule with Asia–Pacific country visits and quarterly leadership meetings in Europe. So they both welcome these opportunities to relax, share some laughs, reflect on their lives and savour their friendship amidst the daily chaos.

Maddie, however, is becoming more concerned about her marriage than about her ability to handle her professional life. The travel, study and workload are beginning to take their toll on her family unit. With Paul lecturing every day and Maddie seldom home, they have hired a nanny to care for their son and to manage the home chores. Maddie feels Paul has become less attentive and increasingly moody, and she is worrying about their future as a family. She has tried speaking with him about their relationship but he is not engaging in the conversation, replying in an offhanded way that everything is fine. Maddie's gut is telling her differently, however. Today she plans to raise the topic with Alan. It is a sensitive topic, but she is feeling a little desperate.

After listening to her concerns, Alan leans forward and says, 'I have two suggestions for you. Seek out a marriage counsellor and convince your husband of the need for it. However, be sure you search for a counsellor with whom you will both feel comfortable as the sessions tend to become very personal. And second, find yourself a good life coach. You're burning the candle at both ends and, eventually, both flames will burn out. You need to act now if you truly want to reignite the relationship with Paul and save your family. I have been blessed in my career to have people around me who could read the signs and pick me up – redirecting me whenever it looked like I would fall into the same trap. This business can be brutal. It will tempt you and then burn you if you let it. It will extract everything from you and offer little other than financial benefits in return. Each year you will feel the push for more and better. I'm pleased that you've shared this with me, but I can't be the person to help you. Those that you find and lean on for support will need to work closely and in confidence as you share your deepest and intimate secrets. Trust me, I have been there and fortunately survived.'

Alan sits back and smiles gently, adding, 'But the best news is that you have taken the first step towards recovery. Now just make sure you don't let other distractions, namely your busy work schedule, prevent you from finishing this important journey.'

Later, Maddie thinks back to her conversation with Alan. Something is puzzling her about something Alan said: 'If you truly want to reignite and save the relationship.' Why is this comment bothering her? Paul has been her whole world for more than half of her life. Could the issue be that she has fallen out of love with him? Has she become so focused on her career, attracted by all the attention and wanting this more than Paul? Surely not, she thinks.

Over the next week, this thought plays regularly on her mind and haunts her dreams. She has watched Paul interact with their son, seeming content to engage and occupy himself in his development. Is he also sensing the same thing between the two of them? Paul was an intuitive person, and many times in their relationship he has surprised Maddie by sharing his observations, which she had been oblivious to herself. She decides then and there that she can't just throw this all away. They have come so far together and are now able to enjoy the financial freedom they both desired. Why is she even considering throwing this away? One night she asks Paul if they could sit and talk after their son is asleep.

Their discussion goes long into the early hours of the next morning and they conclude that their relationship is in trouble. Paul confesses that his attraction to Maddie is beginning to wane, having watched in recent months as Maddie's focus has shifted almost totally towards her career. He has found it more appealing to stay behind and spend time with other faculty staff than to come back to the empty house. He respects Maddie's decision to pursue her career, but he just hasn't prepared himself for the personal loss that has brought with it. Until the moment, Paul says that, Maddie hasn't been the slightest bit aware that she has become the wedge, all this time thinking that Paul is the cause. Maddie shares the thoughts she has had about Paul and the fact that she has spoken with her friends to seek guidance. Not once has she stopped to think that maybe the reason behind the problem is her.

Paul listens but seems disengaged, which Maddie interprets as a bad sign. Is it already too late to salvage this marriage?

'Paul, I would like to fight for our relationship if you are willing. I'm wondering how you would feel about seeing a marriage counsellor?' Paul smiles, realising just how well he knows Maddie. A month earlier, he himself researched family counsellors in Hong Kong and found that this was a vibrant business.

Reaching into his computer bag, Paul pulls out brochures from different counselling websites he has visited. Maddie is surprised by how long their relationship must have been in trouble, and only now is it all coming home to her. They look through the brochures together but agree it's too late in the evening to be making decisions on such an important topic. Best to adjourn and return to this conversation after getting some much-needed rest. Not that either party manages much sleep after retiring to their sides of the bed. Before turning off the light, Maddie looks in on her son. He is the innocent player in this whole mess. She feels her eyes welling up. How did this all happen? A flashback to her conversation at that first networking event at Harvard, where her marketing professor had called her out as trying to become someone that she wasn't. Maddie thought she had learned the lesson intended, but now realises that she had merely heard the warning and failed to heed it.

That next day is one of firsts. She calls in sick for the first time in her career. She is up early and cooking breakfast for the first time since arriving in Hong Kong. She takes her son to school for the first time in almost six months and kisses her husband goodbye as he heads off to work. She has to admit to herself that she feels relieved when she finally sits down for some alone time to reflect and collect herself. Her thoughts return to work. How could she manage everything and devote the right amount of time to her family without risking her career or falling behind with her studies?

As she has done successfully so many times in past years, Maddie puts her thoughts down on sticky notes. She dumps everything she can think of that is important in her life right at the moment. Then reviews her goals and long-term career strategy to see if there is anything she needs to add. As she starts sorting the notes, almost immediately she begins to see the problem. The entire surface of their dining table is now overflowing with notes. She starts sorting them into themes, looking for possible duplication and unnecessary items. Then she starts a second wave of culling. This time she's more ruthless, and it's working. It means she has to let go of some things on her wish list. She reasons that they could return when she has taken care of other priorities.

With her list now somewhat close to what she believes to be realistic, Maddie opens her calendar and starts to align the items on her notes with her schedule. It is a daunting process, but she can see the solution beginning to take shape. After a good two hours and further culling, she sits back, exhausted but pleased. She has cut back on her travel commitments, which she realises are responsible for much of the trouble. Clustering her trips into a solid block means she would be away only one week a month, excluding infrequent flights outside of the Asia–Pacific region. This will enable her to accommodate her study and exercise requirements before heading to the office in the mornings while ensuring she is home for dinner and able to spend time with her son before he goes to bed, plus quality time with her husband. She realises that there will always be unexpected situations requiring her to break from this plan. However, provided she is committed to making it work, she believes it is going to be possible. Maddie is feeling excited to share her plans with Paul as soon as he returns from work.

After dinner they resume their discussion about the need for counselling, which Maddie now feels is less necessary and is surprised that Paul seems to be in favour of it. Checking through Maddie's calendar overview, Paul asks her about some of the assumptions she had made about being able to juggle her office workload, and asks whether she is delegating effectively to others within the department. Paul reminds Maddie that one of the hallmarks of a good leader is that they find opportunities to develop their team, and one of the best ways they can do this is by sharing the workload and giving everyone a chance to stretch and grow. Maddie knows it well.
It's Leadership 101, but she has to admit that she has been so deep in the

middle of the issues that she has overlooked it. She is beginning to realise the need to stop, step back and 'see the trees' all around her. Sometimes the ability to be open to the obvious, to experience that which surrounds us, is as precious as being handed the gift itself, she thinks.

'Thank you.' she says to Paul. 'I needed your wisdom as I have been overlooking this. If I can help my team to grow, then they can take over a portion of my work and allow me time to breathe. Part of my study program has been talking about the need for all leaders to coach their team, and it provides specific guidelines on how we can start to practise this. I'm going to make a point of beginning this tomorrow.'

Paul sits back and considers her carefully as if looking directly into her heart and soul. 'It seems you are trying to salvage things around here. I'm impressed with what you've shown me tonight. My concern is whether it's sustainable, although if you're willing to give it a try, then I'm on board and will support you to achieve it.'

The next day she sits with her boss and lays out her plan for developing their team. With his approval, she plans to speak with the group and discuss this new approach. Of interest to her is the opportunity to coach each individual and to spend time understanding what they want in life and their career. Her boss seems particularly pleased with this idea and says that he doesn't know where she finds the energy to come up with these ideas, but however she is doing it, she should learn to harness it and make it a permanent part of her toolkit. He approves wholeheartedly of the concept and reminds Maddie about similar coaching that they have already engaged in themselves.

'Just follow the lead from what we did and you should be fine. Remember, however, that not everyone will be as excited about this opportunity as what you might be. Take it one step at a time, and don't force the process.' Maddie is feeling confident as this has been her hallmark to success over the years. She works hard to draw people in and create trust, which is so critical.

She thinks back to the near undoing of her family and shudders, reminding herself that even those closest to her haven't always felt the love recently, so she decides to heed her boss's advice and start slowly. She has learned that the crucial ingredient for success in almost every situation lies in the preparation and planning. So, locking herself away in one of the smaller meeting rooms for the remainder of the day, she proceeds to fill in the details of her strategy and arranges for a team meeting tomorrow. As her boss happens to be in Hong Kong right now, Maddie decides that it would be far more effective for him to introduce the idea and open the way for her to roll-out the initiative.

Calling on what she learned in the change management module she recently finished with Harvard, Maddie builds her story. First, she draws on analogies and metaphors to help her team link strategy to their world. Then she carefully crafts a clear 'why' and 'what's in it for me?' statement, mapping out the vision of what this initiative will achieve, or the 'end game'. She sets out the names of each team member and beside each she draws the five-sided SCARF model. Based on Maddie's assessment of the business since arriving in Hong Kong, she identifies the most likely social preferences that motivate the team members – status, certainty, autonomy, relatedness and fairness. Studying the results, she reviews her strategy and story, ensuring that she is able to find something that will resonate with each person. She plans to ask each person to complete the SCARF assessment online, but for now she has to rely on her observations.

Maddie has already identified the immediate tasks she plans to delegate, including sufficient challenge and importance, so it's clear these are not just unwanted jobs to be offloaded onto the team. She also reviews each team member's background, expertise and most recent appraisal to get an understanding of their capabilities. She looks for signs of interest or disengagement, searching for those who may be willing or needing to develop. Comfortable that she has mapped the delegated tasks to the most appropriate person, and remembering to consider their SCARF motivations, Maddie prepares for the first one-on-one coaching session.

She will discuss that plan, outlining the overall task and specific requirements, measurements and timeline. Then she will seek feedback from each member to gauge their level of understanding and commitment. Her preparation is sound. She intends to hold regular team meetings as part of the task review so that the assigned person has an opportunity to demonstrate their progress and receive immediate feedback, even gratitude from their colleagues and supervisor.

Next, she schedules a meeting with the head of HR to understand the guidelines, systems and tools already in place for the team and individual employee development. She is pleased to find that the company is already well advanced in this area. Maddie studies how best to apply this information and discuss her strategy with the HR talent manager, whom she invites to the briefing meeting. Her mentoring and coaching are starting to pay dividends, and the realisation that she can't succeed alone rings loudly in her mind.

For the final piece of the preparation, she plans to ask three simple questions in the meeting:

1. What is currently working for them in their individual positions and within the team?
2. What is not working for them and should be stopped?
3. What do they think they could start doing that would benefit them, the team and thecompany?

Maddie smiles to herself as she types out the questions, thinking that she must remember to share the experience with Alan at their next coffee catch-up.

In the evening, after enquiring about and listening intently to the events in her husband's day, Maddie spends a full thirty minutes sharing her own experience with Paul and asking whether he thinks she has missed anything. The critical message she wants Paul to receive is that she is focused and committed to implementing this strategy following their discussion. By delegating these tasks she is returning to her grassroots; the approach that made her successful in the beginning. She is empowering her team who, in turn, will drive the success of the business. As a side benefit, Maddie's day will be much more manageable, giving her ample time for the other activities in her life, including her family.

In the months that follow, Maddie grows in confidence and becomes as comfortable presenting to senior executives as she is to her colleagues and team. Her customer fandom grows as her influence spreads across countries in the region. By the time she has completed the two-year talent program, Maddie has touched the lives of almost everyone she has encountered. Her aptitude and discipline have resulted in above-average outcomes. On graduating, she is voted most likely to become CEO by her fellow Harvard graduates, for her ability to simplify complex matters and communicate the facts.

Together with her ability to see through the problem and find solutions, perhaps her most endearing trait, Maddie repeatedly demonstrates her ability to stay true to herself without the mirage of being someone she isn't. In her early career it was her strength, and she credits much of her success to it. Then, as she got caught up with the attention and success, this trait had become her weakness, her kryptonite. It took an observant and straight-shooting marketing professor to call her out on it, together with the failure to grasp that her marriage was failing. Since that near-miss, Maddie has taken steps to ensure she never returns to the 'dark side'.

Following Alan's suggestion, Maddie has leaned on her Harvard network to find a life coach. Her genuineness has made her a favourite with many of her professors, who are usually happy to assist those they deem to be worthy. Maddie secures an introduction to a European-born and Boston-based professor considered by many as the 'father of coaching' and often called on to mentor other coaches. After a short period, he introduces Maddie to the process of systemic coaching and the use of a method he refers to as 'constellation coaching'. The systemic process is standard in coaching and emphasises the need to move away from a problem and leverage personal resources in the shift towards the desired outcome. The constellation method enables the coachee to visualise an entire scenario, so they can see the dynamics of the situation and think through the roles and relationships of the different players involved. It highlights what has triggered the issue and, most importantly, what actions are available for a solution.

Maddie stands looking at a purpose-built board, where she has carefully placed nine figures around a central figure to represent herself. The other nine characters represent the vital people in her life – Paul and her son, her boss and two other key executives in the company, Alan, a social media influencer and two professors. Then she places a new figure on the board as the coaching has progressed. This figure represents the future unknown and is neither good nor bad. She walks around the board, looking at the situation and herself from different angles.

She turns the board, which swivels on its base. Now she is able to imagine the issue through the eyes of the others and to witness the scene from different perspectives. Moving the figures and working through a series of compelling questions from her coach, Maddie considers the consequences of various actions and outcomes. Finally, she is clear about her approach. They have repeated the exercise several times in the past 12 months with equally encouraging results.

The coaching engagement concludes after 12th session, when both parties agree that Maddie's progress has placed her on the path to reaching that desired level of satisfaction she identified and targeted in their first session together. It has been a rewarding and fulfilling exchange for her at a time when she most needed some clarity and it has been instrumental in her turnaround, confirming the critical areas of her life she had needed to address for future sustainable happiness. To revisit Alan's metaphor about her candle burning from both ends, she can now say that multiple candles are surrounding her, each providing light for a chosen activity and with many more stored away, awaiting their time to be lit and play a role in the future life of Maddie Agnes.

Over time, Maddie continues to grow and demonstrate her competence as a leader and, on turning 40, she is invited to run her own regional office in southern Europe. She takes over responsibility for nine small countries, stretching from Croatia and Romania in the north to Greece in the south and Bulgaria to the east. It is a dream come true and an opportunity to return to her family's homeland, victorious after conquering the world. Based in Athens, Maddie is able to convince her mother and sister to make the shift as well and to live out their lives in a familiar environment among old friends and relatives. Paul meets relatives he had never known existed. Their son experiences life in Europe for the first time, exploring his ancestry firsthand.

Maddie feels at home, happy and successful, content and eager to conquer her next challenge.

Epilogue

Five years after moving to Europe, Maddie accepts an offer to head-up a global consortium founded by an old friend and in partnership with leading IT giants from Silicon Valley. The corporation is in the process of reshaping the elevator industry using the next generation of technologies to enable a transition away from its labour-intensive, hands-on, service-based business towards a plug-and-play spare parts provider model, supported through distribution and virtual support call centres.

Chapter 15: Tim adds coaching to his growth strategy

Year one of the talent program is drawing to a close, and it has been an action-packed year for Tim and Janet on many levels. The app company is growing apace and generating significant revenue, which enables them to increase the number of full-time employees to five. The growth also comes at some cost to their short-term plans, however. Both Tim and Janet are desperate to find extra time in an already busy schedule. They needed to handle managerial tasks for their company while supporting a product pre-launch outside of Australia. It means they need help in managing their home life, and for this they have hired a part-time housekeeper to assist in taking care of their immediate needs such as cooking, cleaning and the endless washing their son seems to create.

Tim and Harry's relationship has been strengthened further, with Harry continuing to coach Tim on technology topics and communication as a partner in their app company. Tim is feeling a little guilty about the amount of time Harry has contributed to coaching him. Still, Harry remains insistent that until Tim has achieved his long-term goals of learning to code in various languages and is competent with other aspects of technology, his work will remain incomplete. Tim's overall commitments have hampered the speed of achieving these goals, but he is making progress and so remains focused in this area.

Janet and Tim have also been studying. Janet signed on for a commerce degree and Tim is in his first year of six-module leadership program offered through his company. He is now also required to spend more and more time in the office, supporting sales and sitting beside the service operations, to gain a deeper understanding of the overall business. It has been great, and he truly enjoys it; however, he is also still managing his project site, which isn't proving to be as easy as he has hoped. The head of finance seems to have taken a personal interest in Tim's progression, often stopping by to ask for his opinion on different topics. Tim figures it is as much about testing his knowledge and aptitude as it is about wanting his input.

Over these past 12 months, Tim has competed in two group challenges, which were part of the talent program, and the requirement was to complete a computer-based business simulation and achieve the most sustainable, high-performing business outcome. The first simulation was quite basic and realistic, requiring the application of general leadership skills supported by the learnings coming from the first three modules he had studied – First 365 days, Stakeholder Engagement and Executive Safety. His team finished second overall, which he is happy about; however, he observed how competitive many of the participants from the other groups are and is questioning whether he gave the exercise and opportunity enough effort.

Ahead of the second simulation challenge, he ensured that he was clear on what he had learned from the last three modules related to sales, installation and service. He felt very confident in these three areas, given the time he spent on the practical side of the field operations in his day job. He was unprepared, however, for the twist that came from the company hosting the simulation. In each group, a disruptor was introduced whose sole purpose seemed to be to challenge every decision the group made. As a result, Tim's group finished third. Afterwards, the group gathered for a debrief with their assigned program coach. He asked them to describe their feelings at that moment, to which they all admitted to feeling a little deflated and less enthusiastic about the next challenge in six months.

It was, of course, the response the coach had expected. He proceeded to share with them a story related to the performance of one of the past teams. That team had finished last after a similar experience and had attributed the blame to the introduction of the new team member.

That group had come to their post-coaching session with their heads hung low, feeling that they had just received an unexpected and unfair blow. The coach reminded the team that the other three groups also experienced the same level of disruption but had managed the confusion differently. Fast forward to the next two simulations (six and 12 months ahead) during phase two of the program, and after some soul searching, this same team was able to raise its performance, finishing first in both competitions.

The coach shared with Tim's team the secret to the turnaround and success. They began to understand how important it is to become influential people managers, how to effectively introduce new players into their group, just as in real life where we face constant employee churn. They realised that if this disruption occurs every time someone new joins their operation, they would never be successful. So, when that team finished last, they agreed on a course of action, which later catapulted them to becoming unstoppable and able to capture first place. As a side note, no group since has been able to better that team's business results.

It is an inspiring story that has the desired effect of shaking out the negative energy and replacing it with the possibility of success in the next challenge. Everyone is now focused on what has to happen to perform a similar turnaround in six months. The answer the coach gives is simple – study what it takes to build a strong team. You have already touched on the solution during those first six modules. Now you need to rethink your approach during the challenge and, coupled with what you will learn from the coming modules, identify the gaps. With those gaps, consider how to close them out and avoid a repeat occurrence. Even better is how to capitalise on the diversity in your team and to maximise the opportunities. The coach suggests a couple of good movies that might shed further insights in this area as well. The coach concludes that the outcome could have been worse. Had they been successful based on their actions and performance, they would never have had this opportunity to learn from the situation and grow further. The coach hopes the powerful lesson will be one they take with them throughout their career. Tim realises that the experience indeed has been invaluable. the team remains together for a further two hours, exploring what they have learnt and putting together their strategy.

Alan's latest trip to Sydney is perfectly timed as Tim wants to share his experience in the business simulation exercise and sound out his theory of what went wrong. He is interested in obtaining another expert opinion on how they could have approached things differently and achieved a different outcome. Alan listens as Tim outlines the business case, injecting questions at the appropriate time to ensure his understanding of the scenario.

Tim has noticed that Alan never takes notes while listening. Instead, he seems to listen to every word and observes Tim's body language. Alan then repeats to summarise what was said. It is a skill that impresses Tim, who often wonders whether this was a learned skill and if he could ever master that level of engagement.

On this occasion, Alan seems to be even more focused than usual, nodding and leaning in, repeating Tim's comments. As Tim moves, Alan mirrors his movements. Even the words Alan uses seem to strike a chord with Tim. It is almost as if Alan is inside Tim's mind and body. Yet, rather than feeling uncomfortable, it feels very natural and disarming. Tim is relaxed and uninhibited, willing to share everything on his mind regarding the situation. In the end, the two have an in-depth conversation that lasts two hours, concluding with a list of insights and suggestions from Alan. Tim has always been impressed by Alan's business knowledge, but this time it is incredible.

Tim looks at Alan, 'What just happened? Did you hypnotise me or something? I was incredibly present during that entire conversation, but it felt as though you had slipped truth serum into my coffee, and I just couldn't stop pouring everything out to you!'

Alan smiles and confesses that he uses a skill called 'mirroring' to match Tim's movements, and the same sensory language that Tim uses, to make a deeper connection.

'For instance,' Alan explains, 'You speak in a very visual and kinaesthetic way. Would you like me to demonstrate?'

Tim nods.

'If I ask you to explain what you thought about the conversation we've just had, how might you respond?'

Tim thinks for a moment. 'I can see the big picture now, and it appears we failed to induct our new colleague into our team from the beginning, ensuring that he knew us, and we knew him. Instead, we saw him as an outsider and imposter, almost, who we pushed away rather than embraced. As a result, he pushed back and found ways to undermine our efforts. We didn't harness his abilities, which meant we operated at 75 per cent capacity rather than maximising our potential, and mathematically we all know that one multiplied by anything less than one cannot produce one. The lesson for me here is that the team needs to function like a well-oiled machine, with each person playing to their highest ability, but feeling secure in the knowledge that the other members would also be performing their tasks at the peak of their ability. Does that sound about, right?' Tim pauses and looks at Alan for his confirmation.

Alan surprises Tim by placing his mobile phone on the table and hitting the play button. Tim listens to himself speak in the recording. The first time it plays, he misses most of what he said, as he is trying to understand the point Alan is making. Alan replays it a second time, asking Tim to focus on his language. He asks if Tim can hear the descriptive words he used, explaining that someone's style typically draws from three senses: auditory, visual or kinaesthetic (touch and feel).

'Listen to your words and take notice of how often you use visual expressions to describe your thoughts.'

Tim listens and smiles to himself. It's true.

Alan says it is an old tactic commonly used in negotiating, especially by car salespeople.

'If you went in to buy a car and said, "I want to listen to the purr of the engine." And the car salesperson says, "Yes. It comes in a vast range of colours." The buyer's likely reaction is to become frustrated and immediately suspicious, and a disconnect occurs. However, if the salesperson picks up on the language and says something like, "Ah great. You're going to love it! Music to your ears." Then you are likely to feel that this person understands you. The practice comes from neuro-linguistic programming, or NLP. The study has been around for almost 50 years, but the method goes way back.'

Tim is intrigued as he wants to become a better negotiator, and this sounds like an unfair advantage. He thinks back to his most recent client discussion about a contract variation and wonders how much he had given away unnecessarily.

'So, you mean that many people understand this?'

Alan admits that this isn't the only tactic used by negotiators, and suggests that if Tim wants to improve his skills, there are many courses he could take to learn them.

'But, yes,' adds Alan. 'Professional negotiators typically have this among their arsenal.'

Tim is curious. 'What drives your desire to help others? What value do you get from sitting here with me and offering support? I'm guessing it's not a specific job function, so there must be more to it, surely?'

Alan replies, 'That's a good question and one which I"m happy you asked as it demonstrates you're starting to evolve as a leader.' Alan shares his own life story and speaks about how he had been fortunate his father was a successful leader of a large corporation. When Alan himself entered full-time employment, his father sat him down and shared some of his wisdom. He told Alan that there are many unknowns he will likely encounter every day in business. Still, the one constant that will serve as his guiding light throughout that journey comes not only from his own experience but by leveraging the knowledge of others. Alan was encouraged by his father to find himself a minimum of three mentors. Back then, the coaching concept hadn't taken hold as it has today. If it had, Alan suspects his father's guidance would have been to find a balance between the two professions.

Throughout his career, Alan has leaned on the knowledge and skills of advisers, while finding his way and building his library of experience. Therefore, when the opportunity came up some 15 years ago to mentor young leaders, not unlike Tim, it was a natural transition and role for him to play.

'Besides,' he adds. 'We now realise that this practice is one hallmark of good leaders. The coaching world today has an even broader approach not based around sharing their experience. Via the belief that everyone deep down holds the answers to their problems and through the use of powerful questioning, a coach can work with a client (or employee in our case) to find the right solution. In my case, I like to use a combination of both mentoring and coaching. However, an authentic coach doesn't guide or give advice. They rely on the client identifying their own direction and then co-creating the solution together. The approach varies depending on the skills of the coach and the specific area, such as sports coaching, which tends to cross that boundary more often than not.'

This time, it is Alan who notices Tim 'mirroring' his actions, and wonders if it is intentional or just that Tim is so fully absorbed in what he is learning. Either way, Alan is happy to see Tim's engagement. Tim interrupts Alan's thoughts.

'So, would you recommend that I find additional mentors and coaches? In the past, I have engaged with a business mentor for a short period, plus a financial mentor for two years, and both provided a great learning experience. Now, aside from your mentoring, I have a friend and business partner who is coaching me in technology, which is an area of interest and one that's important for the company we operate. Based on what you know of me after this past 12 months, what would you suggest I do to identify mentors and or coaches?'

'It's a very personal decision and depends on the individual's current situation,' Alan responds. 'It's common to have either a business mentor or executive coach. They play different roles, as you already understand. It's also popular these days for people to engage with a life coach. From what you've told me, you're leading quite a full and busy life these days, so it may even be worth looking at some of the niche areas such as confidence coaching. As you have experience with finance and the specific area of technology, I would say those areas are already adequately covered. Still, you can think of almost anything you might like coaching in and search for it online, with a good chance of success.'

Tim likes the suggestion of a confidence coach, even though he is only guessing about their areas of focus. He has delivered presentations to the senior management as part of his talent program and has not liked the experience at all. Immediately after each occasion he made a mental note that this was an area he needed to give more attention to. Perhaps a confidence coach could help shed light on what is going wrong and provide insights on how to make improvements. Besides this, he isn't great with the dreaded slideshow presentation. He has seen some highly professional-looking slideshows, but sadly his never seem to come close to being in the same league.

Tim suddenly realises that he has taken up almost three hours of Alan's time and gasps when he looks at his watch.

'WOW! I'm so sorry!' Tim exclaims. 'Look at the time. I lost track as it's been such an engaging session. I've learned so much and have a lot to take away. Do you have plans for dinner this evening?' Tim adds. 'If not, I would love to introduce you to my wife and son. We live just across the harbour there in Neutral Bay. You can see your hotel from my living room. By the way, where did you live before moving to Hong Kong?' Tim asks. 'I don't think we have ever spoken about that.'

'I'm an eastern-suburbs guy, born and bred,' Alan confesses. 'Grew up surfing off Bondi and Maroubra, went to Marist College Pagewood, while living and playing rugby in Randwick.'

'Right! It's settled then,' Tim says, as he can't bear the thought of missing the opportunity for some rival banter across the dining table with someone from the eastern suburbs. Perhaps he should invite his sister over to join the debate, given that she lives in Coogee.

'What time shall I swing by and pick you up? How is 6:30?'

'Well,' Alan pauses, 'if you don't think it's going to be too inconvenient. It's not often I get to meet the family of those I'm mentoring, and it would make quite a pleasant change from dining alone in the hotel.'

'Excellent. I'll let Janet know to set an extra place. Hope you like leftovers,' Tim says with a grin.

'Thank you. I'll pick up some wine. What's your preference – white or red?'

'Red, please, and thanks, but don't go to a lot of trouble. We drink just about anything. We've indulged in a cardboard carton sitting on a shelf from time to time,' again smiling.

Alan hits back, 'Sounds like I'm in for a treat tonight then! Leftovers and wine from a bladder. Perfect!'

As much as Alan knows that Tim is joking about their food and drink for dinner, he still feels a tinge of relief later, when they step inside the apartment and he smells the aroma of Italian cooking drifting from the kitchen. Tim shows Alan to the living room and points across to the familiar building where Alan is staying. 'Most nights, Janet and I sit here with a telescope, training on the windows in that tower and wondering whether we will get a glimpse of you parading around half-naked or on a secrete rendezvous with a gorgeous blonde,' Tim winks.

'You're perhaps 20 years too late for such possibilities,' Alan says, looking down at his body and touching his greying hair. 'I'm afraid my stays typically consist of meetings or coaching most of the day, and then I might catch some live theatre, take a stroll through Darling Harbour. Sometimes I even vegg out in a bookshop on George Street, as it's still one of my favourite places to visit.' Alan retorts.

As the evening wears on, the atmosphere lightens from courteous pleasantries to typical rival slinging. Fortunately, Tim has secured his sister Rachelle as Alan's support. It is a no-holds-barred affair, as every landmark, politician and sports team are fair game.

Tim is about to serve his ace when the doorbell rings. James and Cynthia Henley are in the doorway, holding a bottle of bubbly. Tim is puzzled, and asks if everything is alright. He wonders whether he and Janet have missed a special occasion. After ushering them in and a short round of introductions, Tim explains that they are in the process of debating the better location across Sydney, believing that he now has the unfair advantage, with his parents sure to favour his northern suburbs.

Sadly, they remain neutral, based on James Henley's reasoning that he'd spent his time working in the eastern suburbs even though he lived not far from Tim, Janet and their son. Of course, it is slightly different for Cynthia, with both her home and place of business close by on the northern shores, although she does hold a soft spot for the family apartment in Coogee. Alan takes the opportunity to explore with the new guests their line of work after explaining that Tim has been careful to keep his entire family at arm's length until this moment.

The three take the chance to get acquainted while the three younger members of the group clear away the dinner plates. Alan introduces himself first, explaining his role and location in Hong Kong. He is fortunate to have the opportunity to travel frequently and mentor young leaders like their son. Cynthia pulls out her business card and hands it to Alan, sharing that she is in fashion design and runs several boutique stores. Alan seems to recall seeing the logo before but can't be sure. Perhaps it is a label he has seen on his wife's clothes, he smiles to himself. James says he's a heart surgeon. Alan, who is still studying the logo, looks up and places the card down. Ah, sadly, I know your hospital and clinic all too well. My mother suffered a massive stroke many years ago and, while the ambulance and later the doctors were able to stabilise her, it seems the initial damage was just too severe, and she passed within a day of the attack.'

James is now busy searching his contacts on his phone. He looks up and asks, 'Was your mother's name Mary? Mary Wright, who passed away in 2009?' Alan nods and looks a little saddened as he recalls the painful memory.

'Alan,' James says, pausing and looking a little perplexed. 'It's truly a small world. I wonder if I could chat with you in private for a moment. I was the attending physician for your mother and was in the room when she passed. We tried to resuscitate her but were unsuccessful as you know. If you're okay, I have something your mother asked me to share with you all those years back.'

Cynthia sees that as her cue to leave the room and moves into the kitchen to assist the others. James waits until Cynthia is out of the room before he continues. 'I remember having a conversation with your mother directly after she regained consciousness from her surgery. Even in her condition, your mother possessed a lively spirit and a great sense of humour. Her first sentence was a joke that heaven or hell looked very similar to the place she had just left. It made everyone in the room laugh, even the priest who was on standby in case your mother requested his help. I can tell you that in my long career, that was a first. Then she looked me directly in the eyes and said, 'Well, I'm guessing by the number of people here in my room that things aren't great. Give it to me straight, Doctor, what's the prognosis?'

Alan listens, speechless, but he can visualise his mother clearly, and James's description matches his mother's character to a T.

James continues that after giving Mary the news, she asked James that if he should ever see her son, to please tell him that he was always in her heart and that she and his father were incredibly proud of everything he had done for them and others. James asked whether he could contact her son, but she had replied that he went to Africa for two weeks every year with his wife to helping children over there, and it wouldn't be practical to reach him.

'Your mother said that she had updated her will not long before and gave us the name of the attorney we should contact, which we did immediately. After your mother passed that evening, I contacted the attorney several times to check whether the message had reached you and she confirmed that it had. I'm hoping that you also received the letter I wrote to you and left with your mother's attorney?'

It takes Alan a moment to digest the news. He then looks up and smiled. 'Thank you for sharing this story, and yes, I did receive the letter. I had carried the burden of not being home when my mother needed me the most, but I'm pleased to know that at least she didn't die alone and frightened.'

A few moments later, Tim's head appears around the corner.

'I'm not sure about you older folk, but I have to get up early in the morning. Would you mind if we have a final round and then call it a night?' His timing is perfect as Alan now needs time to reflect.

James hands Alan his card and invites him to reach out anytime he'd like a chat, and says he would be happy to meet up. Rachelle volunteers to drop Alan at his hotel on her way to Coogee. At the same time, the Henley seniors head home, leaving Tim and Janet to finish up before retiring themselves.

Tim continues to be mentored by Alan over the following year and takes his advice to engage with a confidence coach. The coach's brief is to help build Tim's charisma and presence. They also work on improving his presentation skills a few notches. Janet's validation of Tim's growth comes the night she sits in the audience and watches her husband accept an award for winning the business simulation competition and then deliver a presentation on the winning formula during the closing ceremony. Perhaps he won't be another Steve Jobs, but compared to the man she married only a few years ago, he has grown in confidence and stature immeasurably. She is looking at a real leader standing there proudly on stage. As she glances sideways, she thinks, just for a moment, that she can see a welling up in the eyes of Mr James Henley beside her.

Shortly afterwards, the company honours its commitment and appoints Tim as its newest branch manager. He is ready and capable, looking to get his hands 'dirty' while he calls on the experiences he has amassed through his career so far, confident in the knowledge that he isn't alone. He has the support of his family, the help of his company and an ever-growing group of mentors and coaches. It is a story that Tim has visualised many times since he started working. A day when he would have the opportunity to lean on the shoulders of many, sniff the new air and gaze at the world from an ever-so-slightly elevated perspective. It is a first but critical step on the journey to future successes. Along the way, he has learned so much and is grateful to so many.

With those who are now reporting to him, Tim wastes no time in establishing a branch mentoring program in which anyone who has an interest is encouraged to mentor someone else who has a desire to learn and grow. Tim also begins to coach his direct reports. Nurturing them, rather than pressuring them, to understand the value of being stretched. On the office wall, in clear sight of everyone that enters, he erects a board with the quote attributed to Albert Einstein: 'A mind once stretched can never return to its original size'.

Epilogue

Tim runs this small branch for four years and enjoys tremendous success in his third and fourth years after having stopped the losses in year one and making a small profit in year two. During that period, he continues to learn about business and grow as a leader. Janet and Tim sell their shares in the app company after deciding to branch out in a different direction. In his fifth year, Tim accepts an offer to move to Queensland and run the state operations. Eighteen months into his new posting, he receives a call from an old mentor who says he is pulling together an all-star team for a new business venture and wonders whether Tim has time for a coffee.

Transformational Strategy 5: Coaching

Some key facts about the coaching profession

The world of coaching has exploded in the past 30 years. However, it remains mostly self-regulated, which means the standards can vary considerably between individuals. There are, however, several global professional associations that have defined standards a coach must be able to fulfil to achieve certification.

Associations such as the International Coaching Federation, established in 1995, defines coaching as 'partnering with clients in a thought-provoking and creative process that inspires them to maximize their personal and professional potential' (https://coachingfederation.org).

In 2016, two global coaching associations, the European Mentoring and Coaching Council, and the Association of Coaching, published a Global Code of Ethics (ICF Code of Ethics – International Coaching Federation, at https://coachingfederation.org/ethics/code-of-ethics). It was an important step towards aligning the professionalism and standards of coaching practice.

The range of fields covered through coaching is expansive, from business and executive teams through to life, sports, health, spiritual, political, family and many other fields.

Companies seek external coaches to assist in the development of their executives and executive teams. They often opt to establish a coaching pool from internal staff for everyday coaching of employees. One hallmark of every executive leader today is that they need to coach their team towards improved performance.

One of the more confusing issues for leaders is in determining whom to engage – a mentor or a coach? The following table highlights two core differences in approach and conversation style between the executive and each of these professions. Both have their purpose but approach the situation differently – coaches 'ask' while mentors 'advise'.

Profession	Who is the expert?	What is the method?
Coaching	Executive/ Coaching counterpart	Ask powerful questions
Mentoring	Mentor	Give advice and guidance

Coaches use communication skills and a range of tools and techniques to help executives alter their perspectives and discover different approaches to achieve their objectives.

There has long been a debate in coaching circles about whether everyone is 'coachable'. The reality is that for the coaching process to succeed, it requires commitment and a willingness for change on the part of the person being coached.

You will notice that some of these questions are similar to the mentors' question stack, but I repeat them here as they are important. Ask the following questions before signing a coaching agreement:

- What are your professional credentials as a coach?
- What field of coaching have you practised in, and for how long?
- Do you have associated qualifications in coaching?
- What coaching standards and codes guide your practice?

- What can I expect from you as my coach, and what do you expect of me?
- Is there a standard or a minimum number of sessions you require?
- How long would you recommend for each session, and at what frequency?
- How will we be able to monitor my progress and benefits from the coaching?
- Is there a flat fee per session, or is it based on time?
- Do you charge for the first introductory / evaluation session?
- What happens if I can't make it to a session, do you still charge me?
- Does every session need to be conducted face to face?
- What happens with my private information – during and after the engagement?
- Can I access your notes or any documents we share during our sessions?
- Is any of my information or our discussions offered to a third party?
- Are our sessions recorded?
- Can you explain the overall structure or approach of a coaching session?
- Is there anything else I should be aware of before signing the agreement?

There is a good likelihood that the coach will provide you with details related to many of the above questions without you asking. However, it's essential that the relationship feels comfortable and that this is the right fit for you.

It also provides the coach with an opportunity to get to know you better as the relationship must work both ways. If the coach feels that there isn't a connection, or isn't the potential to develop one, then they should be honest and advise you.

You can expect that the coach will offer you a 'welcome pack' of sorts. Though not compulsory, it may contain:

1. A welcome letter
2. Your coaching agreement
3. A client information sheet
4. A code of conduct
5. One or more questionnaires to complete, such as a life map and pondering questions.

These documents will help to formalise the arrangement and will give you a clear idea of the roles and responsibilities as well as offering the coach an insight into you and your background.

The two most common forms of coaching are one-on-one, or individual coaching and group or team coaching. Each method has advantages and disadvantages, some of which are shown in the table on the next page.

No single style or technique in coaching will suit every individual or group and, therefore, coaches need to be flexible and able to utilise the method most suited to the client's needs. To support them in this endeavour, coaches have dozens of tools at their disposal to handle each topic and situation. Coaches generally spend time, in the beginning, exploring your personality and understanding what approach seems to resonate most with you.

Method	**Advantages**	**Disadvantages**
One-on-one (reverse for team coaching)	• More personal than team coaching • Addresses *your* topics • Works on *your* goals	• More expensive than team coaching • No opportunity to learnfrom others • No networking opportunities

They will try to avoid pre-empting the flow or discussion in a session, instead leaving you to determine what topics you wish to deal with, knowing that they can support you regardless. Typical opening questions you can expect include, 'What's on your mind?' and 'What would you like to discuss today?' or some version of these.

The techniques and tools used will vary according to the field of coaching and the topic, but the full range available means that you can expect great questions, templates and techniques. Each coach will have their favourites and will love the opportunity to put them to use. A good coach, however, is also keen to learn through the encounter, and you might be surprised by how engaged they become. Be prepared to dig deep into topics and not just settle for the first-level response.

There's no better way to experience the benefits of being coached than to try it firsthand. Search online or ask friends if they know anyone in your area. Check out as many as you desire and then take one or more for a test drive and enjoy the ride.

Being present while developing the future

© S4E Publishing

The only certainty is change! And it is accelerating at ever increasing rates.Our not-too-distant future will look considerably different from today, thanks mainly to the convergence of multiple technologies that are feeding off each other to reshape our lives. Leaders who can see this future can become co-creators and agile adopters of the needed changes, rather than simpler responders to change.

Chapter 16: Alan realises a dream

An old copy of a book titled *Trillion Dollar Coach* sits on the coffee table. Alan first read it when it was published decades ago, and at that time, he had no inkling that he would one day be sitting in the foyer of the company owned by two of the book's authors. Alan is there to meet and discuss the next steps in their joint venture. They were introduced by a venture capitalist who had listened to Alan's pitch and suggested they meet.

'If their reaction is half as favourable as I expect, then I'm all in,' he had said.

Alan has already lost count of the number of trips he has made to San Francisco since then. At first, even he had doubts about the concept. It was certainly 'out there', but if they could pull it off, this would be game-changing for the elevator industry, which is home to an estimated 20 million units worldwide. Every single service operation responsible for maintaining those elevator and escalator units would need to dramatically change the way they operate to take advantage of this new approach. The enticement to make this change is a considerable financial windfall. Additional to the bottom line, the technology being introduced also means using significantly safer equipment and faster turn-around times for replacement.

Alan first had the idea while sitting in a Sydney hotel foyer, observing one of his young leadership prodigies interacting with a hotel robot. At that time, robots had just started to become commonplace in hotels and airports, and the elevator industry was building interfaces to communicate with them. Then came the first ropeless elevator, which opened the flood gates for changes to the way the equipment operated. Cloud-based analytics on elevator–escalator equipment has now reached a stage where it is possible to predict with a high degree of accuracy, the need for component maintenance and equipment replacement. That breakthrough has opened the door to a 'just-in-time' servicing policy and revolution in the industry.

These three technologies – all significant in their times – have already reshaped how companies are structured. The considerable change has brought about improvements to bottom-line results and the optimisation of workforces. Now, years later, the industry is experiencing the latest generation of developments, with predictive maintenance taking a quantum leap forward through the use of nano technology and virtual bots to scan and interrogate the entire installation. The bots constantly search for anomalies and feed this information to cloud-based applications using powerful algorithms for analysis. In addition to the developments in robotics, 3D printing and material science are now greatly influencing product design and installation methods. Alan has seen these transitions unfold but had not reacted quickly enough. They did, however, lead him to a decision three years ago to be the one driving the next significant change, and to be firmly on the crest of the wave. After all, this industry is his life, and in his current capacity as adviser to many of the executive consortiums, he has a front-row seat to the future.

Years earlier, he had read a book called Age of Spiritual Machines – Discussing the period when computers exceed human intelligence by Ray Kurzweil. While Alan didn't fully understand the concept as laid out by Kurzweil, the theory of a 'Law of Accelerating Returns' and exponential growth through the doubling of computation did resonate with him.

Over his career, Alan has witnessed how the former laboratory science approach of trial and error was replaced by simulation science and how the pace of progress was accelerating dramatically, to the point at which every single business on the planet has become an 'information-driven business'. The competition quickly came down to how skilfully each company could use that information.

Alan had envisioned this future state almost 15 years ago. Back then, the room was filled with nay-sayers who responded as if they were personally offended by the suggestion. Now, at the moment of realising this vision, Alan knows the industry's response will be even harsher. He is likely to be ridiculed as nothing more than a somewhat 'old' disruptor with too much free time on his hands, trying to play a young person's game. The words of Kurzweil continue to ring in his head – the world will continue to change exponentially, and progress will be perpetually accelerating.

The most significant risk, which Alan has been careful to spell out, is the same risk that seems to make his idea so attractive to his Silicon Valley partners. The threat comes from within the industry as they would likely try to out-manoeuvre their venture before it gets started. The reality is that if the experiment were to be successful, it would remove a significant portion of manufacturing, installation and service revenue generated from current practices. Following the introduction of this modular approach, a company's survival will depend on how quickly they are able to adapt.

Undoubtedly, it will mean significant disruption and require a dramatic restructuring of their operation. But for those who can see the potential through a broadening of collaboration partners, their efforts will be handsomely rewarded.

Alan likens it to the oil and auto company giants' resistance to the introduction of hydrogen and electrically propelled cars several decades ago. While these companies tried for many years to resist the evolving technology, in the end, the technology won through and today we can see the results. As Bob Iger wrote in his book, The Ride of a Lifetime, when Steve Jobs had introduced him to a new product that Apple was working on, one that would allow the world to watch movies directly on their hand-held devices, many people called Jobs crazy, while others believed it would destroy the cinema and send film companies broke. Iger was immediately aligned with the idea and agreed to the use of multiple Disney movies on the new platform.

Alan believes 100 per cent in what they are working on. It promises to be the biggest game- changer the industry has seen since Elisha Otis invented elevator safety gear some 170 years ago. Still, he would be lying if he didn't admit to being a little nervous about the reaction from many of the colleagues he has spent his life working beside. Some of these people, whom he calls his close friends, stand to lose a lot if they ignore this new evolution. Companies that are more progressive and can respond quickly once they realised the merits of this methodology stood to benefit. It is inevitable that there will be those who will resist or even deny the change as possible. For these companies, it could spell disaster.

There is also a real chance that a newcomer could enter the market, a start-up full of ideas and willing backers that could jump ahead of the traditional establishment. So, as he sits there, waiting for his hosts to arrive, Alan realises that while they are definitely riding the crest of the wave and are sufficiently well advanced, they should not rest until they are ready to start production. This will provide a buffer and the ability to set the direction for future entrants or, worst case, to ward off any aggressive intruders.

Until this moment, he has been able to raise seed capital in return for shares, but only with those investors he believes he can trust, with the aid of multiple non-disclosure and non-compete agreements in place and a heavy monitoring of activities. This money has enabled him to play around the fringes, testing concepts and building simulation models on a miniature scale. He has been cautious about working with only those recognised as industry leaders in their field. Also avoiding unnecessary overhead in the form of offices, equipment and human capital.

Cautiously at first, while they implement the business framework as designed – securing agreements in strategic locations with production partners, distribution centres and shipping agents globally, each location will be run by a very lean, locally positioned management team and overseen by a regional expert.

Highly automated distribution centres need to co-exist in collaboration with production and domestic shipping partners. In most cases the three separate companies would operate from the one mega centre. Production quality and logistics management are the most critical aspects that will govern their success, so there is no room for error in this space. Only those suppliers capable of meeting the exacting product standards will be invited on board, and they need to enter into agreements that lock them into collaboration with the mega centres. The search criteria, therefore, has mapped out the need to find companies prepared to take some risk on a start-up, but who can see the medium to long-term potential. Only then will those companies be invited to partner and given the opportunity to set up operations under the same roof. All parties will then be encouraged to study the internal workings of the other partners and continually seek ways to optimise performance and collaboration. Perhaps even reshaping their systems, processes or tooling to work as genuinely invested business partners towards co-creating a successful and sustainable business ecosystem.

Over the years, Alan has worked with plenty of people who thought they were talented, even great at what they did. Usually, letting you know at some point in the discussion about how they rose above the mire to snatch victory from the jaws of defeat. Those with such a profile are precisely the opposite of the ideal candidate for this venture.

Instead, they are seeking people who don't mind rolling up their sleeves and demonstrating their resilience and courage, and who are equally accepting of their vulnerable traits. Those who have the gumption to know which arguments to engage in and which to avoid. They must be a great leader of the younger workforce and able to understand how to create the right environment to extract the best performance possible. In short, they are not your average, run-of-the-mill executive.

The ideal candidate needs to be a new wave leader. It is a given that the leader needs to be able to let go of ego. The ego-centric mindset of past leaders can only remain viable in those unable to make the transition to the contemporary agile world in which collaboration and networked companies dominate the Fortune 500 listing. Today's information-driven business models require leaders who ooze flexibility, tightly coupled with rapid decision-making and problem-solving capabilities. Running diverse, values-based, culturally reliable companies is now as much an art form as it is a learned skill.

In all of Alan's years of mentoring, he has met relatively few individuals who might fit this profile. Still, that is the mandate he is tasked with, and perhaps their recruit will not come from within the industry. The company head needs to be someone senior enough to command the respect of the industry, but young enough to be relatable to the company's employees. Around that person, they plan to assemble a younger greenfield group of vice presidents who are tech-savvy and, if possible, industry-wise. Alan has a shortlist of candidates displayed in front of him on the screen, some he knows well, while others he has never met. He starts with the latter and touches the screen to call up their profiles and hit the call connect button. The hiring process is about to commence.

It proves a gruelling process of countless video calls and in-person meetings. Still, eventually, they shortlist three candidates to run the organisation and 10 potential vice presidents from around the globe. They needed six to run the regional operations. The rest of the structure will be quite flat. Reporting directly to each vice present will be the sub-regional management team across 12 high-density locations and smaller local teams. Excluding the senior partners, the company will commence with a skeleton staff of 45 people. Within the first 12 months, however, their target is set to grow tenfold as the adoption of their technology takes hold.

With the company board meeting scheduled, and the three CEO candidates invited, Alan and the recruitment agency have done their job. It is now time for the board to make the crucial decision. Each interview is spaced two hours apart, leaving ample time for questions and reflection. Alan has purposely placed Maddie as the second interviewee. She is one of two women shortlisted and a strong contender, although the others have also impressed Alan over the past several months whenever he has met with them. He is feeling confident that any of the three could succeed in this role. However, Maddie has the distinct advantage of being the only one from the industry and with a wide-ranging reputation for her achievements in the various roles she has played. Alan will sit in on the interview but won't play an active part in the discussion or decision. He has been responsible for the shortlist selection, and now the other five members of the board must make the final choice.

Each candidate is a true professional, with successful business backgrounds and impressive academic credentials supporting their interests in the role. However, it isn't only the candidate who is on display here. There is also a consideration of the candidate's family. Did the candidate emulate the prized target profile beyond the business environment? The board deems this an important factor as the company's figurehead will likely become highly recognised in the media, an so an almost full family disclosure has become a hallmark of today's technologically informed society.

The decision isn't easy, and several additional rounds of meetings with each candidate in different settings are deemed necessary. Alan is impressed by the diligence displayed from each of the board members. Their attitude toward the selection process and their apparent intellectual competence, gives him a strong sense of pride and, for the first time, genuine confidence that this company will be a force in the future.

One week after commencing, the CEO selection process is concluded and a decision is reached. Alan sits once again, facing his large video screen. This time from his apartment on the 65th floor of The Shard, high above the hustle of London's city streets. Alan greets his colleagues in Silicon Valley.

'You did a great job, Alan. It was such a tough decision to separate the three candidates, but, in the end, there is a defining factor that we just cannot overlook. Maddie comes from and is well-connected in the industry, having worked in many of our regional locations. She has an impressive track record in business and academically. Her family background is impeccable and respected, but the clinching element is her career mentoring by our very own chairman. She, therefore, comes very highly recommended.' There is a pause and, slowly, smiles appear on the faces of everyone on both sides of the screen.

'Have you already informed Maddie of your choice?' Alan asks.

'No, we will advise the others that they weren't successful once Maddie's appointment is locked into place, but we thought you might like the opportunity to give Maddie the excellent news. She is a deserving choice, Alan, and you know her better than anyone here. By the way, when can we expect to see you back here? We have a lot to catch up on before we get started.'

Five minutes later, Alan is reclining in his chair, staring out of the window towards the bridge. It has indeed been a significant journey until this point, and he wonders what the next 12 months have in store. Despite his age, he is feeling as fit and healthy as ever, excited by the challenge laying ahead, and now very content in the knowledge that his star pupil will soon be calling the shots. They have the technology, they have the business framework and they have now snared their CEO of choice. Just a few more boxes to tick and employment contracts to sign and the vision will turn into reality.

He speaks to his computer, 'Call Maddie Agnes for me, please, Simon?'

'Straight away, Mr Wright,' Simon replies. Moments later, Alan and Maddie are locked in conversation. Both are elated by the news, both feeling a sense of gratitude towards the other. After meeting for that first time roughly 10 years ago in a coffee shop overlooking the Yarra River in Melbourne, the journey has led them to this pinnacle in their careers. While it is just the beginning, somehow deep inside both know that the next chapter's success is almost guaranteed. Still, there is no time to waste as news of Maddie's appointment is bound to ruffle a few feathers in the industry.

'How soon can you get back on a plane to San Francisco? We have much to do, and the team is eagerly awaiting your arrival. I said I would personally escort you there myself. Do you think it'd be possible for Paul and Alastair to make the journey with you? You might need to be there for a couple of weeks. We're ready to hit the "activate button" on this operation. It would be great publicity if we could announce our new CEO appointment and have her family standing beside her,' Alan concludes.

'It sounds like I'm about to announce I'm running for public office,' Maddie responds, but Alan can hear the smile in her voice.

'We've had our legal team look over your current contract, and this shouldn't present too much of an issue. The team will represent you and assist with any issues if they arise. Barring any unexpected objections, we believe you could be released inside the next month but be prepared for a negative and somewhat standard reaction of requesting you finish up immediately. Don't worry financially either, as we have your back and will compensate you handsomely in any event. You are officially on our payroll from now. Our legal team has drawn up a letter of resignation for you, and you should find that in your inbox about now. Please read and sign it, then when you're ready, make the call, notify your boss and hand in the letter.
I know you well enough to know that you won't burn any bridges unnecessarily, which will be important for the future of our company. Please keep me informed of developments, and you know you're always welcome to contact me at any time. Once we have a clearer understanding of your availability, we can plan the trip to the States.'

'By the way,' he adds. 'we still need to appoint your six regional vice presidents who'll become your eyes and ears. Once they are on board, we'll immediately start to work with them to select the country teams. Hopefully, inside the next three months we will have our full squad in operation. The good news is that our recruitment agency has already lined up some excellent candidates and there are a few personal favourites whom I've mentored over the years. I'm confident you'll like the line-up, but just as with your appointment, I won't be involved further, so you will make the final decision. If you don't mind, I'll send the files across for your review and consideration; then we can discuss any questions you have.' Alan pauses as he realises he has been speaking far too long, and waits for Maddie's input.

There is an awkward silence before Maddie says, 'Alan, I'm grateful to have this opportunity, and together we are going to achieve great things. However, I confess that I'm feeling a little guilty, as my current company has given me so much.'

Alan smiles, instantly vindicated that his company has made the right choice.

As predicted, several months later the newly assembled team meets virtually from across the globe for the first time. It is a very proud moment for Alan as he stands in the background and watches his most successful prodigy outline the future of a company destined to write a new chapter in the history books. An industry that, until less than a decade ago, has seen very few game-changing breakthroughs. But, as has been demonstrated repeatedly over the past century, progress perpetually accelerates for humanity. We keep getting better in everything we do, and this was the conclusion Alan reached many years ago. As outlined in Kurzweil's book, 'all-new technologies are a combination of existing technologies'. With that, you start to realise that this is just the next logical step in a continuing evolution for this industry. One that Alan has had the foresight to understand and the ability to visualise. One that he has gambled on and been lucky enough to find the right people who share his vision and belief.

Among those gathered for the meeting and standing equally as proud, is Tim Henley, the new vice president of operations for South-East Asia, engaged for his youthful leadership perspective, his detailed knowledge of the industry and his strong business acumen. The sealing of his appointment has come courtesy of a chance discovery of a coding error while he was using the recruitment company's online employment application software. Tim and family are now based in Singapore and he is responsible for distribution in a region spanning Australia in the south, Hong Kong and Taiwan to the north and multiple Asian countries in between. He has met with his new boss a couple of times in person but feels he already knows her well through a shared relationship with their mentor.

Beside Tim stands an older man, whom Alan has met on several occasions and who comes highly recommended by a colleague. Harry Bloom has been engaged as a business partner to act as special adviser on technical development, production and distribution matters. His reputation as an expert for bringing teams together to achieve seemingly impossible deadlines with breakthrough technology and his creative genius in conceptualising and designing out-of-the-box ideas has secured him this partnering role. Harry's own app company has been nominated as one of the 'Top 10 Influential Small Businesses' of the past decade and has been responsible for dramatically improving the efficiency of the construction industry.

As Maddie's presentation reaches an end, three questions appear on the screen, to which she responds, 'These three questions have been responsible for guiding my career and for shaping the businesses I have run. They were shared with me by a very dear friend many years ago, and I would like to share them with you. Please make it your habit at least once every quarter to ask of yourself and your team these same three questions. I will read and share a summarised version of everyone's answers with the board and during our senior management reviews. The answers that you generate to these three simple questions will most likely form the cornerstone of our inspiration. We'll draw from them to keep our business at the forefront of technology and to lead this industry. As we go forward and create this future, regardless of how technologically sophisticated we become, we should always retain the following five core people-centric pillars that serve to support our strategic initiatives:

1. We will operate a mentoring platform that is available through all levels of this organisation. Every employee, regardless of their title or role, can learn from those experienced and novice, whether they have trodden the path before them or just see it from a different perspective. On this platform all will have the freedom to share their thoughts, wisdom and experience.
2. Our company's culture will exist around the desire for feedback, which transcends equally upwards as it does down. In essence, all employees, myself included, will seek and offer feedback to management, peers, colleagues and partners, regularly.
3. Our company must thrive on collaboration. Not only within our circles but by equally valuing the contribution provided by our many business partners. This neural network is crucial to our sustainability and must be developed and strengthened at every level and opportunity in every region.
4. Continuous learning, be it through self-study, company programs or on-the-job opportunities, will be mandated and rewarded. If we wish to stay at the cutting edge of technology and our industry, this is essential. All staff need to desire growth and development, which they then share with their colleagues and boost contribution in their role. All management will be held accountable for development planning and driving sustainable, lifelong learning programs.
5. Finally, the company will commit to engaging certified external coaches who are experts in team, executive and leadership development. Through these coaches, we will build an internal pool of support coaching networks that serve as coaching intermediaries in unison with the experts.'

As the meeting closes and the teams go their separate ways, their phones ping in unison. The message reads:

'While we are separated by distance, we remain bonded through technology and our networks. No question is so silly that it can't be asked, nor is there a bad time to ask it. Never limit your ability, worrying if others will approve. Instead, we want to embrace diversity of perspectives. If you believe in what you are doing and have a vision of what it will create, then pursue it wholeheartedly. Each one of us is embarking on this personal and professional journey, and together we are creating a new chapter in history.'

Closing comments

In this book I have covered five ways to reduce the feeling of isolation as an executive while leading a team, group or even an entire organisation. Additionally, those same five strategies enable us to leverage the strength and support of others, to overcome anxiety and fatigue from our daily efforts. Perhaps, most importantly, they take the underlying cause from dealing with the uncertainty of constant change and channel it to providing opportunities for connection and growth. Yes, the secrets that lie within the strategies contain the potential to launch your career and propel you to new heights of achievement.

The magic of embodying these five simple strategies is that they become your armour in dealing with the ebb and flow – the 'yin and yang' that occurs throughout your career – taking the negative energy that often engulfs us and converting it into positive, forward- thinking possibilities.

By opening our minds and changing our perspectives, we can see beyond the immediate and shortcomings, looking instead to the future and fixing our gaze on that vision with the support needed to guide and perhaps engage with you on the journey. It is possible and surprisingly within everyone's reach.

Abbreviations

AI	artificial intelligence
AR	augmented reality
CHRO	Chief Human Resources Officer
CRM	customer relationship management
FAST	Frequent, Actionable, Specific, Timely
G&A	general and administrative
IP	intellectual property
IT	information technology
JHA	job hazard analysis
MC	main contractor
MD	managing director
MOOC	Massive Open Online Course
NLP	neuro-linguistic programming
NPS	net promotor score
PB	personal best
PHP	Hypertext Pre-processor, an open-source programming language
PMI	Project Management Institute
PPE	personal protective equipment
R&D	research and development
ROI	return on investment
SCARF	Status, Certainty, Autonomy, Relatedness, Fairness
SMART	Specific, Measurable, Attainable (Ambitious), Realistic, Timebound
SME	subject-matter expert
SPRINTS	a series of bite-sized project iterations (work packages)
STEM	Science, Technology, Engineering and Mathematics
SWMS	Safe Work Method Statement
VR	virtual reality

About the Author

Hi, I'm Wayne Brown.

I work with executives to help transform their careers by developing elite talent across four of the most critical needs for any professional today: communication, facilitation, education and coaching.

After 45 years in six companies, living on four continents and working in more than 85 cities, I've engaged with people from diverse cultures and groups, leading, facilitating and coaching thousands of executives on topics from leadership through to operational excellence.

In addition, I have experienced the rigours of starting and running businesses and companies, learning along the way through success and failure. My journey has been supported by mentors and coaches who have helped me to stay focused and dedicated to my purpose of helping others.

As a lifelong learner, I've studied through many of the world's leading institutions and have learned from incredible professors and leaders. Today, I continue to develop and grow alongside my clients as we co-create the future together. From my years of playing competitive sports, I learned early on that life is a team activity and that we cannot succeed alone. It takes encouragement, the perspectives of more than one, and collective effort to reach those lofty goals and heights.

To find out more about my personal story, visit our website, skills4executives.com.

Made in the USA
Monee, IL
04 November 2026

67378319R00148